Contents

Contributors

Anthony Payne is Professor of Politics at the University of Sheffield. He has recently co-authored, with Paul Sutton, *Charting Caribbean Development* (Macmillan/University Press of Florida, 2001), edited *The New Regional Politics of Development* (Palgrave Macmillan, 2004) and authored *The Global Politics of Unequal Development* (Palgrave Macmillan, 2005). He was Managing Editor of the journal *New Political Economy* from 1995 to 2005 and remains one of its editors.

Colin Crouch is Professor of Governance and Public Management at the University of Warwick Business School. He was previously Professor of Sociology at the European University Institute, Florence. His recent publications include *Post-Democracy* (Polity, 2004) and *Capitalist Diversity and Change: Recombinant Governance and Institutional Entrepreneurs* (Oxford University Press, 2005). His current research interests focus on the governance of labour markets and other economic institutions in Eastern and Western Europe.

Mark Rupert is Professor of Political Science in the Maxwell School of Citizenship and Public Affairs of Syracuse University. He is the author of *Producing Hegemony: The Politics of Mass Production and American Global Power* (Cambridge University Press, 1995), *Ideologies of Globalization: Contending Visions of a New World Order* (Routledge, 2000) and, with Scott Solomon, *Globalization and International Political Economy* (Rowman & Littlefield, 2005). He is also the co-editor, with Hazel Smith, of *Historical Materialism and Globalization* (Routledge, 2002). His current research focuses on the intersection of the US political economy with global structures and processes.

James Meadowcroft holds a Canada Research Chair in Governance for Sustainable Development in the School of Public Policy and Administration and in the Department of Political Science in Carleton University in Ottawa. He was previously Reader in Politics at the University of Sheffield. His research interests span a number of areas in political theory and environmental politics. In the latter connection he has co-edited, with

Key Debates in New Political Economy

This book ... the major inte ... es th ... the field o ... mporary political econo ... Each chapter ovid s ... state of the art review of a key area written by a distinguished expert in the field. The introduction locates these debates within the wider intellectual and political context which gave rise to them and provides some pointers to the future direction of the study of political economy. Subjects covered include:

* Models of capitalism
* Globalisation
* The environment
* Gender
* Territory and space
* Regionalism
* Development

In short, pithy, but highly original fashion *Key Debates in New Political Economy* sets out for the reader what the contemporary debate in political economy is all about, making it an essential source for all students and scholars with interests in this area.

Anthony Payne is Professor of Politics at the University of Sheffield. He was Managing Editor of the journal *New Political Economy* from 1995 to 2005 and remains one of its editors.

Key Debates in New Political Economy

Edited by Anthony Payne

Routledge
Taylor & Francis Group

LONDON AND NEW YORK

First published 2006
by Routledge
2 Park Square, Milton Park, Abingdon, Oxon OX14 4RN

Simultaneously published in the USA and Canada
by Routledge
270 Madison Ave, New York, NY 10016

*Routledge is an imprint of the Taylor & Francis Group,
an informa business*

© 2006 Taylor & Francis

Typeset in Times by
RefineCatch Limited, Bungay, Suffolk
Printed and bound in Great Britain by
MPG Books Ltd, Bodmin

British Library Cataloguing in Publication Data
A catalogue record for this book is available from the British Library

Library of Congress Cataloging in Publication Data
A catalog record for this book has been requested

ISBN10: 0–415–39726–X (hbk)
ISBN10: 0–415–39727–8 (pbk)

ISBN13: 978–0–415–39726–1 (hbk)
ISBN13: 978–0–415–39727–8 (pbk)

William Lafferty, *Democracy and the Environment* (Edward Elgar, 1998), with Michael Kenny, *Planning Sustainability* (Routledge, 1999) and, again with William Lafferty, *Implementing Sustainable Development: Strategies and Initiatives in High Consumption Societies* (Oxford University Press, 2000). He is presently preparing a book on the environmental state.

V. Spike Peterson is Professor in the Department of Political Science, with courtesy appointments in Women's Studies, Comparative and Literary Studies, and International Studies, at the University of Arizona in Tucson. She edited and contributed to *Gendered States: Feminist Re(Visions) of International Relations Theory* (Lynne Rienner, 1992) and co-authored, with Anne Sisson Runyan, *Global Gender Issues* (Westview Press, 1993 and 1999). Her most recent book is *A Critical Rewriting of Global Political Economy: Reproductive, Productive and Virtual Economies* (Routledge, 2003). She continues to research in the field of gender, politics and the global political economy.

Saskia Sassen is the Ralph Lewis Professor of Sociology at the University of Chicago and Centennial Visiting Professor at the London School of Economics. Her new book is *Territory, Authority and Right: From Medieval to Global Assemblages*, which will be published by Princeton University Press in 2006. Her most recent books prior to this have been the edited *Global Networks, Linked Cities* (Routledge, 2002) and the co-edited *Digital Formations: New Architectures for Global Order* (Princeton University Press, 2005). She has just completed a five-year research project for UNESCO on sustainable human settlement.

Björn Hettne is Professor in the Department of Peace and Development Research (Padrigu) at Göteborg University in Sweden. He is the author of a number of books and articles on development theory, international political economy, European integration, regionalism and ethnic relations. He was project leader and co-editor of the five-volume United Nations University–World Institute for Development Economics Research series on *New Regionalism* published by Palgrave Macmillan 1999–2001.

Adrian Leftwich is Senior Lecturer in Politics at the University of York in the United Kingdom. His authored books and edited collections include *South Africa: Economic Growth and Political Change* (Allison & Busby, 1974); *Redefining Politics* (Methuen, 1983); *New Developments in Political Science* (Edward Elgar, 1990); *Democracy and Development* (Polity, 1996); *States of Development* (Polity, 2000); and *What is Politics?* (Polity, 2004). He is currently working on a Department for International Development-funded research project concerning institutions for pro-poor growth and development.

Preface

This book is derived from the articles that appeared in Volume 10 Number 4 of the journal *New Political Economy*, which was published in December 2005. This issue marked the journal's tenth birthday and was explicitly designed by its editors to seek to establish the 'state of the debate' in new political economy after a decade of the journal's existence. We were pleased with the quality and range of the articles that we had commissioned and thought it might be useful to students and other readers interested in political economy if they were republished in book form. As outgoing Managing Editor of the journal I have written an additional short introductory chapter setting out the genealogy of new political economy and introducing the main themes of the collection.

I should therefore like to thank all of *NPE*'s other editors during its first decade of existence for all that they have done to help me to bring out the journal on time and in good shape. They are Andrew Gamble, Ankie Hoogvelt, Michael Dietrich, Michael Kenny, Graham Harrison and Nicola Phillips. We all also owe a great debt to our administrator, Sylvia McColm, who has worked tirelessly in the journal's cause over these years. I must further acknowledge the support over the same long period of Dr David Green and all the other staff with whom we have worked in the journal editorial and production departments of the Routledge Taylor and Francis Group. Finally, I must express my gratitude for the enthusiasm and speedy decision making that Craig Fowlie, publisher for Politics and International Studies within the Routledge books division, has latterly brought to this book project.

Anthony Payne
Sheffield

Abbreviations

APEC	Asia–Pacific Economic Cooperation
APT	ASEAN Plus Three countries
ASEAN	Association of Southeast Asian Nations
ASEM	Asia–Europe Meeting
AU	African Union
CEO	chief executive officer
CME	coordinated market economy
DfID	Department for International Development
EC	European Community
ECOWAS	Economic Community of West African States
EPZ	export processing zone
EU	European Union
GAD	gender and development
GATT	General Agreement on Tariffs and Trade
GPE	global political economy
ICT	information and communication technology
IMF	International Monetary Fund
IPE	international political economy
IR	international relations
LME	liberal market economy
NAFTA	North American Free Trade Agreement/Association
NEPP4	Netherlands Fourth National Environmental Policy Plan
NGO	non-governmental organisation
OAS	Organization of American States
OECD	Organization of Economic Co-operation and Development
SADC	Southern African Development Community
UN	United Nations
UNU	United Nations University
US	United States of America
WID	women in development
WIDER	World Institute for Development Economics Research
WTO	World Trade Organization

1 The genealogy of new political economy

Anthony Payne

Political economy is by general consent one of the oldest intellectual orientations in the history of the social sciences. So, what can sensibly be meant by seeking to introduce readers to 'key debates' within something called 'new political economy'? This introductory chapter seeks to answer that question and, in so doing, to set in context the various *tours d'horizon* of key subfields of political economy contained in the remaining chapters of this collection. It does so by exploring the thinking that lay behind the foundation in 1996 of a new academic journal named *New Political Economy* and establishing the full genealogy of the intellectual project that the originators of this new publication sought to sustain, and indeed advance, by the foundation of such a journal.

The first issue opened with an editorial which declared, with what in retrospect seems extraordinary confidence, that 'a new stage in the development of the world economic and political system has commenced, a new kind of world order'. Understanding this new world order was deemed to require 'new modes of analysis and new theories, and a readiness to tear down intellectual barriers and bring together many approaches, methods and disciplines which for too long have been apart'. We boldly labelled the approach to analysis that we sought to promote a 'new' political economy and declared that the methodology we had in mind 'rejects the old dichotomy between agency and structure, and states and markets, which fragmented classical political economy into separate disciplines' and 'seeks instead to build on those approaches in social science which have tried to develop an integrated analysis, by combining parsimonious theories which analyse agency in terms of rationality with contextual theories which analyse structures institutionally and historically'.[1] Such ambitions may have seemed somewhat overblown to many of those who read that first issue. Perhaps they still do. Yet they also give a sense that, in our minds at least, we were embarked upon a genuine intellectual adventure, that we were seeking to contribute to a rebuilding of the field of political economy and that, in that very spirit, we were asking for the support of scholars from all over the world who agreed with the general notion that a new political economy was emerging and needed to be explored in a novel way.

In setting out the project in that way in that opening editorial, the journal's editors in effect revealed that they not only subscribed to a reading of the history of political economy that emphasised its seventeenth and eighteenth century origins, but that they wanted consciously to revive the most fundamental of the classical traits of the field and restore them to prominence again in the contemporary era. In its initial form classical political economy addressed the issue of running a large family household or estate, but, as trade and commerce grew and modern state structures began to be built, it came to focus centrally upon analysis of the economic and political organisation of the emergent nation-state. Early mercantilist theories were thus distinguished by their emphasis on the need for nation-states to accumulate wealth and their expectation that the national interest would always be different from the sum of individual interests. For their part, the French physiocrats argued that agricultural production was the true foundation of economic value, whilst Scottish Enlightenment thinkers preferred to stress the central place of manufacturing and commerce in the economic affairs of states. Classical political economy eventually came of age in 1776 with the publication of Adam Smith's seminal *Inquiry into the Nature and Causes of the Wealth of Nations*. Smith famously showed how the development of a number of important market mechanisms could underpin the emergence of a more specialised division of labour in the economy and thereby bring about greater wealth and prosperity for all.

As Andrew Gamble argued in a separate publication, classical political economy always comprised three key discourses: 'a practical discourse about policy, concerning the best means of regulating and promoting the creation of wealth, and maximizing revenue for the public household; a normative discourse about the ideal form which the relationship between the state and the economy should take; and a scientific discourse about the way in which a political economy conceived as a social system actually operates'.[2] In his estimation Smith was pivotal less because of the originality of his theoretical insights than because the fact that he managed 'to combine all three discourses in an arresting new social vision'.[3] Indeed, Smith had himself defined political economy in *Wealth of Nations* as 'a branch of the science of a statesman or legislator' whose objectives were 'first, to provide a plentiful revenue or subsistence for the people, or more properly to enable them to provide such a revenue or subsistence for themselves; and secondly, to supply the state or commonwealth with a revenue sufficient for the public services'.[4] In good part as a consequence of Smith's influence, political economy continued to display this multi-faceted identity throughout its classical period, advancing further through the writings of David Ricardo and Thomas Malthus and climaxing with the publication in 1848 of John Stuart Mill's *Principles of Political Economy*.

At this point Marx enters into the genealogy of new political economy in a crucial way. It was Marx, in fact, who identified 'classical political economy' as his main intellectual target and, in so doing, coined the term. His original project had been to use his version of Hegelian logic to write a multi-volume critique of the categories of analysis and operating principles underpinning Mill's great work. What was eventually published from 1867 onwards as the first three volumes of *Capital* only partially realised this ambition: the anticipated volumes on the state, on international trade and on the world market never appeared in fully-fledged form. In his efforts to set out the laws of motion of capitalism and the consequent political implications of such a system Marx manifestly confronted all of the discourses of classical political economy – the practical, the normative and the scientific – and there can be no doubt that he assembled over his lifetime a hugely influential new view of political economy that has not only spread all over the world but has given rise to many of the concepts that continue to sit at the centre of social analysis. But at the same time it is very important to note that, for all of his genuine radicalism of thought, Marx did not break from the classical sense of what political economy was, and should be, about. In Gamble's words again, he 'did not dispute the basic conceptualisation of the field'.[5]

Nevertheless, as Michael Krätke and Geoffrey Underhill have recently noted in their brief account of the history of the tradition of political economy, Marx did represent an important turning point. As they put it, 'his revolutionary critique stimulated many to intensify the search for "pure science" removed from the complexities of history and socio-political interaction, generating "Economics" as opposed to the older and discredited term, "Political Economy" '.[6] Feeding off the same core principles that had underpinned Jeremy Bentham's 'utilitarian calculus' in moral philosophy, the so-called 'marginalist revolution' created over the course of the second half of the nineteenth century a new paradigm in economic analysis wherein increasingly abstract, indeed algebraic, calculations were made about the marginal utility of different economic choices in conditions of presumed scarcity. Stanley Jevons in Manchester, Carl Menger in Vienna and Léon Walras in Lausanne each contributed in their different ways to the birth of neoclassical economics and the concomitant ending of the presumed unity of economics and political economy.[7] Economics thereafter took off in its preferred direction, leaving new disciplines like economic history and sociology, and later on political science and development studies, to pick up the historical and institutionalist modes of analysis that had hitherto always been the defining features of political economy.

How, then, was the torch of political economy kept alive in the context of the emerging hegemony of neoclassical economics? Perhaps the best way to understand the various intellectual developments of the first half of the twentieth century in this broad field is to conceive of two such torches that in the end burned brightly enough and for long enough to help spark the major revival of political economy within the academy that has taken place over the last thirty years or so. One represented a continuing institutionalist current within economics, generally functioning as a dissident movement, although enjoying passing phases of prominence as and when economic and political conditions gave it sustenance; the other grew from revolutionary beginnings into a genuinely radical tradition that proposed in turn theories of imperialism, theories of the systemic link between development and underdevelopment, and eventually theories of the 'world system' as a whole. Both bodies of thought were influenced by Marx, the former in a more subtle, sometimes hesitant, way, the latter overtly and self-consciously. Although it is striking, and disappointing, that neither strand of thinking spoke much, if at all, to the other at the time they were being developed, they did at least keep political economy alive over the course of several difficult decades. They now constitute two further bodies of thought, in addition to the classical tradition, on which contemporary 'new political economy' has been able to trespass and build.

The resilience of the first of these two ongoing traditions can be traced back to Joseph Schumpeter. Although his own practical politics were conservative, Schumpeter read Marx and took his analysis seriously. He was also brought up in the immediate aftermath of the *Methodenstreit* – the famous clash between Menger's Austrian school which was promoting its version of neoclassical economics and the German historical school which still remained grounded in nationalist political economy – and deliberately sought in his own early thinking to bridge that fundamental chasm.[8] Schumpeter's cumulative theory of economic development has accurately been described as 'a comprehensive attempt to formulate an integrated theoretical, statistical, institutional and historical analysis of the mechanism and contours of capitalist economic evolution'.[9] In other words, he was as much economic historian and economic sociologist as economist pure and simple. Yet his initial programme of reconciliation and integration was notably unsuccessful, with economics continuing to grow in confidence as a separate discipline and the two sides of the old *Methodenstreit* becoming ever more entrenched in their respective camps during the early years of the twentieth century. Schumpeter himself moved to the United States in 1932 and addressed his concerns more and more to political questions, such as the role of the capitalist state. In fact, two of Schumpeter's contemporaries ultimately had more influence than he ever did in shaping the discourse of political economy, especially during the 1930s and 1940s when unemployment, worldwide war and the emergence of increasingly interventionist states inevitably brought forward new thinking. In these years John Maynard Keynes offered a compelling way of conceptualising *and* managing capitalism that was neither communist nor fascist in inspiration, with the result that, for a long period after the end of the Second World War, his ideas underpinned economic policy making in the advanced industrial world. Karl Polanyi also demonstrated forcefully that economic relations are always embedded in complex social relations without which market economies cannot operate. He famously detected a 'double movement' in this era whereby 'markets spread all over the face of the globe' and yet at the same time 'a network of measures and policies was integrated into powerful institutions designed to check the action of the market relative to labour, land and money'.[10] The influence of both of these strands of analysis has been particularly long lasting, with Keynesians and Polanyians continuing to contribute actively to the political economy debate to this day.

The second tradition has been characterised here as radical in the sense that it has always maintained an explicit or implicit connection to Marxism and, as such, has always taken it for granted that the political and economic domains are intertwined and need to be considered together. It has been widely charted and is generally well understood. It reappeared most strikingly after Marx in Lenin's depiction of imperialism as 'the highest stage of capitalism' in his well-known pamphlet published in 1916, itself a contribution to a passionate debate amongst Marxists of the time about the best way to theorise the new imperialism. It then ran on into the work of Paul Baran, André Gunder Frank and other dependency theorists in and out of Latin America, embraces the wide-ranging 'world system' theories of Immanuel Wallerstein and his followers, includes the French regulation school and feeds finally into the contemporary, highly fashionable embrace of Gramscian political economy in both cultural studies and international relations theory. The point about this tradition is that its contributions have often been ignored by the mainstream, not only in economics but also in other social science disciplines. It has been too easy perhaps for many to condemn this work as either potentially dangerous (in the context of the Cold War), or no longer relevant (in the context of the ending of the Cold War), or as applicable at best only to certain parts of the 'developing world'. Radical political economy of this genre has thus long been part of the intellectual tool-kit of development studies, for example, but for most of the post-1945 era it was kept at the margins of political science and international relations analysis, only being allowed in occasionally as a third, somewhat alien, voice in the latter discipline's so-called 'great debates' between realism and liberalism. However, from our perspective it constitutes a central part of the history of political economy, which again only needed to be recognised for what it was and reintegrated accordingly into the core of the subject.

In sum, as neoliberalism asserted itself across the Anglo-American world during the course of the 1980s, as the Berlin Wall was torn down and communism as a system collapsed, as something called 'globalisation' came to the fore, and, above all, as analysts struggled to make sense of these sea-changes in the world order in which they were living, there still existed a very fruitful, albeit neglected, history of political economy thinking to reach back to and draw into renewed use. It was obvious too that many of the separate disciplines of the social sciences were finding it increasingly hard to comprehend the many different facets of these changes within their conventional remits. As a result, scholars were uncertainly – but, nevertheless, with growing frequency – reaching out beyond the inherited boundaries of their particular disciplines. Economics, predictably, was initially the most hesitant in doing this (it was still generally very confident in the merits of its core methods). But political science was beginning actively to develop new research programmes in state theory, government–industry relations and public choice.[11] International relations was opening up to a new and very popular subfield, dubbed 'international political economy (IPE)', which sought to understand the increased salience of economic issues in world politics.[12] Area studies were also starting to enter more fully into these kinds of debates.[13] In sociology both structuration theory and strategic–relational theory endeavoured to break down some of the traditional gap between structural and agential modes of analysis by viewing structure as only being capable of expression through agency. For their part too, notions of culture and discourse were in the process of being widely imbricated across all the social sciences. In the face of these many manifestations of weakening disciplinary boundaries, even economics fell prey in the end to a reassertion of its dissident other, with the appearance of new Keynesian, Austrian and institutionalist schools.

In essence, this was the moment that *New Political Economy* sought to seize. The explicit aim of the journal was described as the creation of 'a forum for work which seeks to bridge both the empirical and conceptual divides which have characterised the field of political economy in the past'.[14] The core terrain that it set out to explore was defined as embracing four major subfields of political economy, each identified by reference to its key contemporary research agenda:

1 *Comparative political economy* – focusing on regulation and the policy regimes and institutional patterns which characterise alternative models of capitalism.
2 *The political economy of the environment* – focusing on sustainability and the question of which social and economic institutions are needed to reproduce existing patterns of social and economic life in the long run.
3 *The political economy of development* – focusing on inequality and the many structures and processes of the world system that produce distributional outcomes characterised by uneven development and wide variations in the wealth and poverty of particular regions, sectors, classes and states.
4 *International political economy* – focusing on the thesis of globalisation, the claim that there is a quickening pace towards the creation of a global economy and global culture, seeking to clarify both its extent and its impact, and the shape of the changing world order which is emerging through both specific events and long-term trends.

Above all, the editors concluded, 'we want to encourage conversations and exchanges of ideas and experiences across boundaries which in the past have often been unnecessarily fixed'.[15]

This last point has been integral to the whole new political economy project. It was meant to apply with particular force to a dialogue between the four core areas that were picked out as the particular focus of the journal. Thus comparative political economists were implicitly criticised for not showing sufficient awareness of the wider regional and global context within which national models of capitalism operated. Environmental political economists were encouraged to escape from the delusion that there were technical and/or market fixes to environmental problems and invited to set their work more fully within a social and political context. Development political economists were challenged to come in from the ghetto of an ever more unfashionable and declining subfield and place their traditional preoccupation with equality at the centre of a bigger stage. Finally, international political economists were invited to end their fixation with the limitations of conventional international relations theory and their conviction, understandable of course within limits, that IPE offers a 'better international relations' and enter instead an analytical world in which all political economy is by definition international in some sense, thereby rendering the reiteration implied by the prefix redundant. Many IPE scholars still remain reluctant to concede this obvious point, as Nicola Phillips has argued in a recent piece that echoes but also makes more explicit the critique of this subfield made in the editorial of the first issue of *New Political Economy*.[16]

Of course, it is only the journal's readers who can judge how well this admittedly ambitious project has been realised during its first decade. Its editors stand by the words of the original prospectus and can attest to the fact that several other scholars have seemed more than willing to tread the same road. For one thing, no less than 325 'new political economists' have been published in the journal over the course of its first ten volumes. We fully recognise that the field of political economy remains fragile compared to the main monodisciplinary giants of the social sciences, with their professional associations and committed readerships, but we think that it is now stronger within the academy than it was ten years ago and we hope that the journal has helped in some way to support that revival. As indicated in the preface to this book, we chose to celebrate *New Political Economy*'s birthday by preparing a special issue. We selected what we thought were the major intellectual debates with which the journal has been preoccupied over the last ten years and asked a number of distinguished authors (some of whom had previously published with us and some of whom had not) to review the state of those debates as they stood at the end of 2005 – what has lately been said, what has not been said, what ought now to be said. Those seven articles are accordingly reproduced here as guides to the key current debates in new political economy.

The discussion begins with two of the foundational debates in new political economy: those addressing 'models of capitalism' and 'globalisation'. Colin Crouch reviews the former and finds that the extensive neoinstitutionalist literature on capitalist diversity has many achievements to its name, especially the counterweight it has provided to easy arguments predicting convergence amongst the world's most powerful national political economies. Yet he also criticises this literature for adopting a labelling mode that has sought a unique theoretical box to which each individual model of capitalism must be assigned and argues powerfully for its replacement by a new analytical approach that anticipates 'recombinant capitalism' and considers to what extent traces of each of a series of models can be found within any given case. Mark Rupert addresses the study of globalisation by admitting at the outset the impossibility of reviewing this vast literature in anything like a comprehensive fashion, but then proceeds to reflect on what he personally has learnt from engagement with it, which is principally that globalisation is an intrinsically political project still integrally related to the historical process of capitalist social development. He thus prefers to talk of globalising capitalism rather than to see globalisation as a phenomenon *sui generis*. For all that, he ends his chapter by conceding the resilience of state-based forms of politics in reproducing the core structures of globalising capitalism and admitting, in particular, the new relevance of old arguments about imperial power.

As indicated earlier, the journal has always been concerned to embrace within its frame of reference research on environmental political economy and it has also in practice published quite a lot of work within gendered political economy. James Meadowcroft fully demonstrates the enormous range of issues now included within the first of these subfields and considers relevant theoretical perspectives, such as 'ecological modernisation' and 'managing the commons', before turning to address in detail the critical question within contemporary environmental political economy of whether it is possible to seek to steer socio-technological transformation along desired pathways. He concludes that this kind of 'transition management', although not without many difficulties to which he alludes, nevertheless points in the right direction, not least because it overtly engages with technological futures and assigns an active role to states in any serious attempt to come to terms with environmental pressures. V. Spike Peterson shows equally effectively the extent of the continuum of 'overlapping and ongoing' feminist interventions in political economy, revealing how these range from merely 'adding women' to the kind of analytical theory she espouses where gender is understood as a governing code that systematically shapes not only how we think but what we presume to know. On this more constructivist, indeed poststructuralist, basis she advances an extraordinarily rich 'rewriting' of many, many aspects of neoliberal globalisation, in its various productive, reproductive and virtual dimensions, which brutally exposes the impact of the cultural code of feminisation and thereby amply demonstrates the insights that can be derived from a fully-fledged gendering of political economy.

The new political economy of territory and space has been another repeated arena of debate in the journal over the last decade. Accordingly, Saskia Sassen reflects upon and develops further some of the themes of her past work on territory, authority and rights. She organises her argument around the claim that we are now seeing the incipient formation of a type of bordering capability and state practice regarding its territory that entails at least 'a partial denationalising of what has been constructed historically as national'. In particular, she suggests, and shows via a range of examples, that global processes frequently take place at subnational levels, thereby complicating and ultimately undermining more conventional analyses that insist on the mutual exclusivity of the national and the global. For his part, Björn Hettne seeks to move beyond the existing claims of the 'new regionalism' literature in political economy, to which he has himself contributed so much, by emphasising continuities as much as changes in the ongoing role of the regional dimension in global transformation. In particular, he suggests that regionalism might actually shape the unfolding new world order and draws an arresting distinction between the implications for regionalism of what he sees as the current struggle between two contrasting world order models, represented by the United States (US) (at least under the Presidency of George W. Bush) and the European Union (EU). In his take, the former envisages a neo-Westphalian world order grounded in a global concert of regional powers; the latter a post-Westphalian world order built upon a concept and practice of multiregionalism.

The coverage of key debates in new political economy is brought to a conclusion in a final chapter by Adrian Leftwich who reviews in wide-ranging fashion the modern history of the study of development within political economy. He argues trenchantly that announcements of its death have been premature: indeed, that, 'if development studies are dead, then so too is social science'. He shows how the analysis of development has, slowly but steadily, been returned to the traditions of the early, great social scientists wherein it was automatically presumed that economic, political and social institutions interacted over time and, moreover, could only be properly understood by foregrounding this very process of interaction. He is happy to see politics and political economy back 'in command', although fully recognising that understanding the political ideas, interests and practices which shape institutions also requires us to embrace the cultural and the ideological. Leftwich shows, in short, how the study of development, understood as a process that takes place in all societies of all types, can sit at the very heart of future work in new political economy.

Notes

1 Andrew Gamble, Anthony Payne, Ankie Hoogvelt, Michael Dietrich and Michael Kenny, 'Editorial: New Political Economy', *New Political Economy*, Vol. 1, No. 1 (1996), p. 5.
2 Andrew Gamble, 'The New Political Economy', *Political Studies*, Vol. 43, No. 3 (1995), p. 518.
3 *Ibid.*
4 Adam Smith, *An Inquiry into the Nature and Causes of the Wealth of Nations*, original edition 1776 (Allen & Unwin, 1964), p. 375.
5 Gamble, 'The New Political Economy', p. 518.
6 Michael R. Krätke and Geoffrey R. D. Underhill, 'Political economy: the revival of an "interdiscipline" ', in: Richard Stubbs and Geoffrey R. D. Underhill (eds), *Political Economy and the Changing Global Order* (Oxford University Press, 2005), p. 28.

7 For a very good analysis of the roots of neoclassical economics, see Matthew Watson, *Foundations of International Political Economy* (Palgrave Macmillan, 2005), pp. 51–9.
8 See Richard Swedberg, *Joseph A. Schumpeter: His Life and Work* (Polity, 1991).
9 Alexander Ebner, 'Schumpeter, Joseph Alois (1883–1950)', in: R. J. Barry Jones (ed.), *Routledge Encyclopedia of International Political Economy*, Vol. 3 (Routledge, 2001), p. 1369.
10 Karl Polanyi, *The Great Transformation: The Political and Economic Origins of Our Time* (Beacon Press, 1944), p. 76.
11 See, for example, Gamble, 'The New Political Economy', pp. 523–30.
12 See, for example, Craig N. Murphy and Roger Tooze (eds), *The New International Political Economy* (Lynne Rienner, 1991).
13 See, for example, Anthony Payne, 'The New Political Economy of Area Studies', *Millennium: Journal of International Studies*, Vol. 27, No. 2 (1998), pp. 253–73.
14 Gamble, Payne, Hoogvelt, Dietrich and Kenny, 'Editorial: New Political Economy', p. 8.
15 *Ibid.*, p. 11.
16 Nicola Phillips, ' "Globalizing" the study of International Political Economy', in: Nicola Phillips (ed.), *Globalizing International Political Economy* (Palgrave Macmillan, 2005), pp. 1–19.

2 Models of capitalism

Colin Crouch

That capitalist economies might take diverse forms has been long recognised by some scholars. Sometimes this diversity has been seen as a matter of evolutionary development. This was true of Max Weber's ideal-type approach, that of the advocates of postwar modernisation theory, and of those who followed Antonio Gramsci's identification of a Fordist phase of capitalism that was deemed to succeed the classic free-market form. This last idea flourished particularly in the French *régulationiste* school.[1] These approaches, different from each other though they are, all see some forms of capitalism superseding, and as therefore in some sense superior to, earlier modes. Hence these are not theories of a true diversity in the sense of a continuing multiplicity of forms, the historical superiority of any of which might never come to an issue. Analysts willing to adopt a less historicist approach have been rarer. The modern *locus classicus* was Andrew Shonfield's work,[2] which examined the role of various institutions surrounding the economy – various branches of the state, banks, stock exchanges – in a number of Western European countries, the United States and Japan. Although he thought some were more efficient than others – in particular, he was impressed by those that inserted some elements of planning into otherwise free markets – he did not talk in terms of historical transcendence.

When more theoretically inclined political scientists and sociologists returned to considering economic questions in the 1980s, they resumed Shonfield's concern with national politico-economic systems and hence national varieties of capitalism. Occasionally sub-types would be recognised within a national economy (mainly with regard to Italy and Spain), but these sub-types have nearly always been geographically subdivided, so the concept of territorially based economies has been retained. This does not mean that each nation-state has been seen as embodying its own unique form of capitalism; rather, national cases are grouped together under a small number of contrasted types.

This literature has many achievements. It has provided an intellectual counterweight to easy arguments about globalisation, which predict an inevitable trend towards similarity among the world's economies. Neoinstitutionalist accounts of diversity have provided both theoretical arguments and some empirical demonstrations to suggest that these may be great oversimplifications. However, if we are to model the diversity of economic institutions more scientifically, and particularly if we are to study institutional change and innovation, we need to deconstruct the wholes that contemporary institutionalism takes for granted and discover their constituent elements – elements which are able to survive in combinations other than those thus identified.

Acceptance of the value of taking this approach would have considerable implications for the future study of capitalist diversity. It has in particular a major methodological consequence: empirical cases should be studied, not to determine to which (singular) of a number of theoretical types they should each be allocated, but to determine which (plural) of these forms are to be found within them, in roughly what proportions, and with what change over time. This alternative is less ambitious than the current fashion, in that it does not enable us to map the economic world with a few parsimonious categories. But it is also more ambitious, partly because it corresponds more closely to the requirements of scientific analysis, but also because it is able to accommodate and account for change taking place within empirical cases. This is something which most of the neoinstitutionalist literature on capitalist diversity finds difficult to do, leading to the functionalism and determinism of much of its analysis.

The aim of this chapter is to develop this critique of the existing literature, to highlight some promising recent trends and to point towards the new approach indicated above. This last, which involves first deconstructing into constituent elements and then being ready to recombine into new shapes the aggregated forms of currently dominant analyses, is developed more fully elsewhere.[3]

Pitfalls in the formulation of types

The smallest number of theoretical types consistent with the idea of diversity is two. For almost all writers on models of capitalism, one is always the free-market model of neoclassical economics. This constitutes the principal intellectual antagonist for neoinstitutionalists, even when they argue that it accounts for only a highly specific form of capitalism.[4] There must be at least one other form to make a theory of diversity: hence dichotomies. At the other extreme there is no theoretical limit to the number of forms that might be identified, but theories rarely propose more than five or six. Given the relatively small number of empirical cases of advanced capitalism for those tied to a national case approach (currently around 25), it is difficult to sustain more than a handful of types without lapsing into empiricism.

The work of Michel Albert, who made the original contribution to dualistic analysis, is typical.[5] He modelled two types of capitalism, which were seen in an antagonistic relationship. They are labelled in geocultural terms as Anglo-Saxon and *rhénan* (Rhenish). The former defines free-market capitalism, considered to be embodied in the Anglophone countries.[6] The second takes its name from certain characteristics considered to be common to the riparian countries of the Rhine: Germany, the Netherlands, Switzerland, more problematically France. However, not only is the author uncertain whether France's institutions fully belong to this type (an anxiety which was one of his main motives in writing the book), but Japan and Scandinavia are considered to be part of it. The broad institutional range gathered together to form this second type is disconcerting. The essential idea is a capacity to make long-term decisions that maximise certain collective rather than individual goods. But this means ignoring differences among the very diverse forms of collectivism found.

It is important to note that this dualism in the identification of types of economy parallels the debate between political philosophies – neoliberalism and social democracy – which lies behind the analysis and behind most contemporary political debate.[7] This has created some confusion over whether neoinstitutionalism's confrontation is with neoclassical economics, and therefore at the analytical level only; or with neoliberal politics, implying an ideological confrontation; or with all political practices associated with the anti-Keynesian and pro-capitalist forces which came to prominence during the period.

One form taken by both the scientific and the ideological debate has been dispute over which kind of capitalism delivers the best economic performance. As David Coates showed in his study of models of capitalism, this has been an extraordinarily difficult issue to resolve.[8] He unravelled the complexities of the components of economic growth and other indicators of performance, in particular pointing out the importance for comparative studies of where national cases have stood at particular moments in relation to the overall evolution of the world capitalist system. He showed how it had been a mistake for institutionalists to seize at various times on particular national examples as proving the superiority of economies not based on pure markets: the models selected had a tendency to start to underperform. Analysts have been on stronger grounds when making either a weaker or a different claim. The former is that various kinds of institutional economy can do just as well as (not necessarily better than) a pure market one; the latter is the argument that institutional economies enabled the coexistence of high levels of economic performance alongside the pursuit of certain other social goals (for example, a relatively egalitarian incomes distribution) not readily available to purer market economies.

Neoclassical analysis considers how economic actors would behave if a world of perfect markets existed. It usually but not necessarily incorporates the normative assumption that both economy and society would be improved were institutions to take this form, but neoclassical economists are at liberty to consider that this may not always constitute a practical proposition; they are not bound by their analytical approach to any particular policy conclusions, or to consider that the world in reality takes a certain form. It is neoliberalism which, as a political creed rather than a form of analysis, not only definitely adopts a positive normative evaluation of markets, but also believes that they could always be introduced in practice.

But in practice not even neoliberals do this. A by-product of the ideological dominance of neoliberalism since the 1980s, and in particular its association with the most powerful nation-state on earth – the United States – has produced a tendency among even serious analysts to assume that certain practices and institutions constitute part of the neoliberal paradigm just because they are found in the US. The characteristics of the neoliberal model are derived from empirical observation of what is thought to be its main empirical example. But it is logically impossible to derive the characteristics of a theoretical category from the characteristics of an example of it, as the theoretical characteristics have to be known before a case can be considered to be such an example. For example, an extremely powerful, scientifically oriented military sector, tying a number of contracting firms into close and necessarily secretive relations with central government departments, is a fundamental attribute of the US economy, and central to much of its innovative capacity in such sectors as aerospace and computing. The operation of such a military sector has nothing to do with the principles of either neoclassical economics or neoliberal politics. Analysts respond to this in two ways. Some just ignore the existence of this sector and its special characteristics in their account of the US economy. For example, the Organization for Economic Co-operation and Development (OECD) felt able to describe the US as a country lacking any close support from government for industry.[9] Alternatively, it argues that the defence sector is somehow part of the US 'liberal' model, without noting the difficulties of such an assumption.[10] Indeed, as Campbell and Pedersen argue, at the practical level neoliberalism has not been the monolith that both its advocates and opponents set it up to be.[11] Within it have been contained a diversity of practices, some not particularly coherent with others. Kjær and Pedersen point, for example, to clear differences from the normally presented model in the form taken by so-called neoliberalism in Denmark,[12] whilst King and Wood have even demonstrated significant distinctions between the neoliberalisms of the United Kingdom and the United States in the 1980s, two cases normally seen as joint paradigms.[13]

The collection of studies edited by Peter Hall and David Soskice under the name *Varieties of Capitalism* represents the most ambitious and significant contribution to date of the dualist approach.[14] It draws much from Albert, though it barely acknowledges his contribution. Their book has become the emblematic citation for all studies of diversity in capitalist economies. It is also an example of the preoccupation of many neoinstitutionalists with coming to terms with and, in this case, eventually becoming absorbed by, an idealised version of neoliberalism. It seeks not only to allocate every developed capitalist economy to one or other of two categories, but derives from this account a theory of comparative advantage and a list of the kind of products in which the country will specialise.[15] This is achieved with the aid of certain assumptions concerning what constitutes radical and what incremental innovation – a characteristic which is considered to differentiate whole classes of goods and services. It is this factor, combined with its use of this sectoral analysis to account for certain important developments in different national economies during the 1990s, which has made the account so appealing.

Despite some ambiguity about a possible third model, these authors work with an essentially dualist approach along the rationale outlined above. They specify, first, a liberal market economy (LME) identified with neoliberal policies, radical innovation, new sectors of the economy and the Anglophone countries (Australia, Canada, Ireland, New Zealand, the United Kingdom, but primarily the US). Germany is at the centre of a second type, called a coordinated market economy (CME), where social and political institutions engage directly in shaping economic action. This form is linked to social democracy, incremental innovation, declining economic sectors and non-Anglophone countries.

It is odd that the core linguistic uniting characteristic of the LMEs, the only generalisation that really works, is never actually discussed as such. More aware of Irish sensitivities than most authors, Hall and Soskice always talk of 'Anglo-Saxon and Irish' economies. But, perhaps because like others they resist the far simpler and more accurate 'Anglophone', they miss some serious potential implications of this. For example, one of the most impressive pieces of evidence cited by them to support their contention that radical innovation is concentrated in LME countries and only incremental innovation in CMEs is work carried out for them on patent citations.[16] This reveals a strong statistical tendency for patents taken out in Anglophone countries to cite scientific sources, while those taken out in continental Europe and Japan tend to cite previous patents or non-scientific sources. The six leading countries out of 18 studied are all Anglophone (headed by Ireland). *Prime facie* distinction between radical and incremental innovation does seem to be well proxied by that between academic and product citations, and one can see this being related to the character of research in firms, research centres and universities. But it is also possible that firms in Anglophone countries are more likely to cite articles in the overwhelmingly Anglophone literature of global science than those in other countries. Further, liberal market economies are largely defined by their having characteristics determined by common law traditions; these also encourage the use of patenting of innovations to a greater extent than civil law systems. Therefore higher levels of patenting – as a legal device, not necessarily a reflection of actual innovation – will be most widespread in common-law, and hence liberal market, systems. This distortion may help explain why, according to Estevez-Abe, Iversen and Soskice, New Zealand has more radical technological innovative capacity than Germany, Sweden or Switzerland.[17]

The LME type of economy depends on labour markets that set wages through pure competition and permit very little regulation to protect employees from insecurity, and on a primary role for stock markets and the maximisation of shareholder value in achieving economic goals. Such an economy is considered by the authors to be poor at making minor adaptive innovations, because employers make inadequate investment in employee skills which might produce such innovations; but it excels at radical innovations, because the combination of free labour markets and external shareholders makes it relatively easy to switch resources rapidly to new and profitable firms and areas of activity. A CME, featuring corporatist wage-setting, strongly regulated labour markets and corporate financing through long-term commitments by banks, follows exactly the reverse logic.

Hall and Soskice stress strongly that they are depicting two *enduring* forms of capitalism, because each has different comparative advantages. However, those of the CME form are located solely in minor adaptations within traditional and declining industries, while LMEs have assigned to them all future-oriented industries and services sectors. In the end, therefore, this is a neoinstitutionalism that fully accepts the logic of neoclassicism set out above: in the long run, all institutions other than the pure market fail to cope with the future. Since these different forms of capitalism are considered to have been the products of historical *longues durées*, it also means that the German economy never was radically innovative in the past, which requires explaining away many past events in the economic history of such German industries as chemicals, machinery, steel and motor vehicles when these sectors were at the forefront of technological advance.

This brings us to a further fundamental point: typologies of this kind are fixed over time; they make no provision for changes in characteristics. As Zeitlin puts it, approaches like that of Hall and Soskice render learning almost impossible. Or, as Bertoldi says, they ignore any impact of change in the world economy and make no allowance for evolutionary development. As Hay has it, this literature tends to take either a spatialising approach (the elaboration of models, as in the cases we are discussing here) or a temporalising one (identifying historical phases, and therefore probably giving more scope to actors' capacity to change, but ignoring synchronic diversity). It is not necessary for neoinstitutionalist analysis to be as rigid as this.[18]

Hall and Soskice also assume automatically that all innovation within new industries represents radical innovation, while all within old ones can represent only incremental innovation. This is because they use different sectors as proxies for different types of innovation. According to such an approach, when Microsoft launches another mildly changed version of Windows it still represents radical innovation, because information technology is seen as a radical innovation industry; but, when some firms eventually launch the hydrogen-fuelled motor engine, this will only be an incremental innovation, because the motor industry is an old industry. Further, the authors do not confront the leading position of two clearly CMEs (Finland and Sweden) in new telecommunications technologies and the Nordic countries generally in medical technologies.[19] Robert Boyer has shown that the institutional pattern found in the Nordic countries can favour high-technology growth in information and communication technologies as much as the Anglo-American one. This is completely lost in accounts that insist on dualism and an *a-priori* allocation of institutional patterns.[20] Instead of the *a-priori* paradigm case methodology, Boyer used Charles Ragin's Boolean techniques to derive institutional patterns empirically.[21] Booleian algebra assigns category values (not interval ones) to the mass of characteristics that constitute a whole. Individual characteristics are identified as either present or absent. This enables a search for shared characteristics in a number of complex empirical cases, assisting the researcher to determine which characteristics tend to be found together, and which are rarely or never associated.

A further serious flaw in the *Varieties of Capitalism* approach is that it misunderstands the work of individual innovative companies. While engaging in radical innovation, firms usually also need to bring out products with minor improvements in order to sustain their position in markets while they wait for a radical innovation to bear fruit; but, according to the Hall-Soskice model, it is not possible for firms within an LME to succeed at incremental innovation. It is a major advance of the approach that they focus on the firm as an actor, rather than take a macroeconomic approach to the study of economic success. However, many of the advantages of this are vitiated by the fact that their model allows the firm virtually no autonomy outside its national macroeconomic context.

These authors further follow conventional wisdom in arguing that the superiority of American (or Anglophone) firms over German ones results from the fact that in the Anglophone countries all managerial power is concentrated in the hands of a chief executive officer (CEO) who is required to maximise shareholder value, with employees engaged on a hire-and-fire basis with no representative channels available to them. Here they are failing to distinguish between the firm as an organisation and as a marketplace. By seeing the CEO's power as being solely to maximise share values by the use of a hire-and-fire approach to management, they are able to present the firm in an LME as solely the latter and not as an organisation. They can therefore dispense with the knowledge accumulated in the theory of the firm, which distinguishes between market and organisation, and presents at least the large firm as an organisation with personnel policies, and with management having a wider range of discretion and possibilities than just maximising share values.

This is significant. In reality firms differ considerably in the extent to which they construct organisational systems, internal labour markets and distinctive ways of working, even developing specific corporate cultures, rather than simply establishing themselves as spaces where a number of markets intersect. For example, a firm that develops a distinctive approach to work among its workforce as part of its competitive strategy cannot depend on a hire-and-fire personnel policy. Employees need to be inducted into the firm's approach and are likely to demand some understandings about security if they are to commit themselves in the way that management wants. Rapid hire-and-fire meets neither of these needs. This fundamental difference in corporate strategy has nothing at all to do with differences between LMEs and CMEs; both can exist within either, particularly the former. Neglect of the firm as an organisation is thus a weakness of much neoinstitutionalist analysis. It is caused by the obsession already noted with a dichotomy between two mutually incompatible politico-economic ideologies, a dichotomy in which the distinction between firm and market is not at issue. At times Hall and Soskice seem to regard the organisational structure of the firm (or corporate hierarchy) as a characteristic of both LMEs and CMEs, and therefore an irrelevant variable – though it should be conceded that the relevant passage is worded ambiguously, as follows:

> All capitalist economies also contain the hierarchies that firms construct to resolve problems that markets do not address adequately. . . . In liberal market economies, these are the institutions on which firms rely to develop the relations on which their core competences depend.[22]

They seem here to be building into their model a functionalist balancing item, implying that hierarchy will exist to the extent that it can 'resolve problems'. In that case, why does their theory not build into the features of both LMEs and CMEs those that they would respectively need in order to have them cope with the kinds of innovation that their theory says is impossible for them? At the level of type-building one should not pick and choose which institutional features automatically receive compensation and which do not. As Weber originally formulated the concept, ideal types are 'one-sided accentuations', pressing home the logical implications of a particular kind of structure. The aim is not to provide an accurate empirical description, but a theoretical category, to be used in the construction of hypotheses. Again, the authors are not building their theory deductively, but are reading back empirical detail from what they want to be their paradigm case of an LME – the US – into their formulation of the type. It is simply not possible within their methodological approach to ask the question: is everything important that occurs in the US economy the embodiment of free markets?

Hall and Soskice do briefly consider diversity within the CME form. Apart from Germany, they also see Japan, Switzerland, the Netherlands, Belgium, Sweden, Norway, Denmark, Finland and Austria as unproblematic – though differences between what they call 'industry-based' coordination of the German type and 'group-based' coordination found in Japan and Korea are recognised.[23] In an earlier work Soskice fully recognised these two distinct forms of CME: a Northern European model, and the 'group-co-ordinated' East Asian economies.[24] ('Northern Europe' is here defined by Soskice to include Italy but not France.) But not much is made of the distinction in the full development of theory or cases.

A 'Mediterranean' group (France, Italy, Spain, Portugal, Greece and Turkey) is also given some recognition. Like Albert before them, Hall and Soskice accept that France is somehow different, and consider that a so-called Southern European group (including France) probably constitutes a third, state-led, post-agrarian model.[25] This at least makes matters more differentiated, although it produces a type curiously unable to distinguish between the French state and the Italian or Greek ones. Sometimes this 'Mediterranean' group is seen as being empirically poised somewhere between the LME and CME model, which enables the authors to insist that LME and CME remain the only points which require theoretical definition. But elsewhere the Mediterranean countries are treated as examples of CMEs; Thelen, for example, treats Italy as almost unambiguously a 'German-type' 'co-ordinated' economy.[26] One of the starting points of the model was an earlier paper by Soskice criticising the Calmfors and Driffill model of wage bargaining.[27] This model had contrasted economies with centralised and decentralised collective bargaining arrangements, classing the French, Italian and Japanese among the latter. Soskice pointed out that, although these three countries were not as coordinated as Germany or Sweden, one could identify within them various mechanisms that ensured some coordination of wage bargaining. He found (within the sample of countries being considered) that only the UK and the US lacked such mechanisms; therefore, all other cases were classified as CMEs. Both here and in Hall and Soskice, the basic drive of the dichotomy is to confront the neoclassical model with a single rival type.

Beyond dichotomies

Some contributors to the study of capitalist diversity have gone beyond dichotomies. Vivien Schmidt has three models of European capitalism: 'market' (very similar to the LME model), 'managed' (with an 'enabling' state that encourages economic actors to cooperate, more or less the CME model) and 'state' (an interventionist state of the French kind).[28] The last is designed to remedy the neglect of this form by Hall and Soskice. Acknowledging that the role of the state has declined considerably in France in recent years, she points out that its background role and historical legacy remain of considerable importance in enhancing national economic capacity. But, indeed, much the same could be said of the US state, whose role in the vast defence-related sector could well be defined as 'state enhancement' of economic capacity. Schmidt also manages to be sensitive both to change and to its *timing*.[29] She studies how countries embodying each of these types respond to the challenges of globalisation and Europeanisation. A central hypothesis is that these challenges do not lead to simple convergence. Governments of the various countries have responded in complex ways, producing new forms of diversity. If there is any overall convergence, it is mainly towards a loss of extreme characteristics and thus some sharing of attributes from the various models. And these diversities are full of interesting paradoxes: the UK, having had in many respects the weakest economy of the three, was thus the earliest to be forced to come to terms with the pressures of globalisation. As a result, it now appears better prepared to face that challenge than Germany which, being initially the strongest economically, could delay adjustment.

A second hypothesis fundamental to her study is that political discourse has been particularly important in shaping national responses to the challenge. By this Schmidt means, not just that different substantive discourses were adopted, but that these took different forms. She distinguishes between 'communicative' and 'coordinating' discourse forms. The former, more suited to centralised systems like the British and French, inform the public of what needs to be done; the latter, more typical of Germany, are used to develop consensus among powerful actors who cannot be controlled from the centre. This work therefore marks a refreshing shift towards an actor-centred and non-determinist account. Schmidt by no means discounts the existence of very strong structures, within which her actors need to operate. But these are malleable by innovative actors, in particular by politics. She criticises particularly effectively the oversimplified accounts that characterise much rational choice work in international political economy. This, she argues, is a curiously depoliticised form of study of politics, assuming as it does that the interests of nation-states can be modelled in a straightforward way, with fixed, consciously held preferences. She demonstrates effectively how governments in the three countries of concern to her study developed very varied positions in relation to Europeanisation: for example, the UK was quickest to respond to many of the single market initiatives, but slowest to the single currency. This can all be explained, and she provides good explanations, but these require tactical and historically contingent political actors.

But Schmidt still follows the practice of identifying empirical cases as standing for ideal types. This is unfortunate, because her own actual practice is well able to cope with the implications of seeing cases as amalgams of types: her actors are creative political schemers, looking for chances to change and innovate, not automata acting out the parts the theorist has set for them. And, as noted, she succeeds in showing how over time individual countries have moved around the triangular space which her particular model of types of capitalism allows them.

Several other authors present three or more forms of capitalism, or of elements of capitalism, nearly always retaining a geocultural approach. Gøsta Esping-Andersen's analysis of different types of welfare state embodies variables relating to the outcomes of political struggle, or dominant political traditions, which avoids some of the functionalist implications of the *Varieties of Capitalism* model.[30] Again, one starting point is free-market or liberal capitalism associated with the Anglophone group of countries, and another is Germany, producing a conservative 'continental European' model. There is, however, a third, social-democratic pole, geographically associated with Scandinavia. Critics of Esping-Andersen's model have concentrated: on identifying mixed cases (Castles and Mitchell); on stressing how the treatment of women in different systems does not seem to correspond to the simple typology (Daly); or on breaking up the over-extended 'conservative continental' category. A fourth type has now been clearly established, separating Southern European welfare states from this one on the basis of their particularly large role for the family (Naldini) and other informal institutions (Ferrera). Ebbinghaus, concentrating on policies for combatting early exit from the labour market, which he sees as deeply related to the form of the overall welfare regime, adds a fifth type based on Japan. All these works continue to depend on the characteristics of paradigm cases, which can be highly misleading. For example, Viebrock, in a study of different forms of unemployment benefit systems, has shown how Sweden – usually the absolute paradigm case of social democracy – has for reasons of political history retained a role for voluntary associations alongside the state in the organisation of its unemployment insurance system.[31]

A strong move away from dualism, which neither starts from nor privileges the free-market model, is the scheme of Richard Whitley.[32] He builds up a set of fully sociological models of capitalism based on six types of business system (fragmented, coordinated industrial district, compartmentalised, state-organised, collaborative, and highly coordinated), related to a number of different behavioural characteristics.[33] He also presents five different ideal types of firms (opportunist, artisan, isolated hierarchy, collaborative hierarchy, allied hierarchy)[34] and a diversity of links between these types and certain fundamental institutional contexts (the state financial system, skill development and control, trust and authority relations).[35] Significantly, Whitley's main fields of study are Japan, Korea, Taiwan and other Far Eastern economies, rather than either the American or the German cases, and he is therefore further removed from the obsession with neoliberalism and a contrast between it and a model of 'organised capitalism' that sometimes distorts the analysis of those who concentrate on Western Europe and North America.

By far the best and most sophisticated approach to a 'post-dualist' typology of capitalism to date is that established by Bruno Amable.[36] He collected quantitative data on a vast range of characteristics of the national economies of most OECD countries: product markets, labour markets, financial systems and social protection. He uses literally dozens of individual indicators to assess each. He then allows a typology of groups of countries to be formed empirically by these data; he does not start from paradigm cases. This procedure gives him five groups, which, as with other authors, fall into familiar geocultural patterns: market-based (primarily Anglophone), social democratic (Nordic), Asian (Japan and Korea), Mediterranean (Southern European) and Continental European (continental Western European less the Nordic and Mediterranean countries). He further finds (as have others[37]) that this last group does not show much internal coherence, and for some purposes splits it further into two sub-groups: one comprising the Netherlands and Switzerland, the other Austria, Belgium, France and Germany. Moreover, Amable is not afraid to draw attention to further diversity for some of the characteristics, with the result that countries do not always figure within their normal group.

At times Amable lapses from his finely nuanced stance. For example, the book ends with a future- and policy-oriented dialectic between the market-based and a simplified and generalised Continental European model.[38] It seems that engaging in the rhetoric of debate about the future course of capitalism leads always to dualism, even when, as in Amable's case, the best strength of the author's position lies precisely in the demonstration of a far more differentiated world. He also depends necessarily for his data on sources like the OECD which are often constructed with in-built biases. For example, although at one point Amable acknowledges the importance of military-related research and production in many of the high-tech sectors of the US economy, he follows the OECD in excluding all consideration of this from the indicators of the role of the state in the economy and of the regulation of external trade.[39] These minor criticisms apart, Amable has demonstrated that a genuinely scientific approach, using very extensive and diverse kinds of data, produces a useful and coherent typology comprising five or six types, at the same time enabling clear recognition of exceptions within types.

Dichotomisers will argue that they are applying the principle of parsimony and Occam's razor to complex schemes of Amable's or Whitley's kind. They will claim that, while there is clearly a loss of information if one collapses Whitley's 'co-ordinated industrial district, compartmentalised, state-organised, collaborative, and highly co-ordinated' mechanisms into the single idea of a CME, that idea seizes on the essential point that divides all these forms from the pure market one: coordination. But, as Scott and Hay have separately argued, parsimony must not become an excuse for inaccuracy and ignoring important diversity.[40] Is coordination the fundamental attribute of all the types in Whitley's list? On what grounds could this quality be regarded as more fundamental than the other characteristics which divide them, especially since the coordination takes place at very different levels? Recent developments in the governance approach draw attention to the role of collective competition goods provided by various governance modes in local economies, without demonstrating anything remotely strong enough to be called national 'coordination'.[41] This suggests the possibility of analyses more moderate than those addressed at the whole macroeconomy.

Meanwhile, Hage and Alter have convincingly demonstrated analytical distinctions among several institutional forms.[42] In that case, to apply Occam's razor to reduce them all to one idea of coordination is to cut into serious theoretical and empirical flesh. An explanation becomes more parsimonious than another when it uses a smaller number of explanatory variables *while explaining at least as much* as its opponent. For example, it is more parsimonious to model the solar system as heliocentric than terracentric, because the former uses far simpler mathematics to account for at least as many planetary movements as the latter. We should be far less impressed with the heliocentrist if she had to say: 'Forget about the outer planets; this theory is more parsimonious because it just looks at the inner ones'. But contemporary social science often makes use of precisely this kind of argument, using the idea of parsimony as meaning a kind of rough, tough macho-theory that concentrates on the big picture and ignores detail.

As Whitley's formulations demonstrate, the relationships between different forms and different behavioural characteristics present a varied patchwork of similarities and differences, not a set of polar contrasts. This suggests in turn the fundamental point: that individual empirical cases might well comprise more complex amalgams still of elements from two or more theoretical types. Whitley himself treats a fragmented market model of economic organisation separately from one dominated by large firms, and is therefore able to see the US itself as a hybrid of two different forms of capitalism rather than a pure case. This question has considerable practical implications, which are discussed more fully elsewhere.[43] It is often recognised by authors who speak of 'hybrid' forms. For example, Schmidt suggests strongly that some changes in French institutions are making that case increasingly a hybrid, with borrowing from Germany as well as from neoliberal sources.[44] Jackson suggests that hybridisation, as opposed to simple imitation of the exogenous, is the usual outcome of attempts at 'borrowing' institutions, even under extreme periods of transition, such as Germany or Japan under postwar occupation.[45] Other researchers have shown the power of hybrid cases in achieving important reforms in welfare state organisation.[46] Zeitlin discusses various national cases that have become exceptions to their 'types' as the result of mixing institutional forms at the initiative of what I would call institutional entrepreneurs. Considering an earlier period, Windolf discusses how French family capitalism played an important part in the country's postwar modernisation, merging with advanced financial means of control and the strong state to produce a dynamic new model. 'Hybridisation' deals with only one way in which cases may deviate from types, and it is still very close to the idea of clear, macro-level types, because it sees these as the source of the hybridisation. However, it does constitute an important challenge to simple equations of cases and types.[47]

Questioning the centrality of the nation-state

The centrality of the nation-state in most typologies of capitalist diversity also needs to be questioned. This centrality is found in most neoinstitutionalist studies, including those on 'social [that is, national] systems of innovation and production'.[48] It is also central to work from the parallel but distinct literature on 'national systems of innovation'.[49] At one level the case is well made. Very extensive elements of governance in the industrial and post-industrial societies of which we have knowledge do operate at the level of the nation-state: states have been the main sources of law, and most associations and organisations target themselves at the state.[50] Given that markets are framed by law, this means that, of the modes of governance usually discussed in governance theory, the state itself (obviously), markets and various levels of associations are all heavily defined at national level, while community and informal associations exist at a lower geographical level. Even research that explicitly works at comparisons between regional or other substate geographical levels often has to acknowledge the importance of the nation-state as a major instance for the determination of socioeconomic variables.[51]

But many macro-level neoinstitutionalists go further than this and postulate virtually hermetically sealed national institutions – often because they are concerned to address debates about economic and social policy, and these are mainly conducted at national levels. Radice argues that this has perhaps been particularly the case for left-of-centre analysts desiring to 'bring the state back in', leading to an exaggeration of the importance of national policy.[52] More generally, neoinstitutionalists are led to stress the nation-state by their functionalist assumptions, which model discrete, autonomous systems, each equipped with their sets of institutions, like a body with its organs. There are also methodological advantages in being able to treat nation-states as discrete units of analysis, as many economic data are produced at national levels. Theorists of the diversity of capitalism are therefore eager to play down the implications of globalisation, and argue intelligently and forcefully against the naive assumptions of much other literature that globalisation somehow abolishes the significance of national differences.[53]

However, the position of the nation-state as the definer of the boundaries of cases is not so fixed that it should be taken for granted *per definitionem*. This is particularly obvious with respect to multinational corporations. As Beyer shows,[54] large firms draw on resources from a range of different national bases; it is very difficult to identify them with particular national types and to see their institutional possibilities as being constrained by their country or countries of location. As Jackson puts it, national models of capitalism are becoming 'institutionally incomplete'.[55] This seems particularly true where international corporations are concerned, but even firms that are nationally owned and operate primarily within one nation-state have access to knowledge, links and practices existing outside the national borders. Radice similarly criticises the national innovation system literature for a kind of mercantilism, arguing that it does not take adequate account of the fact that technology is always a public/private collaboration, and that the private actors are usually global firms. Something always 'leaks' abroad from national programmes; innovation is at once global and national.[56] He also points out the falsity of the dichotomy between so-called globalising and national forces, as though one could identify them and then establish their relative importance.[57] The phenomena associated with globalisation are brought about at the behest of domestic actors working to influence national governments. As Helleiner earlier made the point: internationalisation is not an independent variable, because it is an outcome of state policy.[58]

Radice demonstrates a different weakness of nation-state-based analysis by pointing out that all states are not equal as units.[59] The US is able to borrow to fund its deficits in a way not available to others, which means that comparing the 'performance' of that economy with others is not a true comparison of institutional capacities. One can move from that observation to point out that nation-states cannot always be treated as a series of unit instances of the same phenomenon; they are also linked together in a hierarchical way to form an overall system, as Wallerstein and other world-system analysts have showed.[60] For example, the units 'Portugal' and 'France' cannot be treated as equal units within which the effects of various independent variables can be independently and comparatively assessed, because they are partly defined by their relationship to each other. Scott stresses the need to consider a range of levels: world system, society (nation-state), organisational field, organisational population, organisation and organisational subsystem.[61] As he points out, different disciplines tend to look at different components of this. Hollingsworth and Boyer are helpfully explicit that their scheme can be used at subnational and transnational, as well as national, levels.[62] We need always to be able to ask: are arguments about the characteristics of national economies limited to specific economic sectors and industrial branches, or do they claim to apply to all? And how far beyond the heartland of the economy does the theory claim to range? If the nation-state is at the heart of the analysis, are political institutions also to be covered by the characterisation? Or does the theory apply even further, to structures like the welfare state, family or religion, for example? As we develop thinking of this kind, we soon come to see that the clear division between endogenous and exogenous that is so fundamental to nation-state-based theories becomes replaced by a continuum of accessibility.

Towards a new analytical approach: anticipating recombinant capitalism

As noted at the outset, most contributions to the literature on the diversity of capitalism conflate theoretical models and empirical cases through a research strategy that seeks the unique theoretical box to which an individual case must be assigned. For example, Goodin *et al.*, while arguing that the US constitutes a pure type of 'market' welfare regime, acknowledge that 80 per cent of US social protection expenditure goes to social insurance schemes of a corporatist nature and not to the means-tested schemes associated with the market model.[63] However, because they consider that this is a smaller proportion than goes to such schemes in other cases, they claim that they are justified in regarding the US as a paradigm of the 'pure' market model. They do not consider the possibility that the corporatist elements of the welfare system might act complementarily to the market process in the US case, and that the US system might operate differently if it really was a pure market one. In fact, the differences that have been identified among neoinstitutionalist theories have major implications for how they relate theoretical models and empirical cases. There are broadly two ways of doing this: the labelling method and the analytical method. The two approaches are analogous to the two different forms of categorisation found on bottles of mineral water: first, the water is labelled as either still or sparkling – the water 'is', unambiguously, one or other of these types; second, there is set out a detailed chemical analysis of elements and compounds, traces of which can be found in the water – the water 'contains' these chemicals.

The neoinstitutionalist researcher following the labelling strategy inspects the characteristics of an empirical case and decides which of a limited number of theoretical models (ideally two) it most closely resembles. The case is then considered to be 'an example' of that model and labelled accordingly, all features of it which do not fit the model being considered as 'noise' and disregarded. A clear example is again the study by Goodin *et al.*, which takes three national cases as examples of three models, then reads back empirical features of these cases into the models. In defence of such procedures Hollingsworth claims that, even if an individual society has more than one social system of production, one will dominate.[64] This is possibly true, but not only should it remain an hypothesis worth testing rather than an *a-priori* methodological assumption, but the role of 'minor' or hidden institutional forms can have major importance. By contrast, the researcher following the analytical approach considers to what extent traces of each of a series of models can be found within the case; there may be no conclusion as to which form it most closely resembles. Even if there is, that information remains framed in the context of the wider knowledge of its attributes. But it is also necessary to recognise weaknesses of the analytical approach. We rarely have in macrosociology or political economy measuring instruments of the kind at the disposal of the chemist analysing the mineral water. If we could say: 'the Californian economy comprises x per cent pure market governance, y per cent basic state support and z per cent immigrant community dynamic effects' – we would be saying something very significant. But we cannot; we can only say: 'the impact of immigrant communities may be important as catalysts for innovation'. The analytical approach thus runs the risk of being wrong-footed as less 'scientific' by an alternative that presents a false scientific precision.

Labelling works best when there is only a limited number of models to which cases can be assigned, but these models embrace a wide range of institutions without worrying about excessive complexity. Conversely, the analytical method is most likely to be found among theories that accept a larger number of types but are less ambitious in their institutional coverage. These theories can best demonstrate their richness when showing how complex an individual case can be, and for that require a large number of models. They are therefore only really feasible when a limited number of institutions is being considered.

The strongest point of the labelling approach is its clarity. The designation of still or sparkling is always far more prominent on the water bottle than the detailed chemical analysis, and it is the only information in which most consumers are interested. Likewise, policy makers, investors and other users of social research into forms of capitalism probably want to know simply: 'is this economy like the US or like Germany?' The labelling model is also of particular value when measuring instruments are crude. We do not have finely tuned ways of measuring elements within a national economy; but we might be able to say what an economy is more or less 'like' – in other words, which simple model does it most resemble?

An analytical approach, in contrast, is able to depict the actors within its cases as confronting an empirical complexity made up of elements of a number of models. A number of recent studies suggest that authors are becoming more willing to accept the degree of complication and apparent incoherence that this implies.[65] If these actors are institutional entrepreneurs, then, unlike the actors within a game theory, they can be presented as having the capacity to try to combine these elements in new ways, making use of serendipitous redundancies embedded in the empirical incongruences of their situation. As theorist and real-world actors interact, the former may be able to develop new theoretical cases out of the recombinant institutions produced by the more successful of these attempts. The two approaches present opposed logics of research. What is noise for the labelling approach becomes grist for the mill of explaining what actors can do for the analytical approach. A high degree of diversity within a case, a problem for labelling theory, becomes for an analytical theory a crucial independent variable for explaining capacity for change. Under the conditions of early twenty-first century capitalisms there is not a question of whether an economy will change, but how it is doing so. The accurate study of this situation surely requires a shift from the labelling to the analytical strategy.

Notes

1 Robert Boyer and Yves Saillard (eds), *Théorie de la régulation: L'état des savoirs* (La Découverte, 1995).
2 Andrew Shonfield, *Modern Capitalism* (Oxford University Press, 1964).
3 Colin Crouch, *Capitalist Diversity and Change: Recombinant Governance and Institutional Entrepreneurs* (Oxford University Press, 2005).
4 Robert Boyer, 'The variety and unequal performances of really existing markets: farewell to Doctor Pangloss?', in: J. Rogers Hollingsworth and Robert Boyer (eds), *Contemporary Capitalism: The Embeddedness of Institutions* (Cambridge University Press, 1997), pp. 55–93.
5 Michel Albert, *Capitalisme contre capitalisme* (Seuil, 1991).
6 It has become routine to use the term 'Anglo-Saxon' here, but it is problematic. It was developed originally to group together the collection of peoples of English, German and Scandinavian origin who inhabited England on the eve of the Norman invasion of 1066; it served to contrast them with both the French-speaking (though originally Scandinavian) invaders and the Celtic inhabitants of other parts of the British Isles. Such a term became useful over 800 years later to distinguish the British and other Northern European (and by now primarily Protestant) inhabitants of the late 19th century US from more recent Latin-language-speaking and Irish immigrants, and by extension also from Poles and

other Catholics as well as from black people and Jews. Its contemporary use by academic social scientists, as well as international organisations like the OECD, seems not only blithely ignorant of these connotations, but also commits the solipsism of using it mainly as a contrast with Germany – which includes the Saxon half of the mythical Anglo-Saxon identity. Its contemporary use also normally includes Ireland – a people explicitly excluded from both the original and subsequent US terms. It is, in fact, used entirely consistently to identify that group of countries where English is the dominant language and the majority population is white-skinned: the UK, Ireland, the US, Canada, Australia and New Zealand. The correct, unambiguous term, which precisely identifies this group of countries is 'Anglophone', and one wonders why this clear and accurate term is not used instead of the more popular, exotic but highly dubious alternative. To insist on this point is not pedantry, but draws our attention to certain possible implications of the fact that the economics literature which finds it far easier to make sense of the Anglophone economies than others is itself almost solely Anglophone.

7 John L. Campbell and Ove K. Pedersen, 'The second movement in institutional analysis', in: John L. Campbell and Ove K. Pedersen (eds), *The Rise of Neoliberalism and Institutional Analysis* (Princeton University Press, 2001), pp. 249–82; and David Coates, *Models of Capitalism: Growth and Stagnation in the Modern Era* (Polity, 2000).

8 Coates, *Models of Capitalism*.

9 Organisation for Economic Cooperation and Development, *The Jobs Study* (OECD, 1994).

10 Bruno Amable, 'Institutional Complementarity and Diversity of Social Systems of Innovation and Production', *Review of International Political Economy*, Vol. 7, No. 4 (2000), pp. 645–87.

11 Campbell and Pedersen, 'The second movement in institutional analysis'.

12 Peter Kjær and Ove Pedersen, 'Translating liberalization: neoliberalism in the Danish negotiated economy', in: Campbell and Pedersen, *The Rise of Neoliberalism and Institutional Analysis*, pp. 219–48.

13 Desmond King and Stuart Wood, 'The political economy of neoliberalism: Britain and the United States in the 1980s', in: Herbert Kitschelt, Peter Lange, Gary Marks and John Stephens (eds), *Continuity and Change in Contemporary Capitalism* (Cambridge University Press, 1999), pp. 371–97.

14 Peter A. Hall and David Soskice (eds), *Varieties of Capitalism: The Institutional Foundations of Comparative Advantage* (Oxford University Press, 2001).

15 Peter Hall and David Soskice, 'Introduction', in: Hall and Soskice, *Varieties of Capitalism*, pp. 36–44.

16 Maria Estevez-Abe, Torben Iversen and David Soskice, 'Social protection and the formation of skills: a reinterpretation of the welfare state', in: Hall and Soskice, *Varieties of Capitalism*, pp. 174–5.

17 *Ibid.*, p. 175.

18 Jonathan Zeitlin, 'Introduction: governing work and welfare in a new economy: European and American experiments', in: Jonathan Zeitlin and David Trubek (eds), *Governing Work and Welfare in a New Economy: European and American Experiments* (Oxford University Press, 2003), pp. 1–30; M. Bertoldi, 'Varietà e dinamiche del capitalismo', *Stato e Mercato*, No. 69 (2003), pp. 365–83; and Colin Hay, 'Common trajectories, variable paces, divergent outcomes? Models of European capitalism under conditions of complex economic interdependence', unpublished paper delivered to Conference of Europeanists, Chicago, March 2002.

19 Bruno Amable, *The Diversity of Modern Capitalism* (Oxford University Press, 2003), ch. 5; and C. Berggren and S. Laestadius, *The Embeddedness of Industrial Clusters: The Strength of the Path in the Nordic Telecom System* (Kungl. Tekniska Högskolan, 2000).

20 Robert Boyer, 'New Growth Regimes, but still Institutional Diversity', *Socio-Economic Review*, Vol. 2, No. 1 (2004), pp. 1–32; and Robert Boyer, *The Future of Economic Growth: As New Becomes Old* (Edward Elgar, 2004).
21 Charles Ragin, *Fuzzy-set Social Science* (University of Chicago Press, 2000).
22 Hall and Soskice, 'Introduction', p. 9.
23 *Ibid.*, p. 34.
24 David Soskice, 'Divergent production regimes: coordinated and uncoordinated market economies in the 1980s and 1990s', in: Kitschelt *et al.*, *Continuity and Change in Contemporary Capitalism*, pp. 101–34.
25 Hall and Soskice, 'Introduction', p. 35.
26 Kathleen Thelen, 'Varieties of labor politics in the developed democracies', in: Hall and Soskice, *Varieties of Capitalism*, pp. 71–103.
27 David Soskice, 'Wage Determination: The Changing Role of Institutions in Advanced Industrialized Countries', *Oxford Review of Economic Policy*, Vol. 6, No. 4 (1990), pp. 36–61; and Lars Calmfors and John Driffill, 'Bargaining Structure, Corporatism and Macroeconomic Performance', *Economic Policy*, Vol. 3, No. 1 (1988), pp. 13–61.
28 Vivien Schmidt, *The Futures of European Capitalism* (Oxford University Press, 2002).
29 *Ibid.*, ch. 2.
30 Gøsta Esping-Andersen, *The Three Worlds of Welfare Capitalism* (Polity, 1990).
31 Frank G. Castles and D. Mitchell, *Three Worlds of Welfare Capitalism or Four?*, Working Paper No. 63, Luxembourg Income Study, Luxembourg, 1991; Mary Daly, 'A fine balance: women's labour market participation in international comparison', in: Fritz Scharpf and Vivien Schmidt (eds), *Welfare and Work in the Open Economy: Volume 11: Diverse Responses to Common Challenges* (Oxford University Press, 2002), pp. 467–510; Manuela Naldini, *Evolution of Social Policy and the Institutional Definition of Family Models: The Italian and Spanish Cases in Historical and Comparative Perspective*, unpublished PhD thesis, European University Institute, Florence, 1999; Maurizio Ferrera, *Le trappole del welfare* (Il Mulino, 1997); Bernhard Ebbinghaus, 'When labour and capital collude: the political economy of early retirement in Europe, Japan and the USA', in: Bernhard Ebbinghaus and Philip Manow (eds), *Comparing Welfare Capitalism: Social Policy and Political Economy in Europe, Japan and the USA* (Routledge, 2001), pp. 76–101; and Elke Viebrock, *The Role of Trade Unions as Intermediary Institutions in Unemployment Insurance: A European Comparison*, unpublished PhD thesis, European University Institute, Florence, 2004.
32 Richard Whitley, *Divergent Capitalisms* (Oxford University Press, 1999).
33 *Ibid.*, p. 42.
34 *Ibid.*, p. 75.
35 *Ibid.*, p. 84.
36 Amable, *The Diversity of Modern Capitalism*.
37 Colin Crouch, *Social Change in Western Europe* (Oxford University Press, 1999).
38 Amable, *The Diversity of Modern Capitalism*, ch. 6.
39 *Ibid.*, p. 200.
40 W. R. Scott, *Institutions and Organizations* (Sage, 2001), ch. 9; and Hay, 'Common trajectories, variable paces, divergent outcomes?'.
41 Colin Crouch, Patrick Le Galès, Carlo Trigilia and Helmut Voelzkow, *Local Production Systems in Europe: Rise or Demise?* (Oxford University Press, 2001).
42 Jerry Hage and Catherine Alter, 'A typology of interorganizational relationships and networks', in: Hollingsworth and Boyer, *Contemporary Capitalism*, pp. 94–126.
43 Crouch, *Capitalist Diversity and Change*, ch. 5.
44 Schmidt, *The Futures of European Capitalism*, ch. 4.

45 Gregory Jackson, 'Varieties of capitalism: a review', unpublished manuscript.

46 Maurizio Ferrera, Anton Hemerijck and Martin Rhodes, *The Future of Social Europe: Recasting Work and Welfare in the New Economy*, Report for the Portuguese Presidency of the European Union, Lisbon, 2000; Anton Hemerijck and Martin Schludi, 'Sequences of policy failures and effective policy responses', in: Fritz Scharpf and Vivien Schmidt (eds), *Welfare and Work in the Open Economy: Volume I: From Vulnerability to Competitiveness* (Oxford University Press, 2001), pp. 125–228.

47 Zeitlin, 'Introduction'; and Paul Windolf, *Corporate Networks in Europe and the United States* (Oxford University Press, 2002), p. 85.

48 Amable, 'Institutional Complementarity and Diversity of Social Systems of Innovation and Production'; and Robert Boyer and Maurice Didier, *Innovation et Croissance* (La Documentation Française, 1998).

49 Christopher Freeman, 'The National System of Innovation in Historical Perspective', *Cambridge Journal of Economics*, Vol. 19, No. 1 (1995), pp. 5–24; Bengt-Åke Lundvall (ed.), *National Systems of Innovation: Towards a Theory of Innovation and Interactive Learning* (Pinter, 1992); and Robert R. Nelson, *National Innovation Systems: A Comparative Analysis* (Oxford University Press, 1993).

50 Colin Crouch, 'Breaking open black boxes: the implications for sociological theory of European integration', in: Anand Menon and Vincent Wright (eds), *From the Nation State to Europe? Essays in Honour of Jack Hayward* (Oxford University Press, 2001), pp. 195–213.

51 Susan Cotts Watkins, *From Provinces into Nations: Demographic Integration in Western Europe 1870–1960* (Princeton University Press, 1991); Andres Rodríguez-Pose, *Dynamics of Regional Growth in Europe: Social and Political Factors* (Oxford University Press, 1998); and Andres Rodríguez-Pose, 'Convergence or Divergence? Types of Regional Responses to Socio-Economic Change in Western Europe', *Tijdschrift voor Economische en Sociale Geografie*, Vol. 90, No. 4 (1999), pp. 363–78.

52 Hugo Radice, 'Globalization and National Capitalisms: Theorizing Convergence and Differentiation', *Review of International Political Economy*, Vol. 7, No. 4 (2000), pp. 719–42.

53 Hall and Soskice, 'Introduction', pp. 54–60; Whitley, *Divergent Capitalisms*, ch. 5; and Paul Hirst and Grahame Thompson, 'Globalization in question: international economic relations and forms of public governance', in: Hollingsworth and Boyer, *Contemporary Capitalism*, pp. 337–61.

54 J. Beyer, 'One best way' oder Varietät? Strategischer und organisatorischer Wandel von Großunternehmen im Prozess der Internationalisierung', MPIfG Discussion Paper 01/2, Max-Planck-Institut für Gesellschaftsforschung, Cologne, 2001.

55 Jackson, 'Varieties of capitalism'.

56 Hugo Radice, ' "Globalization" and National Differences', *Competition and Change*, Vol. 3, No. 3 (1998), pp. 263–91.

57 *Ibid.*, pp. 274–5.

58 Eric Helleiner, *States and the Reemergence of Global Finance* (Cornell University Press, 1994).

59 Radice, ' "Globalization" and National Differences', pp. 273–4.

60 T. K. Hopkins and Immanuel Wallerstein, *World-systems Analysis: Theory and Methodology* (Sage, 1982).

61 Scott, *Institutions and Organizations*, p. 83.

62 J. Rogers Hollingsworth and Robert Boyer, 'Introduction', in: Hollingsworth and Boyer, *Contemporary Capitalism*, p. 4.

63 Robert Goodin, B. Headey, R. Muffels and H.-J. Dirven, *The Real Worlds of Welfare Capitalism* (Cambridge University Press, 1999).

64 J. Rogers Hollingsworth, 'Continuities and changes in social systems of production: the cases of Japan, Germany, and the United States', in: Hollingsworth and Boyer, *Contemporary Capitalism*, p. 268.

65 Amable, *The Diversity of Modern Capitalism*; Glenn Morgan, Richard Whitley and Eli Moen (eds), *Changing Capitalisms? Complementarities, Contradictions and Capability Development in an International Context* (Oxford University Press, 2005); Wolfgang Streeck and Kathleen Thelen (eds), *Change and Discontinuity in Institutional Analysis: Explorations in the Dynamics of Advanced Political Economies* (Oxford University Press, 2005); Wolfgang Streeck and K. Yamamura (eds), *The Origins of Nonliberal Capitalism: Germany and Japan in Comparison* (Cornell University Press, 2001); and K. Yamamura and Wolfgang Streeck (eds), *The End of Diversity? Prospects for German and Japanese Capitalism* (Cornell University Press, 2003).

3 Reflections on some lessons learned from a decade of globalisation studies

Mark Rupert

Notoriously slippery and expansive, potentially encompassing almost every-thing under the sun, interrelating apparently disparate elements into wholes so complex, multi-dimensional, and open-ended as to defy presumptive encapsulation in terms of particular theories or perspectives, the study of globalisation is less a sub-field than an overdetermined meta-field. Even for scholars much more accomplished than I, to write an overview chapter which pretends to anything like comprehensiveness must be to flirt with hubris and delusion, an almost megalomaniacal enterprise akin perhaps to setting out to conquer the world, doomed from the outset to failure if not utter catastrophe. As the United States was sinking deeper into an unwinnable war in Vietnam, Senator George Aiken of Vermont advised that Uncle Sam should declare victory and go home. Confronting the unconquerable field of globalisation studies, I will adopt the converse strategy: declare defeat and proceed. Sur-rendering at the outset any pretence of mastery, I will attempt no seemingly comprehensive or complete god's-eye view. Rather, I set for myself the more modest goal of reflecting on some of the more significant lessons which I have learned from my engagement with globalisation studies over the last decade or so. My discussion here is inevitably limited, partial and perspective-bound, situated at particular intersections of a variety of social and intellectual axes on which others will be differently positioned. Others will surely have learned different things from their own engagements with various aspects of our meta-field. Rather than imagine that my lessons must also be everyone else's, I invite readers to contemplate the ways in which our process of critical engagement might intersect, overlap or converge as well as diverge. I offer this chapter not as a summation of the field, but as the expression of hope that through dialogue differences can be bridged, solidarities constructed, and learning shared as we begin to make a common history.

Here (as elsewhere) I take as my guide the Italian political thinker Antonio Gramsci who acknowledged that no simple, universal, or mechanical model could capture the myriad relations and processes through which concretely situated social actors produce themselves and their world. He noted: 'The experience on which the philosophy of praxis is based cannot be schematized; it is history in all its infinite variety and multiplicity'. Rather, Gramsci understood history as a complex and contradictory story of social self-production under specific social circumstances – a social process of 'becoming which . . . does not start from unity, but contains in itself the reasons for a possible unity'.[1] Gramsci maintained that material social life (not to be confused with narrowly economic activity) entails a diversity of social and political situations and perspectives, but he held out hope for political mediation through dialogue and reciprocal processes of leaning. It is in this spirit that I approach my task here.

Continuity, change and globalising capitalism

A decade ago, not just the significance but the very existence of anything which might usefully be thought of as 'globalisation' was a major focus of scholarly dispute. Some early heralds of globalisation projected a new era of economic-led integration, the coming of a borderless world of almost frictionless flows, a world in which territorially-bound forms of governance such as nation-states would be increasingly anachronistic.[2] Sceptics, among whom Paul Hirst and Grahame Thompson were perhaps in the vanguard, argued that globalisation in this strong sense 'is largely a myth'. On the contrary, they argued that internationalisation and regionalisation are more accurate descriptors of contemporary capitalist tendencies than globalisation, that no major discontinuity exists between the international dynamics we witness today and those which characterised much of the modern period, and that the nation-state retains substantial potential for the regulation of capitalism. They stated: 'such internationalisation as has occurred . . . is well short of dissolving distinct national economies in the major advanced industrial countries or of preventing the development of new forms of economic governance at the national and international levels'.[3]

In retrospect, I take Hirst and Thompson's intervention as a cautionary note of the sort which is useful whenever we are dealing with historical extrapolations. It is certainly possible to exaggerate the extent, depth and social significance of politico-economic globalisation, and to magnify that exaggeration by projecting into the future the tendencies one believes to be operative now. However, from studies of the growth of transnational relations, and various accounts of social forces which have emerged to contest the shape and direction of these open-ended processes, I infer that it is also possible to understate their significance and thereby fail to grasp the potential implications of these tendentially global processes of social self-production.[4] While we may not be entering a wholly new world of placeless, weightless networks and frictionless flows, a world in which political forms such as nation-states and class-related movements are already doomed to obsolescence, I am nonetheless persuaded that there are potentially significant discontinuities involved in the globalisations of economics, politics and culture (although I will have less to say here about cultural dimensions). The partial and uneven de-territorialisations of production and finance; the

restructuring of the 'colonial' division of labour such that some developing
countries are increasingly important sources of manufactured goods in the
global economy while others are relegated to a 'fourth world' of marginalisation, debt and poverty; restructuring gender divisions of labour to incorpor-
ate increasing numbers of women into transnational production chains; the
tendential emergence of a transnational civil society in which new forms of
social identity and political organisation may be emerging as various groups
contest the production of this new world – all of these strongly suggest to me
that there is novelty as well as continuity in the contemporary world. By
referring to globalising capitalism rather than to globalisation as a phenomenon *sui generis*, I hope to suggest this uneasy coexistence of continuity and
change.

Historical materialism enables an analysis of the world-historical forces
underlying (if not determining) these processes of continuity and change.
Among historical social systems, capitalism is uniquely based in the competitive drive for boundless accumulation, accumulation for its own sake. This
core logic of capitalism has compelled market-dependent capitalists continually to seek out new profit opportunities on an ever-broader scale and
with ever-increasing intensity. It is through generalised market-dependence,
the relentless competitive pressures it generates, and the continual reconstruction of social relations it enables, that modern capitalism has produced the
dramatic time-space compression which we recognise as characteristic of
contemporary globalisation.[5] Accordingly, my own analytical strategy has
been to adopt 'a vision of globalisation as an historical process which is not
altogether novel or unprecedented; which is incomplete and uneven, ambiguous and often contradictory in its effects; and which is integrally related – if
not entirely reducible – to the historical process of capitalist social
development'.[6]

Globalisation and the politics of the world economy

While capitalism entails deeply-rooted competitive drives and expansionist
tendencies, this does not imply that globalisation is somehow automatic or
self-actualising; rather, it must be enacted by blocs of social forces pushing
for particular forms of capitalism embodied in particular practices, institutions and ideologies. Since the 1980s, the particular form of globalising capitalism pushed by dominant politico-economic forces has been neoliberalism.
In Kees van der Pijl's incisive summary of the significance of global neoliberalism, 'the core of the new concept of control which expressed the restored
discipline of capital, neoliberalism, resides in raising microeconomic rationality to the validating criterion for all aspects of social life'.[7] In other words,
neoliberalism represents an attempt to universalise and heighten market-
dependence and the 'dull compulsions' of the economic in order to enhance
the powers of global capitalists and facilitate capital accumulation. As an
unfolding political project, this kind of globalising capitalism is sharply con-

tested on a number of dimensions. Viewed from the perspective of the fabled World Economic Forum, the social forces pushing for increasing openness of global markets face 'the challenge of demonstrating how the new global capitalism can function to the benefit of the majority and not only for corporate managers and investors'.[8] Bringing together corporate elites, state managers and much of the media – and with the intellectual support of much of the economics profession – this global power bloc has sought to construct the ideology of a market-based world which Manfred Steger has aptly dubbed 'Globalism'.

According to Steger (and of course he is hardly alone in this), neoliberal globalisation represents a political as much as an economic phenomenon – 'a political project of engineering free markets' on a global scale. Far from the absence of politics or power, the globalisation of neoliberal capitalism entails the construction of multi-scale systems of rule enforcing the sanctity of private property, the primacy of capital accumulation and the disciplines of market-dependence, while containing or excluding potential political challenges. Further, this political project involves the construction of an ideology through which 'the claims of globalism seek to fix a particular meaning of globalisation in order to preserve and stabilize existing asymmetrical power relations'. As Steger put it:

> For business interests, the presentation of globalisation as an enterprise that liberates and integrates global markets as well as emancipates individuals from governmental control is the best way of enlisting the public in their struggle against those laws and institutions they find most restrictive. As long as globalists succeed in selling their neoliberal understanding of globalisation to large segments of the population, they will be able to maintain a social order favourable to their own interests.[9]

Even as it furthers a particular political project, then, the ideology of globalism seeks through its representations to universalise and naturalise, and thus effectively to depoliticise, the neoliberal regime of global capitalism. Globalism represents neoliberal capitalism as the only way to secure individual liberty, efficiency and social prosperity on a global scale. In effect, then, promoting the particular interests of global capitalists becomes the condition of possibility for attaining the social goods of a more generalised liberty and prosperity. Further, this ideology suggests that globalisation (which it simply identifies with the universalisation of neoliberal forms of capitalism, implicitly denying other possibilities) is both inevitable and irreversible. To the extent that globalism becomes a hegemonic ideology, it is able to represent itself as objective truth, reflecting the natural and necessary state of the world. Accordingly, visions of alternative possible worlds can be dismissed as unnatural, impossibly idealistic, the products of ignorant or deluded minds.[10] And globalist ideology achieves this political result even as it claims to speak in apolitical terms, on the basis of sound science.

The economics profession, especially in the United States, has played a crucial role in the propagation and defence of globalist ideology.[11] The authors of a survey of American Economics Association members ask: 'What does it mean to think like an economist?' Their answer indicates that the hegemonic ideology of globalism is firmly anchored in the American economics profession:

> A general conclusion of our study is that U.S. economists embrace the general efficiency of the market approach to society's production and distribution problems. It also appears that the degree of skepticism within the profession toward the potential allocative efficiency of market-based approaches appears to have weakened over the past decade. Nowhere is this more evident than in the area of international economics where the efficiencies of open economies are firmly embraced . . . Specifically there was strong agreement with the propositions that restraints on trade reduce welfare, and that market determined, flexible exchange rates are effective. There was also strong disagreement with the propositions that increasing globalisation threatens national sovereignty in environmental and labour standards, that U.S. trade deficits are a result of non-tariff trade barriers, and that increasing inequality in the U.S. distribution of income is caused by pressures of a global economy.[12]

In accordance with these commitments, mainstream economists have challenged the validity of empirical evidence suggesting that globalisation is bringing increasing inequality.[13] Debates over empirical measures of inequality have not been conclusive, with scholars strongly committed to globalist positions interpreting the data in such a way that inequality appears to be decreasing and scholars of a more heterodox or critical orientation more likely to see a pattern of increasing inequality. This is unsurprising, in so far as data cannot speak until spoken to, and the voice which interrogates the data comes already equipped with a particular conceptual vocabulary, entailing (whether explicitly or implicitly) both analytical and normative commitments.[14] The great debates over globalisation will not be resolved by decisive empirical test, and therefore it is important to examine the ways in which ideological and conceptual frameworks shape the interpretation of evidence in the context of particular positions.

As oracles of globalism, overwhelmingly committed to open markets and free trade, mainstream economists have sought to defend the core project of market-based neoliberal globalisation against popular criticism and political resistance, and to insulate the economic sphere from explicitly political considerations which might undermine the agenda of privatisation and depoliticisation.[15] Jagdish Bhagwati – pre-eminent among international economists – sustains the economists' conventional wisdom that 'economic globalisation is on balance socially benign', that it enhances economic growth and thereby contributes to the diminution of poverty.[16] Bhagwati trivialises resistance to neoliberalism by representing it as rooted in the generational dynamics of late adolescence. Global protests, he implausibly claims, are attributable in large measure to 'the discontent of the young', especially college students of the global North among whom he detects a strong sense of 'empathy for others elsewhere' but also an 'inadequate conceptual grasp of what can be done to ameliorate their distress'. What marks their critical discourse as 'inadequate' is precisely their rejection of the principal axioms of globalist ideology, and their willingness to deploy moral and political discourses in economic life. In particular, these critics and protesters insist on inappropriately applying the 'language of power' to questions of the global economy, and even criticise economics as an academic discipline for rationalising global concentrations of power and wealth. Bhagwati counters that these critics have failed to grasp that economics is a science of means, (putatively) neutral as to ends; and that, in the presence of the Smithian invisible hand, criticising greed is beside the point since, as long as efficient means are chosen, the public good will be served by optimal allocation of resources. For Bhagwati, 'economics is addressed heroically to showing how "man's basest instincts", not his noblest, can be harnessed through appropriate institutional design to produce public goods'. Bhagwati laments that these student-protesters lack the 'intellectual training to cope with their anguish and follow it through rationally in terms of appropriate action' and concludes that this accounts for their 'naive' militance.[17] Alas, these students are taking too little economics and too much literature and sociology, and consequently are susceptible to critical theories of power, knowledge and hegemony. As Bhagwati states:

> Overlaying the entire scene, of course, is the general presumption that defines many recent assertions by intellectuals that somehow the proponents of capitalism, and of its recent manifestations in regard to economic reforms such as the moves to privatization and market liberalization (including trade liberalization), are engaged, as Edward Said claims, in a 'dominant discourse [whose goal] is to fashion the merciless logic of corporate profit-making and political power into a normal state of affairs'.

He dismisses such critical approaches as 'anti-rational' because they 'challenge the legitimacy of academic disciplines, including economics, and their ability to get at the "truth" '. Further, their focus on the 'language of power' ... feeds on the notion that corporations will dominate and exploit the workers under the liberal rules that define capitalism, and by extension, globalisation'.[18]

Of course, any such notion is, in terms of the depoliticising presumptions of globalist ideology, inadmissible. Accordingly, a central target of globalist counter-attack has been the critics' thesis of a global 'race to the bottom' in environmental, social or labour standards, driven by the heightening of market dependence and competitive pressure which is central to the agenda of neoliberal capitalism. Bhagwati not only denies that neoliberal globalisation involves a race to the bottom, but insists that (properly managed so as to encourage efficiency, cope with market failures and externalities, and sustain political support) globalisation will actually produce a race to the top.[19] In the course of making these claims, however, Bhagwati backhandedly reaffirms the very arguments he wishes to discredit. For example, attempting to defend multinational corporations against charges of predatory practices, he comes dangerously close to acknowledging the systemic roots of their global social power and its profoundly consequential nature:

> Multinationals . . . are businesses that must survive by making a profit. Indeed, no corporation ever managed to do sustained good by continually posting losses. If a country wants to attract investment, it has to provide an attractive environment. That generally implies having political stability and economic advantages such as cheap labour or exploitable natural resources.[20]

Gazing at the world through the rose-coloured lenses of globalist ideology, Bhagwati is unable to recognise the engine of accumulation and concomitant structure of power that he just described so succinctly. His subsequent claim that this is simply 'the harsh reality' of capitalist globalisation has the effect of naturalising the social priority of corporate profit, and ratifying its power to maintain that priority at the expense of labour, the environment or other conceivable social values. Its scientific pretensions notwithstanding, this is hardly a value-neutral or apolitical discourse.

   Similar contradictions emerge when Bhagwati turns his attention to charges of heightened labour exploitation and gender inequality in the global economy. In his view, workers are emphatically not being exploited, they are freely choosing to take advantage of opportunities made available to them by international trade and investment. So, for example, that workers are unlikely to be represented by unions reflects not an imbalance of workplace power – facilitated by the apparent mobility of capital and the prevalence of commodity chains and subcontracting relationships which allow employers credibly to threaten workers with job loss. Rather, the relative rarity of unionisation is the result of choices reflecting the 'reduced value' of unions for many workers.[21] Calls for the institutionalisation of labour standards within the global trade regime are not only unnecessary, but are likely to be harmful and should be resisted, for these would unacceptably (re)politicise a global economy presumptively depoliticised by the axioms of the invisible hand: 'the substantial intrusion of protectionist motivation makes the use of trade sanctions less than credible as a tool to be used in advancing labour standards: after all, the public policy scene is marked far too often by lobbies claiming social good while advancing their own self-serving agenda'.[22] On this view, it goes without saying that no such dynamics of self-serving power are intrinsic to the economy.

The same kind of reasoning applies to those workers often portrayed as most vulnerable, the young women disproportionately employed in the export processing zones (EPZs) which anchor emergent global production chains. He writes: 'the proposition that female workers "suffer the worst excesses" makes little sense when the excesses themselves are illusory . . . [T]he young women who work long hours [in alleged sweatshops] are often doing so voluntarily . . . [T]hey are not being exploited; they drive themselves.'[23] Bhagwati trivialises as 'women's fears' the analyses of non-governmental organisations (NGOs) and feminist scholars tracing the ways in which capitalist globalisation interacts with structures of gendered power to place disproportionate costs and burdens on to women and girls – in the household, in the informal sector, and in EPZs, *maquilas* and commercial farms.[24] Indeed, Bhagwati insists that economic globalisation helps women workers, but again, as he explains the mechanisms which produce these (purportedly beneficial) effects, he actually affirms the operation of a race to the bottom. For Bhagwati, social structures and cultural norms of gender hierarchy are reducible to discrimination against women, which in turn can be equated to an unearned wage premium for male workers. The solution to this problem is not, then, to raise the wages of women workers (nor, *a fortiori*, to question the social institutions, structures and norms which embody gender hierarchy and authorise non-payment or underpayment of labour classified as women's work), but to use the competitive dynamics of the market to suppress all wages to the level prevalent for women's work. When the issue of gender hierarchy is reformulated in this way, the race to the bottom-cum-top itself becomes the prescribed remedy: 'faced with increased competition, firms that were happy to indulge their prejudice [for overpaid male workers] will now find that survival requires that any and all fat be removed from the firm; cost cutting will mean that the price paid for prejudice will become unaffordable' and hence 'the gender wage gap will narrow'.[25]

More broadly, in so far as the race to the bottom is actually a race to the top, issues of labour regulation and gender equity can be separated from questions of global governance (since the global economy is allegedly exerting little pressure for nation-states to ratchet their standards downward), the presumed political insulation of the world economy can be preserved, and those who see globalisation as intimately bound up with social power in general and gender power in particular can be dismissed. This is exactly what Bhagwati proceeds to do: 'What has freer trade got to do with it?. . . . These and other implications of women's unpaid work are matters of domestic policy. It defies common sense to attack either the WTO [World Trade Organization] or the freeing of trade for the absence of such policy initiatives by nation-states that are . . . seeking gains from trade by freeing trade. Yet, Women's Edge and other groups do make that illogical leap.'[26] Such a 'leap' is 'illogical' and 'defies common sense' in so far as it deviates from the image of a depoliticised world economy residing at the heart of the ideology of globalism.

I will highlight one more telling ambiguity in Bhagwati's version of globalist ideology. At several points, Bhagwati hints at, without attempting systematically to theorise (for this would undermine globalist axioms), the presence of power structures at work in the world. At one point he tantalisingly suggests that 'globalisation involves issues of the balance of power, and hence also of democratic governance, between groups and between nations'.[27] As a club with which to bash perceived protectionist tendencies, he is happy to take note of power imbalances between NGOs based in rich countries and those from poor countries, and also laments that similar imbalances are at work within the WTO, but pursues no further the potential of his 'balance of power' insight.[28] Bhagwati acknowledges that multinational firms were involved in unfortunate incidents of 'political intrusion' in such places as Congo, Chile and Iran during the 1960s and 1970s, but he suggests that such 'episodes' are 'highly improbable today' due to the global spread of democratic norms and the almost instant availability of information.[29] He recognises as an empirical matter the active presence of particular constellations of power within globalising capitalism – and even claims to have invented the name 'Wall Street-Treasury complex' to describe this 'power elite' – all the while effectively excluding the possibility that the capitalist globalisation he defends might constitute either an imperial structure (reflecting the global dominance of the American state and US-based capital) or a structure of class-based power (reflecting the dominance of financial capital within the globalist bloc).[30] I do not wish to be understood as suggesting that these aporia and elisions are indicators of Bhagwati's own intellectual limits for, on the one hand, Bhagwati has earned an international reputation as a highly capable scholar and, on the other hand, to attribute these contradictions to the oversights of a single individual would be to effectively minimise their larger ideological and political significance. These are not mistakes, they are reflections of the systematic contradictions of the governing ideology of globalism, an ideology which attempts to represent as natural, necessary and apolitical the world of universal market-dependence which it seeks to construct, and, correspondingly, to mystify the interlocking systems of power, from the global to the household, which enable and enforce the discipline of the market. The liberal presumptions which frame the ideology of globalism are not able to suppress these contradictions or to preclude discussion of politics and power as dimensions of capitalist globalisation.

Diversity and complexity of new global politics: lessons and limits of feminist and postcolonial perspectives

If globalising capitalism necessarily involves relations of social power, how ought those relations to be theorised? I remain committed to the basic historical materialist premise that, whatever else it may be or become ('history in all its infinite variety and multiplicity', as Gramsci put it), human social life must everywhere and always sustain a necessary material interchange with the natural world, that socially organised productive activity has been and for the foreseeable future will be an inescapable – if not invariant – aspect of our collective lives, and that human communities cannot reproduce themselves and their world except through more-or-less self-conscious engagement in such activity.[31] From this, it follows that analysis of the relations of social power which structure productive activity is a necessary if not sufficient part of a critical understanding of the processes of social life at work in particular historical contexts. But this is not as simple as it might seem, for class powers must be actualised in various concrete sites of social production where class is articulated with other socially meaningful identities resident and effective in those historical circumstances. Capitalist power over waged labour has been historically articulated with gendered and raced forms of power: separation of workplace from residence and the construction of ideologies of feminised domesticity rationalising unpaid labour; ideologies of white supremacy rationalising racial segregation and inequality; gendered and raced divisions of labour; and so forth. These relations of race and gender have had important effects on class formation. This implies that in concrete contexts class has no actual existence in pure form, that it cannot be effectively determining without itself being determined.[32]

Analyses of global systems of power and production ought therefore to draw upon the perspectives and insights of feminism and postcolonial discourses, and the critical affinities and intersectional politics which these embody. I encountered such arguments a decade ago when studying the politics of the North American Free Trade Agreement (NAFTA). Christina Gabriel and Laura Macdonald argued that women across North America share common aspects of gendered social subordination: 'systematic discrimination gives women unequal access to resources; women's participation in economic activities is largely governed by the sexual division of labour within the household; gender underpins definitions of skills; and women's work in reproduction and production is undervalued'. These commonalities of gendered oppression, they argued, might provide the material basis on which to construct relations of solidarity and mutually supporting struggles. However – drawing on the work of postcolonial feminists who questioned the liberal feminist trope that 'sisterhood is global' – Gabriel and Macdonald cautioned that 'gender, class and race position groups of women differently and mediate the effects of trade liberalizations'. Consequently, they argued, 'there can be no axiomatic unity between groups of women'.[33] Rather, political unification is the product of ongoing negotiation, a problematic process of recognising and mediating these differences in order to realise the potential for solidarity.

This theme was also taken up by Catherine Eschle, who set out to theorise the relationship of feminism to globalisation, social movements and democracy. Eschle argued that, although no facile equation of feminism with democracy was possible, nonetheless second-wave feminist theories and practices involved 'a rejection of restricted notions of politics as a distinctive activity separated from social life, or as limited to a specific realm or social struggle'. Feminism contributed to the construction of an expansive and radicalising 'notion of democratic politics as the contestation of coercive power relations, and the inequalities and marginalisations they produce, in even the most intimate areas of life'; and a corresponding 'feminist formulation of democracy' identified with 'the aspiration to construct more cooperative, inclusive, and participatory relationships between individual women and the community'.[34] Eschle endorsed the critiques of global sisterhood offered by black and Third World feminists, but suggested that these in no way vitiate the democratising project. 'Indeed I propose that the major weakness in second-wave feminist movement democracy was not too much participation but too little. . . . Both the form and substance of democracy were compromised by an aspiration to consensus and an idealization of movement unity that made it very difficult for women to express their genuine differences when participating in dialogue'.[35] Partially overlapping oppressions and opposition to gendered forms of power 'imparts a form of collective agency and identity to feminism, and some coherence to it as a collective actor, but it needs to be recognized that this collective agency and identity is not unitary, stable, or prepolitical but heterogeneous and continually reconstructed through political struggle. Democracy must play a crucial role in such struggle if collective agency and identity is to be negotiated, accountable, and open to change.' Eschle's process-oriented view of social movements implies an expansive horizon of democratisation: 'the construction of connections within and between movements enables more adequate knowledge of the complex ways in which power operates and the development of broader solidarities, thus enabling power relations in society to be tackled more effectively on a variety of fronts'.[36] In so far as globalisation has involved the articulation of gendered systems of power at various scales from the household to the global, the horizon of this democratising feminist project is potentially global. Even if it does not begin from a presumed unity, it holds out hope for a possible unification – grounded in partially overlapping material relations of oppression and processes of constructing a democratic politics in opposition to these.[37]

Also pointing toward a process-oriented and dialogical politics, but motivated by postcolonial commitments, is the important work of Himadeep Muppidi. He taxes much of contemporary scholarship – including rationalist, historical materialist and state-centric constructivist approaches – with 'reproduc[ing] a colonial politics in their conceptualizations of globality'. Quoting Todorov, he identifies the 'primary source of the problem' in 'the inability or unwillingness of the colonizer/liberator to "escape from himself" in its dealings with the Other and to establish a relationship that is more intersubjective than colonial'. I take him to be suggesting that identities and the meanings of the global are continually renegotiated and, to the extent that theorisations of the global take as their point of departure a world and a set of identities already constructed around colonial relations of power, they reproduce implicitly those power relations and foreclose alternative possible worlds. He says that:

Narratives of international relations, for all their provinciality, come, like the marines, from sites endowed with immense coercive power. If they want to establish an ethically defensible engagement with diverse Others in the world, they need to remember, acknowledge and explore the epistemological implications of their historically colonial nature.[38]

To break out of the reproduction of this colonial power relation, Muppidi prescribes a critical constructivist analytic and a politics of dialogue in the co-construction of the global:

> The production of the global is a systemic phenomenon that necessarily has a mutually constitutive relationship with the practices of social actors. In that sense, the systemic production of the global, frequently conceptualized as globalisation, is not outside of individual actors but is constantly reproduced or transformed through their identities, meanings, and practices. Any empirical analysis of globalisation must therefore examine the embedded practices of specifically situated social actors to see how their actions are either productive or transformative of this systemic phenomenon.[39]

While he chastises historical materialism for the Western-centred teleology he sees as implicit in its critical focus on capitalism, Muppidi is not without his own materialist premises, for he insists that the motivation for his critique is the historically unequal power relations of coloniser/colonised which continue to pervade contemporary politics and scholarship, and situates his own epistemological position within the increasingly global flows which allow him to inhabit and exercise 'interpretive competency' in both India and the United States. Yet, on the question of the production of these global flows – which are the material condition of possibility for his analysis – he is strangely silent. Why and how have such flows come into being, and why are they characterised by almost irresistible pressures for economic liberalisation? Without a theory of capitalism, its relationship to the politics of liberalism and its expansive dynamics, it is difficult to see how Muppidi can account for these flows and the interpretive possibilities they generate.

Perhaps a telling example of the untheorised intrusion of capitalism into Muppidi's analysis comes as he discusses the reproduction of colonial globality in US immigration law. In particular, he is concerned with a bill liberalising the flow into the US of foreign high-tech workers (many of whom are Indian). Muppidi analyses the claims of a key supporter of the bill, Senator John McCain of Arizona, to show how McCain's apparent commitment to global openness rested on a deeper commitment to sustaining the competitiveness of US high-tech industries and hence America's supremacy in the global information revolution, incorporating Indian workers only in so far as they are instrumental to this project, and thus reproducing colonial globality in a high-tech world. On Muppidi's account, advocates of the bill prevailed in large part because of the way in which they framed the issue. US information industries allegedly faced a domestic shortage of skilled labour which constrained the ability of these firms to compete globally. If a greater supply of skilled labour was not forthcoming, these firms might well have relocated to where such labour could be found in more plentiful (and less expensive) supply.

> By increasing the quota of H-1B workers allowed into the United States, the U.S. government helped to sustain at least one set of flows between two local spaces in the international system. It also reproduced the social powers of two sets of deterritorialized actors: the corporations that threatened to move and the people who would be entering into the United States on H-1B visas to work for these companies.[40]

Again we may note a deafening silence on the class politics of capitalism and its globalising tendencies, which are inextricably bound up with the issues Muppidi is discussing. It might be fair to ask why employers are driven to seek out labour power which is as productive, plentiful and cheap as possible, wherever that labour power might be found. By means of what social power relations are employers and investors able to threaten to relocate entire industries, and economically devastate the communities where those industries are currently situated, if such conditions are not politically created for them? Can the very emergence of this bill and the discursive strategy of its proponents be understood apart from the structural power of capitalists as owners of means of production enjoying the prerogatives and suffering the competitive compulsions of capitalist owner-investors? Further, are there not issues of class struggle just below the surface of this debate? From the perspective of capital, a 'labour shortage' would find expression in the market through wage rates higher than employers might prefer to pay. This bill would then necessarily involve, and have real implications for, the current employees of these firms whose workplace bargaining power would be dramatically undercut by its passage. Can we adequately understand its politics, and renegotiate more democratic outcomes, without including their voices somewhere in the discussion? Are there potential bases of solidarity, as well as competition, in the relation of Indian and US high-tech workers?

I do not deny the substance of Muppidi's extraordinarily thoughtful analysis of the construction of colonial globality, nor do I take lightly the burden of political responsibility and reflexivity which he urges upon First World scholars in particular, but I do suggest that, in presuming the intrinsic coloniality of all possible versions of historical materialism, Muppidi effectively pulls the rug out from under his own epistemic position and disables critical analysis of the material conditions of possibility on which his analysis implicitly rests. In so doing, he also forecloses an important potential avenue of dialogue and solidarity-building between working people and other non-owners of capital in the formerly colonial and colonised worlds. I conclude that, while feminist and postcolonial critiques may be empowering and enabling of a politics of transnational solidarity, they can also undercut this potential to the extent that they obscure the ways in which capitalism both creates material conditions of possibility for, and also complicates, the very global dialogues which they celebrate. A critical understanding of the politics of globalisation, it seems to me, cannot afford to neglect the contradictory roles of capitalism in these processes.

Empire and the effacement of politics

But how to understand globalising capitalism and its politics? Hardt and Negri's *Empire* has been celebrated as a brave theorisation of new social horizons, a visionary statement of the revolutionary politics of a postmodern global era.[41] An international literary sensation, *Empire* is undeniably a monumental work, an awesome and almost unapproachable edifice of erudition; but, despite its philosophical density, it suffers from a profound political hollowness. A critical analysis of *Empire* suggests that historical materialisms have much to learn from feminist and postcolonial understandings of politics as a (self-)transformative process. To suggest how the substance of such politics is evacuated from the world of *Empire*, I need first to sketch out the overall logic of the argument as I understand it.

Hardt and Negri contend that social life is undergoing a passage of world-historical significance: the transition from territorial systems of rule characteristic of modernity and imperialism to the qualitatively distinct postmodern form of Empire, entailing the decentring and deterritorialisation of rule via the all-encompassing globalisation of capitalism and the emergence of pervasive, information-saturated networks of social production, governance and control. But, by virtue of their commitment to what I will call anarchist-autonomist presuppositions (on which more below), Hardt and Negri infer from the alleged presence of a new global Empire the necessary pre-existence of a globally productive and rebellious form of human subjectivity – the multitude. And, if Empire necessarily presupposes the multitude – imbued not only with socially productive powers but also with a primordial will to resist the containment of those powers – can revolutionary global emancipation be far off? This is at one level a badly needed message of encouragement and hope for globally transformative politics, but the very vehicle of that message – the articulation of anarchist and autonomist premises – carries a disabling effacement, in effect, a de-theorisation of global politics.

Empire is animated by the activist commitments characteristic of the autonomist strain of Marxian thinking, insisting that, after all and before anything else, our world, social life itself, is a product of human social subjectivity, of associated human producers 'autonomous from the dictates of both the labour movement and capital'.[42] In Simon Tormey's admirably clear summary, autonomism emphasises the 'open' nature of historical process and thus the importance of political struggle over economic forces. . . . The significance of such a move theoretically is that it leads to an 'open' account of how resistance to capitalism arises, and thus to a less doctrinaire account of who as well as what can be considered 'progressive' from the point of view of developing anti-capitalist resistance. . . . Autonomists argue that it is the concentration of political and economic power that has to be combated, whether this power be in the hands of the capitalist class or 'representatives' of the working class itself such as trade union leaderships or communist party bosses.[43]

Thus they celebrate the capacity of ordinary people for self-organisation and anti-capitalist struggle in a variety of contexts and note the historical significance of such resistances in driving the development of social institutions.

For Hardt and Negri this historical subjectivity takes the form of a pluralised, postmodern, globalised proletariat – the multitude: 'the subjectivity of class struggle', they assert, 'transforms imperialism into Empire'. They also state:

One might say that the construction of Empire and its global networks is a response to the various struggles against the modern machines of power, and specifically to class struggle driven by the multitude's desire for liberation. The multitude called Empire into being.[44]

Emphasising the historical priority of the multitude's socially productive powers, and hence its transformative potential, Hardt and Negri affirm: 'the multitude is the real productive force of our social world, whereas Empire is a mere apparatus of capture that lives only off the vitality of the multitude'.[45] This implies that the multitude, as producers of the postmodern world of Empire, is capable of transforming global Empire into global liberation.

The struggles that preceded and prefigured globalisation were expressions of the force of living labour, which sought to liberate itself from the rigid territorializing regimes imposed on it. As it contests the dead labour accumulated against it, living labour always seeks to break the fixed territorializing structures, the national organizations, and the political figures which keep it prisoner. With the force of living labour, its restless activity, and its deterritorializing desire, this process of rupture throws open all the windows of history. When one adopts the perspective of the activity of the multitude, its production of subjectivity and desire, one can recognize how globalisation, insofar as it operates a real deterritorialization of the previous structures of exploitation and control, is really a condition of the liberation of the multitude.[46]

This argument leaves me deeply ambivalent. On the one hand, Hardt and Negri aspire to de-reify the social world in order to enable an ontological politics of social self-determination practised by ordinary people in their communities and their daily lives, and this I find not just laudable but exciting. Yet, on the other hand, in their extrapolation of a deterritorialised global politics they appear, paradoxically, to abstract and to re-reify the agent of that politics and thus to efface the real political processes through which any such agency would need to be constructed. Despite *Empire's* apparent commitment to an insurgent global politics, the presumed globality of the multitude – the producers and gravediggers of Empire – has the effect of flattening politics to correspond with Hardt and Negri's flattened and smoothed imagination of Empire. In so far as it represents 'a superficial world' of diffuse and omnipresent power, they suggest, 'the construction of Empire, and the globalisation of economic and cultural relationships, means that the virtual center of Empire can be attacked from any point'.[47] In the postmodern world of Empire, politics is always already global. In effect, then, the politics of concretely situated social agents becomes redundant in so far as it is subsumed within the multitude's already global struggle against an already constituted global enemy.

> Imperial power can no longer resolve the conflict of social forces through mediatory schemata [such as territorial states] that displace the terms of conflict. The social conflicts that constitute the political confront one another directly, without mediations of any sort. This is the essential novelty of the imperial situation. Empire creates a greater potential for revolution than did the modern regimes of power because it presents us, alongside the machine of command, with an alternative: the set of all the exploited and the subjugated, a multitude that is directly opposed to empire, with no mediation between them.[48]

For Hardt and Negri, the omnipresence of power and resistance implies the possibility of globally transformative politics. But it seems to me that this formulation presumes what must be explained: it supposes the pre-existence of a rebellious global subjectivity on the cusp of self-emancipation, and in so doing it begs the question of politics.

In this regard, Hardt and Negri's autonomist perspective has a deep affinity with anarchism and, perhaps ironically, this is a key source of the political hollowness of their text.[49] Having imagined globalisation as seamless and omnipresent Empire, they look for sources of political hope and claim to find it in a curiously transhistorical and effectively asocial abstraction – one beloved of anarchists – the impulse to resist.

> One element we can put our finger on at the most basic and elemental level is the *will to be against*. In general, the will to be against does not seem to require much explanation. Disobedience to authority is one of the most

natural and healthy acts. To us it seems completely obvious that those who are exploited will resist and – given the necessary conditions – rebel.[50]

But can resistance and rebellion be abstracted in this way from historical grounding in the complexity of concrete social relations, specific articulations of economic and political, public and private, global and local, coloniser and colonised? For (self-)transformative politics is not just a function of resisting oppression as such, but of concrete processes of building solidarities on the basis of overlapping (if not congruent) oppressions, and the construction of these solidarities requires the negotiation of difference and in particular the ways in which people are differentially situated on multiple axes of social power and privilege. From the perspective of a potentially (self-)-transformative politics, it matters a very great deal how these potentially rebellious communities are socially situated within particular contexts, how they understand themselves, their oppressions and their resistances, how they negotiate with others in order to begin to envision and move toward common horizons of action, creating what Gramsci referred to as an historical bloc, a collective agency capable of enacting a transformative political project.[51] In other words, if politics is a process of collective self-production by concretely situated social agents, then their presumed will to resist or rebel cannot substitute for the complexities of politics concretely enacted and understood. If progressive forces are unable creatively to confront the political problems of transnational solidarity, the abstract possibility of global transformative politics will be moot. For the purposes of such an emancipatory political project – entailing the problematic self-construction of a global social subject (potentially unified but hardly uniform) – I find a neoGramscian approach, incorporating some of the political questions of feminist and postcolonial scholarship, much more challenging and much more promising than the postmodern global nostrums of Hardt and Negri.

Further, such a neoGramscian understanding of politics helps to illuminate the multiple and contradictory political possibilities resident within popular common sense in various concrete contexts, and to point up the dangerous forces which can and do insinuate themselves into broad-based resistances to globalisation: should progressives fail in their project of transnational solidarity building, the degeneration or corruption of global Empire which Hardt and Negri foresee could as easily lead to victories by reactionary forces representing themselves in the guise of anti-globalisation.[52] Neither in theory nor in politics can progressives afford to bypass the problem of building social solidarity and collective agency across manifold contexts and multiple scales, as Hardt and Negri do.

Globalisation and imperialism

I must end on a confessional note. Over the last decade I have been excited by the possibilities potentially prefigured in the emergence of a transnational political space encompassed neither by the global economy nor by the world of state-centric or interstate politics. I saw in the emergence of such a trans-national civil society a potential site for the kinds of political processes I have sketched out above, a transformative politics negotiating social differences while mediating capitalism's structured separations of the economic and the political so as to create new global possibilities obscured by the reified social forms of capitalism. While I do not now believe that such analyses were wrong, I am compelled by the brute force of recent history to acknowledge that I substantially underestimated the resilience of state-based forms of politics reproductive of the core structures of globalising capitalism, especially imperialism.[53]

At the level of the US-led global order, the balance of coercion and consent has moved sharply toward the former. While the market-oriented liberal vision continues to animate US world order policy, it is no longer represented by key US policy makers to be presumptively natural or spontaneous – that is, voluntary, cooperative and multilateral – but is now portrayed more explicitly as the product of the global assertion of unilateral US power, especially military force. Coercion was never absent from neoliberal capitalism, of course, but to the greatest extent possible the exercise of power underlying this system was hidden or disguised. During recent decades the most significant coercive mechanisms prying open the global South for neoliberal capitalism and (re-)subjecting working people to the discipline of capital were the structural adjustment programmes administered by multilateral international financial institutions, their exercise of power simultaneously mystified and legitimated by the scientific aura of neoclassical economics. Now, however, there has been a shift in the balance of coercion/consent at the core of US global policy, with the unilateral and directly coercive elements officially fore-grounded in ways which they have not been in recent years. The most hawkish and hardline elements in the George W. Bush administration (the Cheney-Rumsfeld-Wolfowitz axis) exploited the atmosphere of jingoism and fear in the US following the terrorist attacks of 11 September 2001 to put into effect their long-cherished vision of US global military supremacy, unilateral action, and the pre-emptive use of military force deployed to create a world in which the American model of neoliberal capitalism and liberal democracy is unquestioned.

Made public in September 2002, Bush's *National Security Strategy for the United States* clearly and explicitly outlines a long-term vision of US global predominance based upon military power, a world in which the US would face no serious military competitors and tolerate no challenges to its interests and its authority, and in which the US government would feel free to use pre-emptive military strikes against those perceived to be potential emergent challengers or who deviate from the administration's putatively universal model of 'freedom, democracy, and free enterprise'.[54] The institutional forms associated with neoliberal capitalism are explicitly integrated into US national security strategy: 'pro-growth legal and regulatory policies to encourage business investment'; 'lower marginal tax rates'; conservative fiscal policies (no small irony here); free trade and international capital flows.[55] Whereas for much of the preceding decade, the core rationale of neoliberalism had been to use (primarily if not exclusively) multilateral and cooperative means in order to separate politics from economics to the greatest extent possible and thus to mystify the workings of power within the global capitalist economy, the new national security strategy directly and explicitly links neoliberal capitalism with American global military dominance. Under the guise of a 'global war on terror', neoliberal forms of globalising capitalism have been integrated into a project which seeks explicitly to impose global order on the basis of military supremacy. The US conquest of Iraq and the pursuit of military-strategic dominance in the oil-rich Persian Gulf region may be understood as expressions of this global imperial project.[56]

In this context, I have been gratified to see an outpouring of new critical scholarship on imperialism and globalisation.[57] As we reintegrate imperialism into the conceptual vocabulary of our sub-field, I hope we are able to do so in such a way that we neither abstract globalisation and imperialism from the relations and processes of capitalism, nor that we reduce the former to the latter in such a way that we lose sight of the political struggles and ideological representations implicated in these questions. Rather, I suggest, critical analyses of global politics should situate neo-imperial power structures within the nexus of relations and processes – at once material and ideological – constituting globalising capitalism and its articulations with relations of nationalised, racialised and gendered forms of subjectivity and power. Accordingly, in the years ahead I hope for critical theorisations of the neo-imperial moment which link it to the energy-intensive historical forms of post-Fordist globalising capitalism, which articulate this latter with historical processes of imperial domination and the construction of global hierarchies, as well as the gendering of global politics such that those subordinated under these global structures are ideologically feminised and dominant social forces represent themselves as quintessentially masculine. These representational themes, and the material relations of social power they invoke, are evident in the brutal images of sexual subordination and humiliation inflicted upon Iraqi prisoners at Abu Ghraib, and the carefully constructed spectacle of George W. Bush landing on an aircraft carrier at sea, emerging from a military jet in full pilot's regalia to strut manfully across the flight deck and declare 'mission accomplished' after the initial conquest of Iraq. Representations more-or-less explicitly featuring such themes have saturated the American media since before the Iraq war began, and speak to the potentially problematic bases of social consent which have enabled the administration to conduct a war which most of the rest of the world sees as blatantly imperialist.

On this view, a necessary condition for the emergence of a post-imperial global politics is the embedding within popular common sense of a culture of transnational solidarity, mutual responsibility and reciprocity, a culture which would foster more dialogic and democratic forms of politics incompatible with globalising capitalism and its forms of subjectivity. The movements for global peace and justice have, in my view, begun the process of constructing such a culture; but further progress is retarded or even blocked by the polarising politics of the neo-imperial moment. To get beyond this conjuncture, and re-energise the process of transnational political renewal and potential transformation, progressives will need conceptual vocabularies with which to attack imperialism, the manifold material relations of social power and the ideological representations which support it. These vocabularies must not neglect the material grounding of global power relations, but must at the same time remain open to dialogue which recognises and seeks to bridge (if not to dissolve) manifold meaningful social differences.

Conclusion

A decade of globalisation studies has changed my thinking about some things, but not about others. Critical analyses of the neoliberal forms of globalising capitalism have demonstrated to my satisfaction that globalisation is an intrinsically political project, involving manifold relations of social power and interlocking systems of rule. Unpersuaded by claims of an immaterial, de-territorialised global economy of flows, I retain an important place in my thinking for the necessary material interchange between human communities and the natural world. I remain committed to a critical theory of global politics focused upon the historical social relations through which people produce and reproduce themselves and their social lives. I have been chastened somewhat by the interventions of feminists and postcolonial scholars, who have persuaded me that a progressive global politics must entail the recognition and negotiation of manifold significant social differences, even as overlapping material relations of oppression and exploitation generate potential grounds of solidarity and perhaps enable a (self-)transformative political project. Further, I have been horrified by the overtly neo-imperial turn in US global strategy and embarrassed by my neglect of theoretical resources which foreground the relationship of globalising capitalism and imperial power. However, this latter realisation will not lead me back toward mechanically economistic interpretations of imperialism since these embody analytical and political limitations which may be counterproductive in the context of a potentially transformative politics of transnational solidarity building. My hope is that, in the coming decade, scholars of globalisation can develop conceptual vocabularies both to understand and to enable a politics of solidarity in a world of imperial power and globalising capitalism which is nonetheless a world of plurality.

Notes

1 Antonio Gramsci, *Selections from the Prison Notebooks* (International Publishers, 1971), pp. 428, 355–6. For an exposition of my interpretation of Gramsci and his

relevance for contemporary global politics, see Mark Rupert, 'Reading Gramsci in an Era of Globalizing Capitalism', *Critical Review of International Social and Political Philosophy*, Vol. 8, No. 4 (2005), pp. 483–97.

2 These were termed 'hyperglobalizers' by David Held, Anthony McGrew, David Goldblatt and Jonathan Perraton, in: *Global Transformations: Politics, Economics and Culture* (Polity, 1999), pp. 3–5.

3 Paul Hirst and Grahame Thompson, *Globalization in Question: The International Economy and the Possibilities of Governance* (Polity, 1996), pp. 2, 4–5.

4 For studies of large-scale changes in the global political economy, see, *inter alia*, John Agnew and Stuart Corbridge, *Mastering Space* (Routledge, 1995); Held *et al.*, *Global Transformations*; Ankie Hoogvelt, *Globalisation and the Postcolonial World* (Johns Hopkins University Press, 2001); Peter Dicken, *Global Shift* (Guilford, 2003); V. Spike Peterson, *A Critical Rewriting of Global Political Economy* (Routledge, 2003); and William Robinson, *A Theory of Global Capitalism* (Johns Hopkins University Press, 2004). Studies of the social and political forces which contest these processes include, among many others: Stephen Gill, 'Globalisation, Market Civilisation, and Disciplinary Neoliberalism', *Millennium: Journal of International Studies*, Vol. 24, No. 3 (1995), pp. 399–423; Manuel Castells, *The Power of Identity* (Blackwell, 1997); Kees van der Pijl, *Transnational Classes and International Relations* (Routledge, 1998); William Robinson and Jerry Harris, 'Towards a Global Ruling Class? Globalisation and the Transnational Capitalist Class', *Science and Society*, Vol. 64, No. 1 (2000), pp. 11–54; Christa Wichterich, *The Globalised Woman* (Zed, 2000), especially ch. 6; a special issue of *New Political Economy*, Vol. 2, No. 1 (1997), republished as *Globalization and the Politics of Resistance*, edited by Barry Gills (Palgrave, 2000); Leslie Sklair, *The Transnational Capitalist Class* (Blackwell, 2001); Catherine Eschle, *Global Democracy, Social Movements, and Feminism* (Westview, 2001); Catherine Eschle and Bice Maiguashca (eds), *Critical Theories, International Relations, and the 'Anti-Globalisation Movement'* (Routledge, 2005); and Louise Amoore (ed.), *The Global Resistance Reader* (Routledge, 2005).

5 On time-space compression, see David Harvey, *The Condition of Postmodernity* (Blackwell, 1989), pp. 242, 293. On capitalism as an historically unique system of market dependence and competitive accumulation, see Ellen Meiksins Wood, *The Origins of Capitalism* (Monthly Review Press, 1999).

6 Mark Rupert, *Ideologies of Globalisation* (Routledge, 2000), p. 43; see also Mark Rupert and M. Scott Solomon, *Globalisation and International Political Economy: The Politics of Alternative Futures* (Rowman & Littlefield, 2005).

7 van der Pijl, *Transnational Classes*, p. 129; see also Agnew and Corbridge, *Mastering Space*, especially ch. 7; Stephen Gill, *Power and Resistance in the New World Order* (Palgrave, 2003); and Robinson, *A Theory of Global Capitalism*; and, for the saga of an insider turned apostate, Joseph Stiglitz, *Globalisation and its Discontents* (Norton, 2002); and Robert Wade, 'US Hegemony and the World Bank: The Fight over People and Ideas', *Review of International Political Economy*, Vol. 9, No. 2 (2002), pp. 215–43.

8 Klaus Schwab and Claude Smadja, quoted in Rupert, *Ideologies of Globalisation*, p. 135; see also Jean-Christophe Graz, 'How Powerful are Transnational Elite Clubs? The Social Myth of the World Economic Forum', *New Political Economy*, Vol. 8, No. 3 (2003), pp. 321–40.

9 Manfred Steger, *Globalism*, second edition (Rowman & Littlefield, 2005), pp. 58, 52, 59–60. For others who would see in neoliberalism the political project of a particular constellation of social power, see the references in notes 4–7 above. For my own attempt to sketch out this nexus, see Mark Rupert, 'Class power and global governance', in: Michael Barnett and Raymond Duvall (eds), *Power in Global Governance* (Cambridge University Press, 2005), pp. 205–28.

10 It is important to note that, although hegemony operates primarily through consensual forms of power, it does not do so to the exclusion of coercive power. On the coercive aspects of neoliberalism, see Jutta Weldes and Mark Laffey, 'Policing and global governance,' pp. 59–79, in: Barnett and Duvall, *Power in Global Governance*, pp. 59–79.

11 On the role of professional economists within the bloc of political forces pushing for economic globalisation in the US during the 1990s, see Rupert, *Ideologies of Globalisation*, especially ch. 3.

12 Dan Fuller and Doris Geide-Stevenson, 'Consensus among Economists: Revisited', *Journal of Economic Education*, Vol. 34, No. 4 (2003), p. 382.

13 Compare United Nations, *Human Development Report* (Oxford University Press, 1999), p. 3; Jagdish Bhagwati, *In Defense of Globalisation* (Oxford University Press, 2004), pp. 66–7; and Robert Wade, 'Is Globalisation reducing Poverty and Inequality?', *World Development*, Vol. 32, No. 4 (2004), pp. 567–89; a useful introduction to this debate is Laura Secor, 'Mind the Gap', *Boston Globe*, 5 January 2003, p. D1.

14 For 'critical realist' expressions of this basic post-positivist premise, see Andrew Sayer, *Method in Social Science* (Routledge, 1992); and Andrew Collier, *Critical Realism* (Verso, 1994).

15 For prominent examples, see Gary Burtless, Robert Z. Lawrence, Robert Litan and Robert Shapiro, *Globaphobia* (Brookings Institution, 1998); Douglas Irwin, *Free Trade under Fire* (Princeton University Press, 2002); and Bhagwati, *In Defense of Globalisation*. To the extent that such authors have expressed support for political reforms, they have done so not on grounds of social justice or economic democracy (considerations which remain anathema in economic discourse) but instrumentally, as concessions necessary to secure political support broad-based enough for the neoliberal project to proceed.

16 Bhagwati, *In Defense of Globalisation*, pp. 30, 53–4.

17 *Ibid.*, pp. 14, 18, 16, 17, 19 and 15 respectively. For evidence that Bhagwati badly underestimates the global scope of resistance to neoliberal capitalism, see Emma Bircham and John Charlton, *Anticapitalism: A Guide to the Movement* (Bookmarks, 2001); Eddie Yuen, George Katsiaficas and Daniel Rose (eds), *The Battle of Seattle: The New Challenge to Capitalist Globalisation* (Soft Skull, 2001); Notes from Nowhere (ed.), *We are Everywhere: The Irresistible Rise of Global Anticapitalism* (Verso, 2003); William Fisher and Thomas Ponniah (eds), *Another World is Possible: Popular Alternatives to Globalisation at the World Social Forum* (Zed, 2003); and Tom Mertes (ed.), *A Movement of Movements* (Verso, 2004).

18 Bhagwati, *In Defense of Globalisation*, pp. 20, 16.

19 *Ibid.*, pp. 30, 32, 123, 132, 150, 164–5.

20 *Ibid.*, p. 162.

21 *Ibid.*, p. 84. Bhagwati's argument here entirely ignores very substantial evidence that globalisation is integrally related to a historic shift in workplace power in the US and elsewhere: see, for example, Kim Moody, *An Injury to All* (Verso, 1988) and *Workers in a Lean World* (Verso, 1997); Kate Bronfenbrenner, 'We'll Close!', *Multinational Monitor*, Vol. 18, No. 3 (1997), available at http://multinationalmonitor.org/hyper/mm0397.04.html; and 'Raw Power', *Multinational Monitor*, Vol. 21, No. 12 (2000), available at http://multinationalmonitor.org/mm2000/00december/power.html. Further, Bhagwati contradicts his own subsequent argument that it is the enduring strength of US institutions – including unions and their political clout – which prevents the race to the bottom from occurring in America: compare Bhagwati, *In Defense of Globalisation*, pp. 129, 131.

22 Bhagwati, *In Defense of Globalisation*, p. 245.

23 *Ibid.*, pp. 82, 175; see also pp. 172, 193. Even as he dismisses the possibility of power and exploitation in global production chains, Bhagwati acknowledges that

'what does seem to emerge persistently from many studies is that the work in EPZ factories is subject to more discipline and may not be suited to all', p. 84. Further, we are left to wonder why it is disproportionately young women who seem to be 'suited' to such workplace discipline.

24 For examples of such gendered analyses of globalisation, see Cynthia Enloe, *Bananas, Beaches and Bases* (University of California Press, 1989), especially chs 7–8; Jeanne Vickers, *Women and the World Economic Crisis* (Zed, 1993); Jan Jindy Pettman, *Worlding Women* (Routledge, 1996), especially chs 8–9; Wichterich, *The Globalized Woman*; Oxfam, *Trading Away our Rights: Women Working in Global Supply Chains* (Oxfam, 2004); and Peterson, *Critical Rewriting of Global Political Economy*.

25 Bhagwati, *In Defense of Globalisation*, p. 76.

26 *Ibid.*, pp. 81, 79.

27 *Ibid.*, p. 46.

28 *Ibid.*, pp. 46–8, 246–7.

29 *Ibid.*, pp. 167–70.

30 *Ibid.*, pp. 204–6.

31 I do not intend here to deny the reproductive labour of the household, but rather to affirm that critical analysis of the processes of social self-production should include the integral relation of productive and reproductive labours.

32 However, this is not to say, in some pluralist sense, that class is only one of a number of possible social identities all of which are equally contingent. In so far as productive interaction with the natural world remains a necessary condition of all human social life, I would maintain that any account of social power relations which abstracts from the social organisation of production must be radically incomplete.

33 Christina Gabriel and Laura Macdonald, 'NAFTA, Women and Organising in Canada and Mexico: Forging a Feminist Internationality', *Millennium: Journal of International Studies*, Vol. 23, No. 2 (1994), pp. 539, 536, 539 respectively. Gabriel and Macdonald were inspired by the seminal work of Chandra Mohanty; see, for example, 'Under Western eyes: feminist scholarship and colonial discourses', in: B. Ashcroft, G. Griffths and H. Tiffen, *Post-colonial Studies Reader* (Routledge, 1995), pp. 259–63.

34 Eschle, *Global Democracy, Social Movements, and Feminism*, p. 92.

35 *Ibid.*, p. 121.

36 *Ibid.*, pp. 123, 141.

37 Although I see potential affinities between my own (admittedly somewhat hetero-dox) Gramscian-inflected interpretation of historical materialism and the materi-ally grounded 'weak postmodernism' with which Eschle identifies herself, I must note that she is pessimistic about reconciliation of feminist projects with historical materialism (which, alas, she understands in relatively reductivist terms): see Eschle, *Global Democracy, Social Movements, and Feminism*, pp. 166–70; compare Rupert, 'Reading Gramsci in an Era of Globalizing Capitalism'.

38 Himadeep Muppidi, *The Politics of the Global* (University of Minnesota Press, 2004), pp. xviii, 17.

39 *Ibid.*, p. 28.

40 *Ibid.*, p. 83.

41 Michael Hardt and Antonio Negri, *Empire* (Harvard University Press, 2000).

42 Steve Wright, *Storming Heaven: Class Composition and Struggle in Italian Autonomist Marxism* (Pluto, 2002), p. 3; pp. 152–75 are specifically devoted to Negri's position within these currents; see also Alex Callinicos, 'Toni Negri in context', in: Gopal Balakrishnan (ed.), *Debating Empire* (Verso, 2003), pp. 121–43.

43 Simon Tormey, *Anticapitalism: A Beginner's Guide* (Oneworld, 2004), p. 116; see

also John Holloway, *Change the World without Taking Power* (Pluto, 2002); and 'Autonomy', in: Notes from Nowhere, *We are Everywhere*, pp. 107–19.

44 Hardt and Negri, *Empire*, pp. 235, 43.

45 *Ibid.*, p. 62; for similar statements of the autonomist premise, see also pp. 51–2, 210, 234–5, 256, 261, 268–9 and 360.

46 *Ibid.*, p. 52.

47 *Ibid.*, pp. 58, 59.

48 *Ibid.*, p. 393. On the untenable claim that globalising capitalism entails the effacement of the state or its displacement by a globalised sovereignty, see Ellen Meiksins Wood, 'A Manifesto for global capital?', in: Gopal Balakrishnan (ed.), *Debating Empire* (Verso, 2003), pp. 61–82. For an earlier intervention which argued strongly for the continuing significance of nation-states within globalising capitalism, see Leo Panitch, 'Rethinking the role of the state', in: James Mittelman (ed.), *Globalisation: Critical Reflections* (Lynne Rienner, 1996), pp. 83–113.

49 For a critical engagement with anarchism as an animating impulse in crucial segments of the Global Justice Movement, see Mark Rupert, 'Anti-capitalist convergence? Anarchism, socialism, and the Global Justice Movement', in: Manfred Steger (ed.), *Rethinking Globalism* (Rowman & Littlefield, 2003), pp. 121–35; for a learned and thoughtful, but also elegantly clear and accessible, discussion of similar themes, see also Tormey, *Anticapitalism*.

50 Hardt and Negri, *Empire*, p. 210. Note that more philosophically astute critics such as Callinicos and Tormey attribute this feature of Hardt and Negri's thought to the intellectual influence of Deleuze. I associate Hardt and Negri's 'will to resist' with anarchism because I believe it is this affinity which accounts for the strong resonance of their work within the global justice movement.

51 See Rupert, 'Reading Gramsci in an Era of Globalizing Capitalism'.

52 On the active contestation of popular ideology and the politics of transnational solidarity-building as opposed to proto-fascist reaction, see Rupert, *Ideologies of Globalisation*; and Steger, *Globalism*. For political critiques of Hardt and Negri in some ways convergent with my own, see Michael Rustin, '*Empire*: a postmodern theory of revolution', in: Gopal Balakrishnan (ed.), *Debating Empire* (Verso, 2003), pp. 2–18; and Leo Panitch and Sam Gindin, 'Gems and baubles in *Empire*', in: Balakrishnan, *Debating Empire*, pp. 42–60; and, from a feminist perpective, Mary Hawkesworth, 'Global containment: the production of feminist invisibility and the vanishing horizon of justice', in: Steger, *Rethinking Globalism*, pp. 51–65. For an Althusserian-inspired perspective which foregrounds the politics of pluralism in globalising capitalism and thus offers a more promising approach than Hardt and Negri, see Mark Laffey and Kathryn Dean, 'A flexible Marxism for flexible times', in: Mark Rupert and Hazel Smith (eds), *Historical Materialism and Globalisation* (Routledge, 2002), pp. 90–109.

53 For a particularly egregious expression of hubris on my part, see Mark Rupert, 'Democracy, peace: what's not to love?', in: Tarak Barkawi and Mark Laffey (eds), *Democracy, Liberalism, and War* (Lynne Rienner, 2001), p. 172, where I straightforwardly equated the politics of transnational civil society with 'the global politics of the twenty-first century'. I do not wish to be misunderstood here: I stand by the substance of my critique of mainstream American international relations scholarship in general and the democratic peace thesis in particular, and I continue to believe that a neo-Gramscian analysis of the politics of transnational civil society holds promise for understanding the dynamics and possibilities of globalisation from below; but I acknowledge that the critical alternative I envisioned was insufficiently attentive to the ways in which interstate politics, warfare and conquest continue to be entwined with the relations and processes of globalising capitalism. For the wisdom of accomplished scholars of historical materialism suggesting (years before the Iraq invasion) that globalisation had not displaced

imperial forms of power, see Peter Gowan, *The Global Gamble* (Verso, 1999); and the following essays in Rupert and Smith, *Historical Materialism and Globalisation*: Ellen Meiksins Wood, 'Global capital, national states', pp. 17–39; Bob Sutcliffe, 'How many capitalisms?', pp. 40–58; and Fred Halliday, 'The pertinence of imperialism', pp. 75–89.

54 White House, *National Security Strategy for the United States* (17 September 2002), available at http://www.whitehouse.gov/nsc/print/nssall.html

55 *Ibid.*, p. 12.

56 For a more substantial elaboration of this analysis, see Rupert and Solomon, *Globalisation and International Political Economy*, especially ch. 5 entitled 'Globalisation, imperialism and terror'. Strongly critical of imperial militarism, placing it in a longer-term politico-cultural context but without explicitly linking it to the structures and processes of globalising capitalism, is Andrew Bacevich's book, *The New American Militarism* (Oxford University Press, 2005).

57 For recent works untangling the relationship of neo-imperial power and globalising capitalism, see among others Perry Anderson, 'Force and Consent', *New Left Review*, No. 17 (2002), pp. 5–30; Alex Callinicos, *The New Mandarins of American Power* (Polity, 2003); David Harvey, *The New Imperialism* (Oxford University Press, 2003); Leo Panitch and Sam Gindin, 'Global capitalism and American empire', in: Leo Panitch and Colin Leys (eds), *Socialist Register 2004: The New Imperial Challenge* (Merlin Press, 2003), pp. 1–42; Ellen Meiksins Wood, *Empire of Capital* (Verso, 2003); Neil Smith, *The Endgame of Globalisation* (Routledge, 2005); and Steger, *Globalism*.

4 Environmental political economy, technological transitions and the state

James Meadowcroft

Over the past decade environmental concerns have increasingly been integrated into the management routines of both states and corporations. This is not to suggest that global environmental problems are becoming any less acute. On the contrary: despite some real accomplishments in controlling pollution, improving resource efficiency, preventing habitat destruction and protecting public health, the overall burden humans place on the global ecosphere continues to rise.[1] On many fronts pressures already exceed critical ecological thresholds.[2] Patterns of greenhouse gas emission, water use, biological resource harvesting, chemical release and soil degradation appear unsustainable. And yet environmental issues are more manifest in societal discourse, and better anchored institutionally, than ever before.

Since the mid 1990s there has been an impressive growth in the literature of environmental political economy. This chapter will reflect on some recent developments in this field. After a brief overview, the bulk of the analysis will focus on one of the more dynamic areas of contemporary scholarship – the debate over technological system change and transition management. This area is of particular interest because the transformation of existing technological systems is critical to addressing contemporary environmental problems – such as human-induced climate change – and understanding how such a transformation can be brought about constitutes an important challenge. The discussion will conclude with some general observations.

Issues and currents

The last decade witnessed a dramatic expansion and diversification of environmental political economy. There is more writing, by more authors, on a wider array of topics, using a broader range of approaches, than ever before. But this is true across the social sciences and humanities. As late as the mid 1990s an individual scholar could aspire to keep abreast of developments in environmental analysis across the social disciplines. But by the early years of the new century this had become virtually impossible. The range and the specialisation of discussion had become too great.

Over the past ten years a series of new and politically salient issues has attracted the attention of analysts. 'Trade and the environment' is one of these concerns. Virtually absent from the 1992 Rio Earth Summit, trade and the environment had become politically charged within just a few years. Environmentalists fretted that trade regimes were weakening national capacities to protect environmental goods and/or trumping international environmental accords, while their opponents complained that environmental regulation could serve as a thinly disguised barrier to trade. Researchers began to explore environment-related trade disputes, as well as the relationship between trade organisations such as the World Trade Organization and the North American Free Trade Association and multilateral environmental accords.[3] Indeed, the trade/environment/development nexus was problematised more generally, with attention turning to issues such as the environmental and social impacts of internationalised production chains, export-led agricultural and industrial development, agricultural subsidy regimes, and the transfer of waste and polluting industries from the rich countries to the poor.[4]

Another emergent locus of inquiry has been the changing role of government in relation to environmental problems. The move from direct regulation towards market-based solutions; experiments with informational instruments, voluntary codes and negotiated initiatives; and the greater involvement of non-governmental actors in policy design and implementation were central here. The economic efficiency, environmental effectiveness and political practicality of these new approaches – from emissions trading and environmental taxes, through certification and disclosure schemes, to covenants and cooperative management – have been hotly debated.[5] And considerable progress has now been made in untangling the characteristics of different classes of measures, establishing the conditions where specific instruments are likely to prove more or less useful, and designing portfolios of complementary instruments to achieve specified policy aims.[6]

'Business, innovation and the environment' has been another growth area. Of course, the performance of firms has been at issue since the dawn of the environmental age. And there is continued interest in the environmental impacts of corporate restructuring, the liberalisation of markets and the expanding commodification of societal interactions. But much recent work has focused on how companies are explicitly engaging with environmental and social issues, and with strategies for 'greening' production by increasing materials and energy efficiencies, reducing wastes and toxic emissions, and redesigning products and services. 'Corporate responsibility', 'eco-efficiency', 'industrial metabolism', 'greening production chains', 'natural capitalism', 'the next industrial revolution' – these are typical preoccupations of this strand of research.[7] Many companies – including some of the largest and most dynamic multinationals – have moved well beyond the 'clean-up and compliance' mentality to assess systematically the environmental impacts of their operations and develop strategies to transform products and services.

But the implications of this development among industry leaders for the bulk of business operations, and indeed for the economy as a whole, remain to be determined.

Climate change also worked its way up the research agenda over the long years during which the Kyoto accord was negotiated, given operational form, ratified, and finally entered into force. Although some scholars continue to view the topic as a distraction from more pressing economic and environmental problems (typically emphasising the specific interests that stand to gain by exaggerating this threat, such as 'big science', an army of consultants and rich-country governments),[8] many researchers have explored the dynamics of the international climate change negotiation process, the evolution of national policy approaches to abatement and adaptation and the strange coalitions to which the politics of climate change is giving birth.[9] Sharply rising oil prices, concerns over the security of energy supply and the debate over 'peak oil' have put energy issues back on centre stage. And the interconnection between the themes of climate change and energy will become a still more important focus for investigation in coming years.

Finally, and less obviously, there has been a gradual awakening of interest in the 'consumption' side of the environmental conundrum. Long a forbidden word in government circles (with politicians nervous of anything that might appear to question 'consumer sovereignty' or economic growth), 'sustainable consumption' has begun to be discussed in the policy arena.[10] Scholarship in this area remains exploratory.[11] The challenge is to develop accounts that combine individual and structural dimensions of consumption. Tentative links are being made across the social sciences to existing work in anthropology, psychology and economics. But much more needs to be done to bring this into the centre of environmental analysis.

Over the past decade these issues have often been linked through three overarching conceptual lenses: 'globalisation', 'governance' and 'sustainable development'. The first provides a way to approach the reordering of economic and political space, where developments in the environmental sphere can be linked to wider patterns of international change. The second taps into the shifting place of government within modern social formations, recognising new modes of governmental intervention, the role of institutions outside government in ordering social relations and the fragmented and multilayered character of contemporary authority. The third, while appreciating ecological limits, locates the management of environmental problems within the context of evolving societal development trajectories. Taken together, these lenses have brought a distinctive flavour to thinking about the environment over the past decade, linking concerns about politics and economics, environment and society, and government and broader societal forces.

Yet in theoretical terms the field remains heterogeneous and fragmented, with researchers typically applying frameworks favoured in their subdisciplinary home-corners. Perhaps the strongest claim to the status of a 'general' theory could be made for 'ecological modernisation'. Starting as a sociological perspective with roots in modernisation theory, this approach began by emphasising the emergence of the environment as an autonomous societal sphere, pointing to a greening in industrial production in countries of the developed world.[12] But the concept was also applied to a policy paradigm which gained favour from the mid 1980s, which approached the environment as an opportunity for innovation, competitive advantage and profit – rather than simply as a cost to firms and to the economy.[13] Here 'ecological modern-isation' could be understood as an attempt to reform capitalism in an eco-logical direction, without undermining the basic axioms of the system.[14] For political and corporate leaders the focus was on win/win scenarios and the creation of new business opportunities. Subsequent analysts suggested that ecological modernisation could be more or less consequent (coming in more or less 'reflexive' varieties),[15] ending with a typology of lesser or deeper changes, that paralleled earlier distinctions between (reformist) 'environ-mentalism' and (more consequent) 'ecologism', or between 'deep' and 'shal-low' green ideological perspectives. Thus, despite the rather broad claims made by some of its proponents,[16] 'ecological modernisation' remains more of a common idiom to explore changing responses to environmental problems in developed societies, than a theory in the traditional sense.

A more focused attempt at theorising can be found in the research pro-gramme on managing 'the commons' (or 'common pool resources') closely associated with Elinor Ostrom and her collaborators.[17] Ostrom's own work combines elements of rational choice theorising with neoinstitutional eco-nomics to model interactions in open access resource systems. Sceptical of both privatisation and centralised state control as successful strategies for managing such resources, the research has explored systems of local com-munity and producer control. The historical and theoretical results have been intriguing, revealing that traditional communities around the globe have independently evolved strategies for managing common pool resources and avoiding slippage towards 'the tragedy of the commons'. Yet, with its exten-sion from an initial focus on biological resource systems (especially fisheries) to much broader 'commons' issues such as the atmosphere (air pollution, climate change), and the integration of more heterogeneous theoretical per-spectives into the programme, an element of coherence in the original effort has been lost.[18] On the other hand, to the extent that what is important is achieving a practical understanding that will allow the design of better management structures in the future, any ideas that can fruitfully be applied from this diverse theoretical toolbox are to be welcomed.

These two approaches are peculiar because their emergence has been so closely grounded in the specificity of environmental political economy. More typically, bits of theory are borrowed from other subdisciplinary niches and extended into the environmental realm. A good example here is 'regime theory' which was originally applied to economic and security interactions, but has found a fertile application in relation to multilateral environmental agreements. Work by a number of writers has extended this approach, identifying the characteristics of key environmental regimes, analysing their formation and assessing their effectiveness.[19] Analysis of different environmental negotiating processes has allowed the formulation of some general principles in this area, and much of the most recent scholarship seeks to apply such understanding to the establishment of a viable climate change regime. Similar sorts of enterprise have been carried out in other areas, such as the extension of security discourses into the environmental realm and the application of social movement theory to environmental groups.

Yet the theoretical fragmentation and eclecticism that marks the domain of environmental political economy provides no real cause for complaint. Human interactions with the environment are not separate from other social behaviours. So why should theories that contribute to understanding alternative dimensions of social interaction not also contribute to making sense of environmental issues? Moreover, in political and economic terms 'the environment' is not one thing. Rather, it is a fractured and multidimensional mosaic that touches social life at many points. So perhaps our theories are similarly destined to remain fragmented and partial, as well as borrowed and contested.

'Transition management'

One of the more interesting strands of research to develop over the past decade relates to technological innovation and 'transition management'. This work engages with the problem of understanding and orienting change in large socio-technical systems. Starting from the insight that 'system innovation' (rather than just incremental improvement) will be required to make practices in key economic sectors sustainable, questions relate to the extent to which it is possible, and the techniques that might be employed, to steer socio-technological transformation along desired pathways. Initially developed by Dutch researchers, the idea was given political expression in the Netherlands Fourth National Environmental Policy Plan (NEPP4), which argued that in relation to environmental objectives:

> Continuing or intensifying current policies will not produce satisfactory solutions as they ignore obstacles preventing sustainable solutions. In fact, these obstacles are system faults in the present social order, in particular in the economic system and in the institutions functioning at the present time.[20]

The document went on to explain that:

> Solving the major environmental problems requires system innovation: in many cases this can take on the form of a long-drawn-out transformation (often lasting longer than one generation) comprising technological, economic, socio-cultural and institutional changes, which influence and

reinforce each other. The period until such a transformation is complete can be seen as a transition. During the transition, objectives are formulated and modified and interrelated policy instruments are applied. Transition requires kinds of planning and transition management.[21]

Distinctive elements of this policy approach include: the identification of major obstacles to further progress on environmental issues as 'system faults'; the contention that 'system innovation' is required to circumvent such obstacles; the expectation that this will involve long-term change to complex social practices; a strategic focus on key problem 'clusters'; an emphasis on the role of national government in managing transition processes; and a commitment to involve major social partners in defining and actualising necessary transitions. Here 'transformation' denotes a significant system change; 'transition' refers to the period of movement from one relatively stable system-state to another; and 'transition management' describes the activity of consciously orienting such transitions in the public interest. Note the strong assumption that transitions can successfully be steered by deliberate policy intervention.

The theoretical articulation of 'transition management' is primarily associated with the writings of Jan Rotmans, René Kemp, Frank Geels and their co-workers involved with the NEPP4 process.[22] They have defined 'transitions' as 'processes in which society or a complex subsystem of society changes in a fundamental way over an extended period (more than one generation, i.e. 25 years or more)'.[23] Key features of this perspective include the following:

- Transitions are understood as 'non-linear' processes, with 'multiple causality and co-evolution', where one dynamic equilibrium gives way to another. The character and rate of change differs over the course of a transition, which typically passes from a 'pre-development' stage to 'take-off', 'breakthrough' and finally 'stabilisation'.[24]
- A three-level model captures the context within which transitions occur: first, there are 'regimes' ('dominant practices, rules and technologies' that frame particular societal domains); then, there are 'niches' (localised areas where innovation can first take root); and, finally, there is the 'socio-technical and economic landscape' (that forms the wider context within which specific regimes operate).
- Transitions are important in relation to sustainable development as they can open the door to radical improvements in environmental (and economic and social) performance. Although transitions cannot be controlled in any absolute sense, they can be influenced (encouraged, re-oriented, or speeded up) through deliberate intervention. The relevant steering perspective is described as 'goal-oriented modulation'. 'Transition management' is 'a deliberate attempt to bring about long term change in a stepwise manner, using visions and adaptive, time

limited policies'. It is understood as a 'two pronged strategy' that is 'oriented towards both system improvement (improvement of an existing trajectory) and system innovation (representing a new trajectory of development)'.[25]

- The long-term perspective is embodied in 'goals' and 'visions': goals represent broad social objectives, defined through public debate and political processes. With respect to the energy system, for example, goals might be defined in terms of the need for 'cheap, safe, secure and environmentally benign energy'. 'Visions' represent particular ideas on how these goals could be achieved, presenting 'inspiring images of the future state of that specific sector or theme'.

- Reference is made to 'transition paths' (trajectories to achieve specific visions), 'programmes for system innovation' (experiments with different avenues of reform in a given sector) and 'transition arenas' (networks to explore innovation). Interim objectives, monitoring progress, and the periodic reviews of objectives, visions and goals are emphasised. The exercise is supposed to be 'adaptive', combining 'bottom-up' initiatives and 'top-down' orientation, and to involve both 'learning-through-doing' and 'doing-through-learning'.

- Interactions among concerned stakeholders are central to the iterative processes at the heart of transition management. Concerned parties are drawn into continuing discussions about goals and visions, the identification of interim objectives and the assessment of progress. Thus transition management appears as a further extension of the interactive approach to environmental governance already institutionalised in the Netherlands.

The intention is to bring long-term social objectives and the potential for immediate gains into contact, and to draw together the logics of system transformation and of incremental improvement. In a recent discussion Kemp and Loorbach have traced the affinities between transition management and other politico-administrative perspectives, including 'incrementalism', 'adaptive governance', 'interactive governance' and 'multi-level governance'.[26] They suggest that as a policy orientation transition management shares features with each of these approaches, but is reducible to none of them.

As this brief exposition should have made clear, 'transition management' can be viewed from several angles: as a policy perspective, a theoretical approach and a research agenda. In policy terms it presents a mechanism for encouraging movement towards sustainable development. Distinctive features include its sectoral orientation, its emphasis on socio-technical regimes, its long-term perspective and its process-oriented character. Transition management privileges experimentation and interaction with actors that want to innovate; and it discourages the attempt by governments to pick 'winning' technologies or firms. In theoretical terms it rests on a series of insights regarding the significance of social-technical regimes, the complex forces influencing their stability and change, and the impossibility of accurately predicting future trajectories. Yet there is a belief that policy can alter the course of events and that, by experimenting now, societies can better appreciate, and adjust to, developments that are less amenable to control. Recognition of scalar differences (niche, regime and landscape), the co-evolution of socio-technological systems and path dependence are also critical theoretical elements. As a research agenda, transition management is interested in policy initiatives that can be deployed actually to influence the path of socio-technological development. Critical questions relate to defining 'goals' and 'visions', identifying appropriate problem-spaces, creating interactive networks, establishing the kinds of experiment that are likely to succeed, allocating scarce public resources, and reconciling national and international initiatives. But there are also broader issues, including deepening the understanding of the extent to which it is possible to anticipate socio-technological change and to steer it along desired pathways.

So what does 'transition management' imply in practical terms? A key element is the establishment of 'transition arenas' – spaces where actors concerned with a particular domain can interact to define goals and visions, and establish coalitions to explore different technological and social options. Emphasis is placed on gaining experience through practical experiments, establishing indicative targets, keeping options open and encouraging a plurality of potential trajectories. In the Netherlands the preparation of a report presenting energy scenarios through to 2050 provided the basis for identifying five strategic transition 'routes' (green and efficient gas, enhanced production chain efficiency, green raw materials, alternative motor fuels and sustainable electricity) that are robust across varied scenarios.[27] Further consultation with stakeholders allowed the formulation of aspirational goals ('ambitions'), transition paths (strategies for change) and specific options (technological and social innovations) for each strategic route. The Dutch Ministry of Economic Affairs has funded a broad array of projects (organised by coalitions of stakeholders) to explore different dimensions of these transition paths. One project, for example, has focused on reducing energy usage in the paper and board sector by 50 per cent by 2020, while another engages with energy usage in the agricultural glasshouse sector. Innovation networks composed of actors from different societal sectors have been established. An evaluation of existing research funding from the perspective of transition management has been undertaken, and the government has established a 'frontrunners desk' to cut through 'red tape', reduce the regulatory burden on innovative firms and identify bureaucratic obstacles to novel experiments.

The idea of a 'transformation' of existing social practices and structures is not in itself new: rather, it resurrects some of the original impetus of early environmental campaigners. What is needed is a fundamental break with existing practices and routines. But the notion of 'transition' is drawn primarily from literatures on technological change – where particular technological systems are seen to give way over time to newer configurations: moving from sailing ship to steamer, from gas to electric lights, or from typewriter to word processor. There is secondary reference to political 'transitions' – such as transitions from authoritarian rule to democracy, and/or from a state-run to a market and private property-based economic system. But the structure of the theory is really based on research into technological change. These origins are particularly evident in the idealised phases of the transition process (with inflection points, differing growth rates and the replacement of one equilibrium by another) and the emphasis on 'strategic niche management', encouraging the creation of specialist enclaves where a new technology can acquire maturity (accumulating experience and driving down costs) and prepare for a break-out.

Although students of technology may once have had a tendency to confine their investigation to the scientific and technical realm, or to dwell on the history of individual artefacts, the field now articulates a more socially grounded approach, where technologies are understood to be embedded in complex networks of knowledge and power. The economic, but also the regulatory, the social and the cultural dimensions of technological evolution are increasingly appreciated. Thus issues as apparently distinct as the operation of capital markets, the practices of the insurance industry, the character of regulatory regimes, consumer tastes and concerns, as well as contingent circumstances (such as fire in a manufacturing facility, the death of an entrepreneur or the discovery of financial irregularities in a company), can influence the relative success of specific technological ventures. Recognition of such complexities and contingencies is a central concern of transition management.

Yet 'transition management' is not without its critics. To commentators outside the Netherlands the approach can appear hopelessly unrealistic. Even in a country known for its consensus-oriented political system and strong traditions of planning and environmental policy innovation, one can wonder whether actors with divergent economic interests (for example, firms representing rival technological approaches) can be expected to agree on pathways of socio-technical change, and whether the political system can be expected to provide a sufficiently stable context to orient transitions that may last decades.

In an interesting paper Berkhout, Smith and Stirling develop a critique of the 'niche-based model of regime transformation' which they understand to be 'at the heart of this *transition management* project'.[28] They suggest transition management places too much emphasis on a 'bottom-up' (enterprise-driven) model of socio-technical change, and on a policy approach focused on encouraging innovation in protected niches. They point to the variety of ways in which socio-technical regimes shift, and to differences depending on whether change is planned or is more or less uncoordinated, and whether it relies on resources internal or external to the existing regime. Moreover, they argue that, with respect to 'normatively driven, purposive socio-technical transitions' (such as those related to sustainable development), top-down drivers may be of more significance. Thus the environmental movement has been particularly successful when it has explicitly 'targeted the incumbent regime' (for example, campaigns against the nuclear industry, or waste incineration), rather than attempting to promote a particular successor; they argue that this 'represents a direct antithesis of the bottom-up niche based model'.[29]

These authors are also sceptical of the 'guiding visions' articulated within the transition management framework. First, they point to 'a disjunction between the historically-informed niche-based model of regime transformation and the normative policy aspirations of transition management'. For the 'visions' that are so central to transition management are absent from the empirical examples of transitions from which the theory of niche-induced change was drawn, where 'an over-arching, consensual vision of the future socio-technical regime was largely absent'. Second, they argue that 'guiding visions' will be more contested, and consensus will be more difficult to achieve, than transition theorists allow. Indeed, 'not only the process of consensus building, but the very notion of public interest itself is highly problematic'.[30] Key issues here are the uncertainty and indeterminacy surrounding decision making, the conflicts of interest bound up with different socio-technological alternatives, and the impossibility of unambiguously ranking public preferences. Moreover, such unreflective usage of the idea of a public interest 'raises the prospect' that 'even the very concept of transition management itself . . . might simply constitute further political resources and arenas for the interplay of the contending interests embodied in competing socio-technical regimes'.[31]

These critics are clearly right about the complexities surrounding socio-technical change, as well as the importance of deepening our understanding of the factors that influence such change. Their point about the disjunction between the evidence on which theory is based (mainly spontaneous change) and the conscious ambitions of the theory itself is particularly pertinent. Broad and consensual visions of the future have not characterised technological development. The potential of emergent technologies has typically only been appreciated by a handful of visionaries; often the really critical applications are not those initially foreseen; and unintended consequences abound. Conflict is typically rife, with technological and economic rivals disputing the course of development and resistance coming from those on whom the costs of change are to be imposed (lost jobs, environmental externalities, regional decline, and so on). But this does not mean that establishing societal goals, or driving technological development to meet particular functional objectives, is impossible. Indeed, governments have often done so, although admittedly on a much more modest scale than envisaged under transition management.

On the other hand, it is not evident that transition management is as dependent on a 'niche-based strategy' as the critics, or even some of its proponents, suggest. The approach attempts to encourage both 'system improvement' and 'system innovation', leaving open the extent to which radical regime change will be required to achieve desired goals in any given context. The encouragement of niche-based innovation is intended to cultivate promising alternatives to existing practices: this may prepare the way for a regime shift, but it also exerts pressure on existing regimes to adapt to meet policy goals. Indeed, transition management can be largely indifferent to which technologies (and which associated actors) deliver the desired performance gains – provided the gains are *actually* secured. Moreover, it explicitly accepts that an array of policy tools (not just niche management) may be deployed to encourage movement in the desired direction, as the discussion of transition in the energy system in the NEPP4 documentation illustrates.[32]

Nor is it clear that a policy orientation that encourages niche-based innovation should be seen as 'the antithesis' of a non-governmental organisation strategy of 'targeting the incumbent regime'; with the one representing a 'bottom-up' and the other a 'top-down' approach to socio-technological change. In fact, this juxtaposition involves several dimensions – relating to different types of actors, modes of political and economic intervention, and phases of the policy cycle – which the 'bottom-up'/'top-down' dichotomy fails to capture. From one perspective the expansion of niche-nurtured innovation to overturn an existing socio-technical regime appears to be 'bottom-up' (or outside-in); but state intervention to stimulate such a processes is very much 'top-down'. Discrediting an established socio-technical regime (and so changing consumer and government behaviour) can be presented as a 'top-down' strategy; but to the environmental campaigners doing the discrediting it feels very much a 'bottom-up' initiative.

Different forms of social organisation can be expected to make varied contributions to socio-technological change. Considering their institutional endowments, it is hardly surprising that environmental movements have had more impact in undermining the legitimacy of current regimes than in building up alternative systems of provision. Governments, too, can 'declare war' on existing technological regimes, but they do so more rarely – because they must represent a broader range of social interests and concerns, and generally seek to avoid serious economic dislocation. A policy stance can apply pressure to an existing regime, and in exceptional cases it may be explicitly directed toward its extinction – consider the phase-out of nuclear power in Germany. But in such cases governments must pay attention to the viability of alternatives and perhaps to cushioning the impact on groups disadvantaged by the change. In fact, the public discrediting of existing practices can be understood as a political move that prepares the way for a shift in the state's posture towards prevailing practices (leading to a tilt in the regulatory balance against the incumbent regime, or to other policy initiatives such as 'niche management'), rather than as constituting an alternative to them.

With respect to the idea of 'visions', tremendous problems are associated with anticipating technological futures and with orienting technological development along pre-imagined lines. In contexts of great uncertainty and indeterminacy, with powerful established interests, it is difficult for political authorities to make wise decisions. But transition theorists are not totally blind to these problems: the desired 'goals' focus on the functional perform-ance of the system rather than the particular technology; and the 'visions' (which do relate to specific technological options) are spoken of in the plural. This acknowledgement of a multiplicity of 'visions' is presented as a strategy to avoid premature 'lock-in', when costs and benefits of different techno-logical alternatives are not yet clear and there is pervasive uncertainty about broader political, economic and technological developments. But it can also be understood as a political strategy to draw groups linked to diverse technological alternatives into transition programmes.

One must also take care when deriding ideas of consensus and the public interest. Certainly, notions of 'public interest' or the 'common good' are problematic. Indeed, democratic politics is characterised by continual strug-gles over the content of these terms, and consensus in any given social sphere is always relative and transitory. But doing without such notions is even more problematic – for it suggests a politics predicated entirely upon the claims of particular interests and focused on the aggregation of existing preferences – so robbing the political realm of the potential to seek creative solutions that reach beyond existing conceptions of interest and identity. Neither political actors nor publics are going to abandon such notions, which ground political authority and focus the contestation that always lies at the heart of democratic politics. So, if transition theorists are to be charged with being somewhat 'naive' in their understanding of consensus and the public good, they might legitimately accuse their critics of the contrary error of assuming that one could ever escape arguments over the public interest, or that transition management might avoid becoming a focus for contending interests.

So the idea of 'transition management' appears to be fruitful, but not without difficulty. Indeed, there are underlying tensions associated with the notion of 'transition' itself. A 'transition' is a movement from one condition to another: it is a process of change linking 'before' and 'after'. It implies a period of flux, the passage of time and endpoints with respect to which the transition is defined. We might not characterise every change as a transition; although by altering the perspective from which phenomena are examined many changes can be understood as components of transitions. Scale is criti-cal here: two 'stable' states linked by a transition might, in a broader context, appear as merely incremental components in a more profound transform-ation. Thus sustainable development (like societal evolution more generally) is composed of countless parallel and sequential, overlapping and nested, 'transitions' occurring on different spatial and temporal scales in which estab-lished social forms (including socio-technical practices) continuously give way to new configurations.

Two concerns arise here. The first relates to the open nature of the transi-tions that 'transition management' manages. The idiom of transition seems to promise closure: the idea that, although the effort may take several decades, the transition will eventually draw to an end as the transformation becomes complete and the problem is solved. Canals are replaced by railways; the horse and plough give way to the tractor: end of story. Well, perhaps. Certainly, such decisive shifts can be observed in some socio-technological systems. But it is not clear that this is always the case. 'Old' technologies may survive in 'niches', just as potentially emerging ones do. More importantly, it is not clear that the macro systems with which transition management is concerned can be modelled in the same way as specific socio-technical subsystems. In political systems the situation is typically even more messy, with some 'transitions' left hanging as new ones begin. With respect to major environmental issues it is not clear that even several decades of effort will have cracked key problems, particularly when one is thinking in terms of broad sectors such as agriculture, natural resource use or energy systems. Here, the (partial) completion of one transition is likely to become intertwined with other emergent 'transitions' as change at all levels in society conspires to redefine the original problem-space. Thus talk of 'transition' can make these processes appear more bounded and finite than they are likely to prove to be. The second (and connected) issue relates to the definition of the problems, in particular how to define the scale or reach of the social-technical practices that are to be transformed. This links to an observation made by Berkhout, Smith and Stirling about the difficulty of identifying what is to count as a 'regime' and when to conclude it has been transcended: is the electricity regime determined by fuel type, turbine technology, the transmission network, or what? This can be considered a problem of specifying appropriate 'levels of analysis' (and intervention). For different definitions of the offending socio-technological regime would presumably entail different constellations of relevant actors and different approaches to their 'management'.

These sorts of difficulties suggest that it is important to maintain an open textured notion of transition, while focusing efforts on change within specific subsystems. The 'levels' issue is less likely to be resolved through an appeal to some general theory of socio-technological change than it is by exploring the detailed physiognomy of the particular socio-technological systems that are judged problematic from the point of view of the environment. In this context, empirical action – exerting pressure on existing regimes to induce change – is critical to extending understanding of exactly how they operate, and how brittle they are in the face of stress. And in defining the parameters of the relevant regimes it is probably best to start from the perspective of the environmental burdens that must be brought under control, and then work backwards to offending socio-technical practices and their cross-connections into established regimes.

Two other potential difficulties with transition management deserve mention: the linkage between domestic and international initiatives, and between political leadership and stability. The socio-technical systems of interest are increasingly international in scope. Production is organised internationally, multinational firms are key actors, and in many cases the scale of necessary innovations surpasses the economic/technological capacities of even the largest states. Consider the challenge of effecting change in the automotive sector. Indeed, strengthening the international component of transition management was a key recommendation of a high level review of Dutch policy conducted in 2004.[33] Moreover, transition management appears to make rather stringent demands on political systems, for substantial policy stability and resilient political coalitions would be required to keep reform from being derailed by changes in political personnel and a turbulent conjuncture.

Technology, growth and the state

Whether transition management can fulfil the expectations of its proponents remains to be seen. But there are grounds for thinking that with respect to policy it points in the right direction, adding a new dimension to the environmental management strategies that have emerged in developed countries over recent decades. Lengthening time horizons; building networks among innovative stakeholders; focusing on sectoral dynamics (evolution, adaptation, investment, restructuring); integrating economic, social and environmental considerations in product, process and policy design – all are critical for the future. Two other elements of more general significance that are prominent in transition management are the engagement with technological futures and the active role assigned to government.

Technology is a central component of environmental problems and solutions. But political debates and policy initiatives relating technology and environment are often skewed. Some green critics dismiss the bulk of established environmental policy as a mere 'technological fix' that fails to appreciate that genuine social change is required if humans are to reduce pressures on natural systems. Emphasis on technological innovation is seen as a distraction when basic values, ways of life and the whole system require urgent change.[34] On the other hand, vocal critics of environmentalist concern with 'natural limits' express a quasi-mystical faith in the efficiency of markets and the power of human ingenuity to deliver technological solutions to environmental ills.[35] Their point is that, when problems of pollution and resource scarcity reach the point that they really matter (relative to other social needs), solutions will be forthcoming. Although rarely encountered in their most extreme variants, these divergent perspectives – that what is needed is not technological innovation but system change, or that markets and technological dynamism will automatically provide solutions – permeate discussion of environmental issues. For their part, governments have typically adopted a more pragmatic approach, either funding research and development in environmental technologies (through public laboratories, universities or tax incentives for business), or using regulation to drive performance improvements. More recently, they have seen environmental technologies as a growth opportunity which can win profitable markets for national industries.

The problem with the first perspective which juxtaposes technological solutions and social change is that the two are not alternatives. Emergent technologies can open and close societal opportunities, just as social evolution can encourage or discourage particular patterns of technological advance. Technological innovation can be as much a strategy to drive social change as a strategy to resist it. The question is not about changing one or the other, but about the orientation of these changes. The problem with the second perspective is that it is based on assumptions of perfect information and competitive markets. It ignores the distribution of costs and benefits, and the practical evidence that suboptimal technological solutions are readily locked in. And it fails to hedge against the risk that the environment proves to be more sensitive to disruption than previously thought. The problem with the traditional government approach to environmental technological development is that it lacks long-term visions and remains confined to a top/down and expenditure/regulatory framework. Moreover, environmental innovation has been divorced from more general policies for economic and social development.

If we are to control and eventually reduce human impacts on the global ecosphere, radical innovation in socio-technical systems will be essential. The scale of the necessary change can be appreciated with respect to climate change, where Intergovernmental Panel on Climate Change scenarios suggest that stabilisation of the climate system will one day require a decline in global carbon dioxide emissions to a small fraction of current levels.[36] To secure such gains societies will have to transform existing patterns of production and consumption. Technological change lies at the dynamic edge of economic development, where science and business meet, and options are explored and decisions are made that open alternative trajectories. Through the development and uptake of new technologies it is possible to integrate environmental considerations with issues of function, quality, convenience and price. We do not (and cannot) know in advance which technological solutions hold the most potential. But we do know that we need to accelerate the development of alternatives. Since various technological approaches will produce different mixes (and distributions) of social goods and bads, society as whole has an active interest in the path of technological evolution. Thus this domain must be a privileged area of intervention for those concerned to move society on to a more ecologically sensitive pathway. Transition management suggests some ways to engage in this process.

With respect to the role of governments, there is little doubt that in recent years there has been a tendency to depreciate their capacity to manage societal problems. The turn towards the market – exemplified by privatisation, contracting out and the import of private sector practices into public administration – has been taken as evidence of a long-term decline in the state's capacity to govern.[37] The internationalisation of economic activity (and the corresponding growth in the bargaining power of corporate actors), together with the increasing influence of international trade organisations

(WTO, NAFTA) and the closer integration of the European Union, are seen to represent erosions of sovereignty.[38] 'Regionalisation' has further diminished the authority of the central state. Traditional steering strategies are thus held to be increasingly ineffective in face of the sheer complexity of the modern world. So how could one expect such an enfeebled leviathan to act on behalf of the environment?

To claims about the sclerotic state one can add other sorts of argument that are profoundly sceptical of the state's capacity to take the environment seriously. One approach emphasises bureaucratic/administrative rationality. Here the instrumental and managerial logics typical of the modern state appear as deep-seated obstacles to constructive engagement with ecological issues.[39] Another perspective points to the economic imperative. States require a continuous flow of resources to support their activities, and governments must manage the economy successfully if they are to survive. Thus maintaining business confidence and conditions favourable to capital accumulation become key state concerns. So growth always trumps the environment. The pernicious dynamic of the state system – particularly, military and economic competition which drives environmentally damaging activities – provides another line of argument against the state's environmental potential.[40] Accordingly, in green circles the notion that hierarchy and domination are in some sense inherent characteristics of states (a view absorbed from the anarchist tradition) retains significant allegiance.[41]

Notwithstanding such arguments, however, at the outset of the twenty-first century states still appear central to any serious attempt to come to terms with environmental pressures. As a number of analysts have recently argued, claims about state powerlessness have been exaggerated.[42] States still command impressive financial and organisational resources. They remain the foundation of civil authority and the principal actors on the international stage. Moreover, states possess established democratic structures that provide a critical context for taking and legitimising collective decisions, including decisions about the environment. Even within the European Union, states remain gatekeepers to implementation, and play the decisive role in making policy and determining the course of future integration. Moreover, one could argue that, to the extent that member states cede authority to the Union, the EU itself acquires state-like characteristics. It is also worth noting that many of the reforms introduced over the past two decades (jettisoning failing industries, reducing subsidy programmes, cutting public deficits) have actually enhanced state capacity for societal intervention, while others (for example, public-private partnerships) can be understood as experiments with exercising influence in altered circumstances.

As the new governance literatures have shown, modern societies are changing, and so too are patterns of state/societal interaction.[43] Increased complexity means that emergent problems are often more easily approached either in collaboration with societal groups (businesses, civil organisations) or 'obliquely' (by putting in place conditions that allow publicly desired ends to be achieved by the activities of private parties).[44] To use Kooiman's terms, there is more 'co-governance' and 'self-governance' in contrast to 'hierarchical governance'.[45] Transition management represents exactly this type of approach: for, on the one hand, it foresees an active and interventionist role for government; while, on the other, it defines that role in interactive rather than directive terms.

To argue that states remain important is not to claim that governments have all the answers. On the contrary, partnerships are necessary precisely because in many areas solutions are not obvious, but require pooled knowledge, collaborative learning and joint initiatives. It is true that activities of business and civil society are often more dynamic and change-oriented than those of government.[46] Businesses introduce new products and services, and modify production processes, altering the material burden imposed on the environment. Moreover, when the corporate sector commits at the highest level to engage with issues such as energy efficiency, life-cycle analysis, or greening production chains, the pace of change can be dizzying. For their part, NGOs articulate public concerns over the environment and mobilise social concern to force politicians and the bureaucracy to act. Increasingly too, direct collaboration between these sectors (for example, forest certification schemes) is having tangible effects.[47] And yet the state remains a critical mechanism for taking collective decisions, giving effect to collective choices and mobilising societal resources for societal ends. Indeed, the insistence upon interactive governance and new policy instruments does not imply that more traditional state approaches do not still have a vital role to play. Good 'old fashioned' regulation remains the most straightforward way to address many environmental problems, with cooperation often eased by the spectre of legislation. Again, to argue for the importance of the state does not mean abandoning the international sphere. But it does mean recognising that states still hold the key to driving change in international institutions and to implementing accords concluded at that level.[48]

With respect to the more radical arguments about states and the environment cited earlier much could be written. Perhaps the most pertinent observation is that precisely because the state is so closely entangled with forces that augment human pressures on natural systems it has the potential to play a critical role in bringing some of these under control.[49] Short of a global cataclysm, there is no way that a world of autonomous small-scale communities, or of functionally (rather than territorially) differentiated units of authority, or an integrated system of global government can take shape in coming decades. In short, we are stuck with states for the foreseeable future. Considering recent experiences with societies where the civil power has faltered, most of us will probably take some comfort from that fact.

Ultimately, the most potent of the sceptical arguments is the one that focuses on the economic imperative confronting states. There is no doubt that the stability of modern societies – with their market economies, representative democratic institutions and welfare distributionist mechanisms – has

depended upon the maintenance of steady economic growth. But the indict-
ment of the state to which this points really rests on a specific claim about the
modern (capitalist) economy – that economic advance can only be purchased
at the expense of the environment. And there are grounds for doubting the
validity of this contention.

Certainly, firms are used to making money by expanding production – by
selling more commodities. This happens every day, and as production grows
so does the environmental impact. But companies can also make money by
selling better products, by increasing energy and materials efficiencies, and
by providing services instead of goods. This can lead to a decreased, rather
than an increased, environmental burden. If such gains are sufficiently large,
the scale of production can even rise as the absolute environmental burden
declines. After all, what matters from the environmental perspective are not
financial magnitudes (sales growth, profit figures, or gross national product)
or end-use utilities. What matters is the physical impact on the natural
world. The problem is the disruption of ecological systems and natural
cycles.

Environmental limits are real. Beyond a certain point it is not possible to
keep increasing the rate at which a biological resource is harvested or waste is
dumped without provoking ecological change. But there are different limits,
operative at different spatial and temporal scales, in different natural systems.
Human activity confronts these limits in different ways, in different places, at
different points in time. The environmental burdens societies impose vary, as
does the vulnerability of local ecosystems. So far the most significant global
limit we confront appears to be related to the climate system, with the emission of greenhouse gases figuring as a universal in contemporary societies
(although gross and per capita emission levels vary by several orders of mag-
nitude across nations). Thus the key is the way that economic activity relates
to critical limits at the local, regional and global levels.

This is why the Organisation for Economic Cooperation and Development
and others have spoken of the urgency of 'decoupling' economic growth
environmental burdens.[50] This is in part what the 1987 Report of the World
Commission on Environment and Development meant when it referred to
changing the 'quality' of growth.[51] This implies generating significant materials and energy efficiencies. It requires actually reducing environmental pressures in many areas. Some analysts have spoken of the need for a four- or
even ten-fold increase in resource efficiency in coming decades.[52] But even
change on such a scale will not ensure environmental sustainability unless
attention is paid explicitly to maintaining environmental pressures within the
assimilative capacity of natural systems and to enhancing the integrity of
ecosystems.

Now we already know that 'decoupling' can be achieved with respect to
individual firms. There are many companies that have dramatically decreased
their environmental impositions, while improving their financial returns and
services to clients. We know that it can be achieved across whole industrial

sectors. For example, the forest products industry in some countries has successfully reduced energy consumption and increased biodiversity protection, while improving its financial position. We also know it can be achieved across national economies, with respect to certain substances (for example, sulphur dioxide or mercury emissions), at least for certain periods of time. What we do not know is whether it can be achieved across a whole national economy, across a range of issues, and for the long term. Above all, we do not know the extent to which it can be achieved globally.

Yet there is no reason in principle to believe such 'decoupling' is impossible, although it will require a radical transformation of existing patterns of production and consumption and significant reform of economic, social and political institutions. But, precisely because environmental limits are diverse, it is not necessary to do everything at once. Instead, efforts can concentrate on the most critical issues first, with feedback being used to adjust the ultimate direction and scope of reform. In this respect the state will have a central role to play.

To say that such a transformation is possible does not mean that it is inevitable. There are many ways to respond to environmental limits, including social and technological options that displace burdens in time (on to future generations) and in space (on to other countries), or that redistribute impacts on to disadvantaged socioeconomic strata, or that redefine 'normality' to accommodate deteriorating surroundings and degraded ecosystems. Technological change has long been a political battleground. But in coming decades political conflicts over the sorts of technological futures towards which society aspires are likely to become much more acute. To take just one illustration from the recent literature – will chemicals policy continue to focus on regulating toxics exposures and on cleaning up when harm to human health and ecosystem vitality becomes undeniable, or will the stance shift to one that actively encourages the 'detoxification' of production/consumption systems and thus embodies a precautionary approach?[53] A real change here will involve a clash of powerful interests and competing ideas, and protracted political controversy.

Thus there will be many challenges for environmental political economy over the coming decade. In a broad sense the goal must be to achieve a deeper understanding of processes of transformation as societies seek to improve their environmental performance while meeting other social aspirations. In this regard key questions need to be answered concerning the links between environmental protection, economic restructuring and the adjustment of welfare systems in the developed states; about the integration of environmental concerns into the political and economic life of the rapidly industrialising states, and the achievement of human development goals in the poorest countries; and regarding democracy, civic life and the continued internationalisation of environment problems and solutions across all states.

Notes

1 Organisation for Economic Cooperation and Development, *OECD Environmental Strategy for the First Decade of the 21st Century* (OECD, 2001).
2 European Environment Agency, *Environment in the European Union at the Turn of the Century* (European Environment Agency, 1999).
3 Carolyn Deere and Daniel Esty (eds), *Greening the Americas* (MIT Press, 2002); Eric Neumayer, *Greening Trade and Investment: Environmental Protection without Protectionism* (Earthscan, 2001); and Richard Steinberg, *The Greening of Trade Law: International Trade Organisations and Environmental Issues* (Rowman & Littlefield, 2002).
4 See, for example: Michael Rock, 'Pollution Intensity of GDP and Trade Policy: Can the World Bank Be Wrong?', *World Development*, Vol. 24, No. 3 (1996), pp. 471–9; Brian Hocking and Steven McGuire (eds), *Trade Politics: International, Domestic, and Regional Perspectives* (Routledge, 1999); Marie-Claire Cordonier Segger, *Trade Rules and Sustainability in the Americas* (International Institute for Sustainable Development, 1999); and Shahrukh Khan (ed.), *Trade and Environment: North and South Perspectives and Southern Responses* (Zed, 2002).
5 For example, Jonathan Golub, *New Instruments for Environmental Policy in the EU* (Routledge, 1998); Arthur Mol, Volkmar Lauber and Duncan Liefferink, *The Voluntary Approach to Environmental Policy: Joint Environmental Policy-making in Europe* (Oxford University Press, 2000); and Thomas Sterner, *Policy Instruments for Environmental and Natural Resource Management* (Resources for the Future, 2001).
6 Marc De Clercq, *Negotiating Environmental Agreements in Europe: Critical Factors for Success* (Edward Elgar, 2002); Winston Harrington, Richard D. Morgenstern and Thomas Sterner, *Choosing Environmental Policy: Comparing Instruments and Outcomes in the United States and Europe* (Resources for the Future, 2004); and Organisation for Economic Cooperation and Development, *Voluntary Approaches for Environmental Policy: Effectiveness, Efficiency and Usage in Policy Mixes* (OECD, 2003).
7 Consider: Braden Allenby, *Industrial Ecology: Policy Framework and Implementation* (Prentice Hall, 1999); Robert Ayres and Udo Simonis (eds), *Industrial Metabolism: Restructuring for Sustainable Development* (United Nations University Press, 1995); and Audun Ruud, 'Partners for progress? The role of business in transcending business as usual', in: William Lafferty (ed.), *Governance for Sustainable Development: The Challenge of Adapting Form to Function* (Edward Elgar, 2004), pp. 221–45.
8 Sonja Boehmer-Christiansen and Aynsley Kellow, *International Environmental Policy: Interests and the Failure of the Kyoto Process* (Edward Elgar, 2002).
9 For just a few examples from this immense and growing literature, consider Michael Grubb, Christiaan Vrolijk and Duncan Brack (eds), *The Kyoto Protocol: A Guide and Assessment* (Royal Institute of International Affairs, 1999); Urs Luterbacher and Detlef Sprinz (eds), *International Relations and Global Climate Change* (MIT Press, 2001); and Barry Rabe, *Statehouse and Greenhouse: The Emerging Politics of American Climate Change Policy* (Brookings Institution, 2004).
10 See, for example: Tim Jackson and Laurie Michaelis, 'Policies for Sustainable Consumption', a Report to the Sustainable Development Commission, 2003; and 'Changing Patterns: UK Government Framework for Sustainable Consumption and Production' (UK Department for Environment, Food and Rural Affairs, n.d. [2003]).
11 Michael Redclift, *Wasted: Counting the Costs of Global Consumption* (Earthscan, 1996); Thomas Princen, Michael Maniates and Ken Conca, *Confronting Consumption* (MIT Press, 2002); and Jacquelin Burgess, Tracey Bedford, Kersty

Hobson, Gail Davies and Carolyn Harrison, '(Un)sustainable consumption', in: Frans Berkhout, Melissa Leach and Ian Scoones (eds), *Negotiating Environmental Change* (Edward Elgar, 2003), pp. 261–91.

12 Arthur Mol and Gert Spaargaren, 'Environment, Modernity and Risk Society: The Apocalyptic Horizon of Environmental Reform', *International Sociology*, Vol. 8, No. 4 (1993), pp. 432–59; and Gert Spaargaren, *The Ecological Modernization of Production and Consumption* (Wageningen University, 1997).

13 Albert Weale, *The New Politics of Pollution* (Manchester University Press, 1992).

14 Maarten Hajer, *The Politics of Environmental Discourse: Ecological Modernization and the Policy Process* (Clarendon Press, 1995).

15 Peter Christoff, 'Ecological Modernization, Ecological Modernities', *Environmental Politics*, Vol. 5, No. 3 (1996), pp. 476–500.

16 Arthur Mol and David Sonnenfeld, *Ecological Modernization around the World: Perspectives and Critical Debates* (Frank Cass, 2000).

17 Elinor Ostrom, *Governing the Commons: The Evolution of Institutions for Collective Action* (Cambridge University Press, 1990).

18 Nives Dolsak and Elinor Ostrom (eds), *The Commons in the New Millennium: Challenges and Adaptation* (MIT Press, 2003).

19 Oran Young, *The Effectiveness of International Environmental Regimes: Causal Connections and Behavioural Mechanisms* (MIT Press, 1999); and Edward Miles, Arild Underdal, Steinar Andresen, Jorgen Wettestad, Jon Birger Skjaerseth and Elaiane Carlin, *Environmental Regime Effectiveness: Confronting Theory with Evidence* (MIT Press, 2002).

20 *Where There's a Will There's a World*, The Netherlands Fourth National Environmental Policy Plan (Ministry of Housing, Spatial Planning and the Environment, 2002), p. 63.

21 *Ibid.*, p. 72.

22 Jan Rotmans, René Kemp and Marjolein van Asselt, 'More Evolution than Revolution: Transition Management in Public Policy', *Foresight*, Vol. 3 (2001), pp. 15–31; and Frank Geels, *Understanding the Dynamics of Technological Transitions: A Co-evolutionary and Socio-technical Analysis* (Twente University Press, 2002).

23 Rene Kemp and Jan Rotmans, 'Managing the transition to sustainable mobility', in: Boelie Elzen, Frank Geels and Ken Green (eds), *System Innovation and the Transition to Sustainability: Theory, Evidence and Policy* (Edward Elgar, 2003), pp. 137–67.

24 *Ibid.*

25 *Ibid.*

26 René Kemp and Derk Loorbach, 'Dutch policies to manage the transition to sustainable energy', in: *Jahrbuch Ökologische Ökonomik 4: Innovationen und Nachhaltigkeit* (Metropolis Verlag, 2005), pp. 123–50.

27 *Ibid.*

28 Frans Berkhout, Adrian Smith and Andy Stirling, 'Socio-technological regimes and transition contexts', Science Policy Research Unit Electronic Working Paper Series 106, University of Sussex, 2003, p. 3, available at http://www.sussex.ac.uk/Units/spru/publications/imprint/sewps/sewp106/sewp106.pdf. Emphasis in the original.

29 *Ibid.*, p. 18.

30 *Ibid.*, p. 14.

31 *Ibid.*

32 *Where There's a Will There's a World*.

33 J. Bruggink, *The Next 50 Years: Four European Energy Futures* (Energy Research Centre of the Netherlands, 2005).

34 For a discussion, see Neil Carter, *The Politics of the Environment: Ideas, Activism,*

Policy (Cambridge University Press, 2001); and Andrew Dobson, *Green Political Thought*, 3rd edition (Routledge, 2000).

35 For a discussion, see John Dryzek and David Schlosberg, *Debating the Earth*, 2nd edition (Oxford University Press, 2005).

36 Intergovernmental Panel on Climate Change, *Third Assessment Report* (IPCC, 2001).

37 For example, Rod Rhodes, 'The Hollowing out of the State', *Political Quarterly*, Vol. 65, No. 1 (1994), pp. 138–51.

38 For example, see Susan Strange, *The Retreat of the State* (Cambridge University Press, 1996).

39 Consider Robert Paehlke and Douglas Torgerson, *Managing Leviathan: Environmental Politics and the Administrative State*, 2nd edition (Broadview Press, 2005).

40 See Mathew Paterson, *Understanding Global Environmental Politics: Domination, Accumulation, Resistance* (Palgrave, 2000).

41 For a discussion, see John Barry, *Rethinking Green Politics: Nature, Virtue and Progress* (Sage, 1999).

42 Consider Linda Weiss, *The Myth of the Powerless State* (Cambridge University Press, 1998).

43 Jon Pierre (ed.), *Debating Governance: Authority, Steering and Democracy* (Oxford University Press, 2000).

44 Consider James Meadowcroft, 'Planning for Sustainable Development: Insights from the Literatures of Political Science', *European Journal of Political Research*, Vol. 31, No. 4 (1997), pp. 427–54.

45 Jan Kooiman, *Governing as Governance* (Sage, 2003).

46 Peter Driessen and Pieter Glasbergen, *Greening Society: The Paradigm Shift in Dutch Environmental Politics* (Kluwer, 2002).

47 Benjamin Cashore, Graeme Auld and Deanna Newsom, *Governing through Markets: Forest Certification and the Emergence of Non-State Authority* (Yale University Press, 2004).

48 For recent discussion of the state's relationship with environmental problems, see: Robyn Eckersley, *The Green State: Rethinking Democracy, and Sovereignty* (MIT Press, 2004); John Barry and Robyn Eckersley (eds), *The State and the Global Ecological Crisis* (MIT Press, 2005); and John Dryzek, David Downes, Christian Hunhold and David Schlosberg, with Hans-Kristian Hernes, *Green States and Social Movements* (Oxford University Press, 2003).

49 For an argument about the state's potential to manage environmental problems that draws parallels with contemporary welfare states, see James Meadowcroft, 'From welfare state to ecostate?', in: Barry and Eckersley, *The State and the Global Ecological Crisis*, pp. 5–23.

50 OECD, *OECD Environmental Strategy for the First Decade of the 21st Century*.

51 World Commission on Environment and Development, *Our Common Future* (Oxford University Press, 1987).

52 Ernst von Weizsacker, Amory Lovins and Hunter Lovins, *Factor Four: Doubling Wealth, Halving Resource Use* (Earthscan, 1997).

53 Kenneth Geiser, *Materials Matter: Toward a Sustainable Materials Policy* (MIT Press, 2001).

5 How (the meaning of) gender matters in political economy

V. Spike Peterson

> Work cannot be understood without examining how gender is embedded in all social relations.[1]

> Our collective fear [is] that the new political economy will fail to adopt a gendered analysis at its core, and will implicitly accept the androcentric bias that has characterized the discipline to date.[2]

What is the state of debate regarding gendered political economy? Answering this question depends on the existence of a debate, who is presumed to be participating and, especially, how we understand 'gender'. Among self-proclaimed feminist scholars we can readily identify a range of positions on 'gender and political economy'. While disciplinary locations prompt some of the variation,[3] the most telling differences – or points of debate – reflect varying theoretical (epistemological, methodological) orientations to the study of gender. The range of feminist research constitutes a continuum of overlapping positions that (as clarified below) reflects varying positivist and constructivist (also postmodernist/poststructuralist) orientations. The former mixes feminist and traditional political economy tools to study how men and women – gender understood empirically – are differently affected by, and differently affect, political economy; the latter foregrounds the feminist tool of 'analytical gender' to study how masculinity and femininity – gender understood as a meaning system – produce, and are produced by, political economy. Hence, there is a range of positions, which means that, while feminists share a commitment to the centrality of gender, they do debate *how* to study it.

It is more difficult to assess how and to what extent less visibly 'feminist' scholars participate in the debate. While we see little evidence that political economy scholars assume the *centrality* of gender, in the last 10 years we do observe more attention to the category of 'women' (for example, in labour markets and social movements) and more references to 'gender' in a variety of publications. We also observe the inclusion of 'gender-thematic' articles in journal special issues,[4] as well as 'gender' chapters in edited volumes that are devoted to encompassing topics (e.g. globalisation). In this sense, even scholars who do not self-identify as feminist have increased their awareness of and references to women and/or gender in the context of political economy. This is obviously a welcome development, especially as it is neither an insignificant nor easily won gain.

It is, however, a surprisingly limited – arguably superficial – engagement from the perspective of feminist claims and achievements. In the past decade feminists have exponentially increased knowledge about women's and men's lives and how gender both structures and differentially valorises masculinised and feminised identities, desires, expectations, knowledges, skills, labour, wages, activities and experiences. They have built professional associations, launched feminist journals, published widely, advanced crossdisciplinary scholarship, pioneered theoretical insights and promoted critical and transformative teaching, research and academic activism. In spite of these successes, feminists note continuing resistance to the breadth, depth and specifically *theoretical* implications of feminist political economy scholarship.[5] What explains the vitality, achievements, and sophistication of feminist/gendered political economy and, at the same time, its limited impact on mainstream and even most critical political economy scholars?

Some, perhaps a great deal, of the resistance is presumably due to individual investments and ideological factors that fuel resistance to feminisms in general.[6] However significant these may be, they are difficult to document and relatively unresponsive to critique. What is more productive, and relevant to the 'state of the debate', is examining how epistemological differences (among non-feminist as well as feminist scholars) shape one's understanding of gender and, hence, where one is positioned on the continuum and how one participates in the debate. To anticipate the argument: in so far as positivist/rationalist/modernist commitments continue to dominate in mainstream, critical and even feminist political economy, gender can only be understood empirically and tends to become a synonym for women, who as a category can then be 'added' to prevailing analyses. More constructivist or poststructuralist commitments are required for understanding gender analytically (as a signifying code); these remain marginalised in economics, international relations (IR) and international political economy, with the systemic effect of reducing non-feminist participation in, sustaining resistance to, and obscuring the most significant claims and insights of feminist political economy.

With these points as background, this chapter first reviews the continuum of feminist positions, indicating the significance of epistemological differences and gesturing toward a literature review of developments in gendering political economy. I argue that the most productive and transformative gendered political economy entails systemic engagement with *analytical* gender and its hierarchical implications (privileging that which is masculinised and devalorising that which is feminised). The next section attempts to demonstrate the value of this orientation (and cites additional literature) by providing a 'big picture' overview of gendered global political economy

(GPE). The objective is to substantiate theoretical claims and illustrate how gender is central to advancing political economy scholarship.

A continuum of (overlapping and ongoing) feminist knowledge-building projects

Across disciplines, feminist interventions have typically begun by exposing the omission of actual women and their activities, while also documenting how women and feminised activities are represented as inferior to male-as-norm (androcentric) criteria. In economics and political economy, feminists have exposed how men dominate the practice of and knowledge production about (what men define as) 'economics'; how women's domestic, reproductive and caring labour is deemed marginal to (male-defined) production and analyses of it; how orthodox models and methods presuppose male-dominated activities (paid work, the formal economy) and masculinised characteristics (autonomous, objective, rational, instrumental, competitive). As a corollary, 'women's work' and feminised qualities – in whatever sphere – are devalued: deemed 'economically' irrelevant, characterised as subjective, 'natural' and 'unskilled', and typically unpaid. For most economists, social reproduction through heterosexual families and non-conflictual intra-household dynamics are simply taken for granted; alternative household forms and the rising percentage of female-headed and otherwise 'unconventional' households are rendered deviant or invisible.[7]

Mounting evidence of systematic exclusions prompts a new strategy: correcting androcentric bias by *adding women* and their experiences to existing analytical frameworks. New questions emerge regarding what counts as relevant data (marriage patterns, family budgets), appropriate sources (church records, personal diaries) and germane topics (caring labour, shopping, food preparation, sex work). From this expanded inquiry we learn more about women and everyday life, but also more about *men* and conventional topics. That is, rather than a masculinist focus exclusively on 'the main story' of men's activities, we attend as well to the 'background' story that is rarely visible but which underpins and enables men's activities. Not only do women's lives become more visible, but the interdependence of both stories is illuminated, which also improves our understanding of the featured story and its primarily male protagonists. Hence, this 'project' not only adds women, but expands into investigating relationships among women's and men's identities, activities and inequalities of power.

The most extensive and familiar feminist research emerges from noting the omission of women and adding them – as an empirical category – to prevailing narratives. This may seem methodologically simple, but often produces surprising results. Recall how Boserup's 1970 study of the effects of modernisation policies on Third World women undercut claims that development benefited everyone. Subsequent 'women in development' (WID) research documented both how policies and practices marginalised women *and* how their exclusion jeopardised development objectives.[8] Numerous subsequent and ongoing studies demonstrate how a focus on women and gender improves our analyses. For example, feminists produce more accurate analyses of intra-household labour and resource allocation; move beyond quantitative growth indicators to improve measurements of human wellbeing; and document the value of 'women's work' and its centrality to 'development', long-term production of social capital and more accurate national accounting. They investigate gender patterns in wages, migration, informalisation, sub-contracted 'home-working' and foreign remittances. And Third World women especially demonstrate the importance of local, indigenous and colonised people's agency in identifying problems and negotiating remedies.[9]

Making women empirically visible is thus an indispensable project. It inserts actual (embodied) women in our picture of economic reality, exposes how women and men are differently engaged with and affected by political economy, and reveals women as agents and activists, as well as victims of violence and the poorest of the poor. But adding women to existing para-digms also raises deeper questions by exposing how the conceptual structures themselves presuppose masculine experience and perspective. For example, women/femininity cannot simply be 'added' to constructions that are *consti-tuted* as masculine: reason, economic man, breadwinner, the public sphere. Either women as feminine cannot be added (that is, women must become like men) or the constructions themselves are transformed (namely, adding women as feminine alters their masculine premise and changes their meaning). In this sense, the exclusions are not accidental or coincidental but required for the analytical consistency of reigning paradigms.[10]

The implications of this insight move us along the continuum, from more positivist/rationalist epistemological commitments limited to understanding gender empirically to more constructivist and poststructuralist insistence that gender is also analytical. In effect, we move beyond critique to reconstruction of theory, and this has been particularly fertile terrain in the past decade. We also move beyond the dichotomy of men and women to the hierarchy of masculinity over femininity.

Understood analytically, gender is a governing code that pervades lan-guage and hence systemically shapes how we think, what we presume to 'know', and how such knowledge claims are legitimated. Epistemological and ontological issues are more visible at this 'side' of the continuum because conventional categories and dichotomies are not taken for granted but problematised. Here we find more attention to discourse, subjectivities and culture, and more interrogation of foundational constructs (rationality, work, production, capital, value, development). Consistent with this, there is typically more evidence of theoretical discussion and debate, and more self-consciousness about analytical assumptions and how they frame the questions we ask, the methods we adopt and the politics they entail. At the same time, as a governing code gender systemically shapes what we *value*. In particular, gender privileges (valorises) that which is characterised as masculine – not all men or only men – at the expense of that which is stigmatised (devalorised) as feminine: lacking agency, control, reason, 'skills', culture, and so on. To illustrate how a focus on analytical gender shifts the terms of debate I briefly consider two developments in gendered political economy.

WID scholarship initially sought more effective inclusion of women in the practices and benefits of development and argued that this would also improve development. But this orientation was gradually challenged as feminists questioned underlying assumptions, registered in a shift from WID and its liberal (and positivist) inclinations to gender and development (GAD), with its more constructivist, critical and structural orientation. It was increasingly clear that 'adding women' left the most significant problems intact. It did not address the denigration of feminised labour, the structural privileging of men and masculinity, the depoliticisation of women's subordination in the family and workplace, or the increasing pressure on women to work a triple shift (in familial, informal and formal activities). In contrast, GAD problematised the meaning and desirability of 'development', interrogated the definition of work and how to 'count it', examined gender ideologies to explain unemployed men's reluctance to 'help' in the household, challenged constructions of feminism imposed by Western elites and criticised narratives of victimisation for denying agency and resistance. These studies indicate an opening up of questions, an expansion of research foci and a complication of analyses.[11]

At the same time, diversity among women forced feminists to reflect critically (and uncomfortably) on the meaning of feminism, definitions of 'woman', the politics of representation and the dangers of universalising claims. 'Sisterhood' aspirations have always been in tension with differences of ethnicity/race, class, age, physical ability, sexuality and nationality, and especially so in the context of globalisation. Politics and analytics merge here as actual differentiations – including hierarchies – among women contradicted the positivist claim of homogeneous categories (empirical males and females); more complex analyses were required. However one assesses their efforts, I believe that feminists have taken the challenges of theorising 'difference' more seriously, and moved more responsibly to address them, than most oppositional groups. On the one hand, feminisms have transdisciplinary and complex analytical resources for investigating and theorising about identity, difference and historically specific hierarchies of oppression (heterosexism, racism, classism and so on). On the other hand, feminist claims to political relevance and critique have 'forced' them to address embodied differences of power: feminist scholars are expected to 'walk' their (egalitarian) 'talk'. In short, contestations of theory and practice that are specific to recent (especially postcolonial and queer) feminisms have, I believe, generated the most incisive and inclusive analyses of power, privilege and political economy available at this juncture.[12]

Prevailing trends and the state of debate

In the past decade feminists have continued to expose masculinist bias and its effects on the theory/practice of political economy and have vastly increased the evidence corroborating (and complicating) early feminist critiques. They have also expanded from an initial interest in more obviously gender-differentiated effects of microeconomic phenomena to interrogate the less direct effects of macroeconomic policies, including how gender operates even in the abstracted realm of financial markets. Similarly, feminists investigate linkages among sectors and levels of analysis, focus less on national/ territorial boundaries and more on transnational/global dynamics, analyse globalisation/neoliberalism as masculinist and racist, and emphasise women's agency and resistance.[13]

As a generalisation regarding theoretical developments, feminist scholars increasingly subscribe to constructivist orientations, where masculinist assumptions are problematised and feminist alternatives explored.[14] Constructivism means different things to different people, especially in different disciplines. Without engaging complex definitional debates, I simply note minimalist claims: constructivism recognises that agent and structure are not categorically separate (as in a positivist binary), but interact to construct social reality. By acknowledging the social construction of agents, identities and ideologies, constructivism opens inquiry to new questions, not least for present purposes, of how masculinist (and other) ideologies shape what we study and how we study it. On the continuum posited here, this goes beyond simply adding women as an empirical category and has the potential for altering existing theoretical frameworks. (Whether and to what extent it does so depends on the particular research issues and epistemological commitments of the researcher.)

In addition, constructivism has two important and overlapping strengths. Analytically, it has the advantage of insisting on the centrality of shared ideas, or intersubjective meaning systems, in constituting social reality; it thus accommodates cultural coding and subjective dimensions that (I argue below) have particular force in today's political economy. Moreover, in contrast to poststructuralism, it has the strategic advantage of making sense to, and being accepted by, a growing audience; it thus reaches across more thematic and disciplinary boundaries and facilitates conversations along and across the continuum of gendered political economy. Constructivism is thus crucial to feminist (and other critical) interventions as it significantly expands the terrain of inquiry and provides an important 'bridge' across epistemological divisions.[15] To address an expanding agenda and critical commitments, feminists draw on a variety of approaches – Marxian, heterodox, institutionalist, neoGramscian, social economics, world systems – and currently favour heterogeneity and pluralism over adherence to any single paradigm.

This suggests perhaps the most significant trend in gendered political economy: away from making feminisms 'fit' orthodox approaches (decreasing dependence on them) to generating unique and unapologetically feminist methodologies and theories. This has been fuelled by an expansive critical literature that rejects 'absolute objectivity', 'decontextualised rationality', rigid boundaries and monological explanations as masculinist and modernist preoccupations, in favour of the holistic, the historical, 'thicker description' and institutional embeddedness. This maturation in confidence involves moving beyond critical, corrective orientations to production of alternatives, demonstrating their efficacy and benefits, and generating visions of economics that include ethical, more humane concerns. Arguably the most fundamental and widely accepted shift among feminists is the rejection of neoclassical models of abstract rationality and 'choice' in favour of a more relevant and responsible model of 'social provisioning'.[16]

This is not to suggest homogeneity among feminists. For analytical as well as strategic reasons, many feminists are wary of adopting what they understand as 'too' constructivist, and especially poststructuralist/postmodernist, orientations. The argument briefly is this: from more positivist starting points gender remains dichotomised and can only be understood as a homogeneous empirical category; women can (at best) be added as such a category to existing frameworks; this will amend and presumably improve analyses, but (because empirical categories and analytical framing are presumed separable) this addition need not have any theoretical implications. One can 'add women' or refer to gender without disrupting orthodox methods or altering foundational questions. As a corollary, simply 'adding women' tends to have little impact on the core of mainstream scholarship, where the gender of bodies, or ratio of male-to-female workers, is presumed not to have epistemological consequences. In other words, as long as theories and methods are not deeply affected, it is relatively acceptable and easy enough to add (empirical) women/gender. This is what many feminist – and apparently an increasing number of non-feminist – scholars are doing.

From more constructivist and especially poststructuralist starting points, gender is understood as a governing code and its inclusion in our analyses necessarily has epistemological/theoretical implications. On this view, gendering political economy entails a questioning of orthodox methods and foundational inquiries in so far as these rely on gendered assumptions and biases. This raises the theoretical stakes dramatically: it threatens to be systemically disruptive, which decreases receptivity and increases resistance to more complex understandings of gender. It is important to note that, in the absence of constructivist or poststructuralist insights, the meaning of operational 'codes' (gender or otherwise) is neither obvious nor readily comprehended. Hence, the systemic, intellectually transformative work of feminists is effectively 'invisible' because it exceeds what the mainstream can see or comprehend through positivist/modernist lenses. In this sense, the marginalisation of constructivism and poststructuralism in economics, political economy and IPE significantly limits how gender is understood, and goes some way in explaining both the variation among feminists and the relatively superficial engagement of non-feminists, who cannot (or do not want to) 'see' the profound implications of taking gender seriously. In other words, epistemological commitments shape receptivity to feminist work, and especially *which* feminist insights/claims are deemed comprehensible, acceptable and/or compelling.

What does this mean for the state of debate? I have indicated a variety of feminist positions and how these contribute to gendering political economy. Debates among feminists are manifested in differing research priorities and differing practical strategies for promoting feminist political economy. Both are shaped by epistemological and ideological differences. Regarding the former and as indicated by the continuum, feminists disagree on what topics are most important to investigate. For example, sexuality and heterosexism are relatively neglected, in part because their relevance is obscured when gender is understood as a synonym for the unproblematised category of 'women'.[17] Similarly, resistance, especially to poststructuralist insights, limits feminist political economy engagement with culture, subjectivities, the politics of representation and postcolonial critiques. This is spurred by a widespread (but I believe mistaken) perception that poststructuralism entails elevating symbolic/cultural/literary phenomena at the expense of material processes and conditions. This is obviously unacceptable to feminists who study political economy 'not just to understand the world but to change it'. Feminists are rightly wary of approaches that minimise 'the material', and at present the most visible poststructuralist work cultivates this perception; I argue instead that poststructuralism potentially offers the most incisive analyses of culture and materiality as *mutually produced* (co-constituted).[18] Rejecting this approach impedes efforts to address diversity, theorise the interconnectedness of hierarchies, analyse how power operates, pay more attention to subaltern voices/perspectives, and take seriously knowledge/theorising from marginalised locations.

Strategically, some feminists advocate relatively more acceptable, 'doable' and presumably efficacious reforms from within – or not far outside of – conventional thinking. For example, through a variety of activities – gender mainstreaming, global networking, women-oriented non-governmental organisations – feminists have expanded their capacity to influence policy-making, inform development strategies, direct research agendas and promote 'women's issues'. Feminists utilise Amartya Sen's capabilities approach to enhance awareness of gender, deploy human rights discourse to promote women's economic rights and advocate microcredit lending to empower poor and especially rural women.[19] While most feminists recognise the need for and support these strategies, some also question their efficacy in terms of securing systemic gains for women and/or transforming structural conditions that reproduce hierarchies not only of gender but class, race, sexuality and nationality. In short, feminists debate familiar trade-offs between 'safer', shorter-term and typically localised 'practical' gains, and more disruptive, longer-term and systemically transformative strategies. The latter, of course, are perceived as 'threatening' to careers as well as to conventional knowledge production and political strategies. Like research priorities, these differences in strategy are shaped by epistemological and ideological commitments. In particular, taking analytical gender seriously exceeds piecemeal reforms (which leave 'too much in place') and implies more systemic transformation of subjectivities, analytical frameworks and institutional structures.

In sum, I argue that epistemological differences are key to understanding the state of debate regarding gendered political economy. Among feminists, analytical and strategic considerations shape what is debated. Among non-feminists, participation in the debate is constrained by epistemological (and strategic?) commitments that impede taking analytical gender seriously, and focus instead on 'adding women/gender' in relatively safe and acceptable terms, thus obscuring the import and systemic implications of feminist theory. In this sense, feminists have little company in debating gendered political economy; rather, they (like feminists in IR) appear to be forging ahead with their own agendas and debates, but in relative – and presumably regrettable – isolation from mainstream and even critical political economy. The point, again, is not to disparage the increased attention to women/gender, as this is a considerable achievement and an indispensable starting point. But in the face of feminist research and transformative theoretical insights, this limited engagement is problematic. The continued resistance to, or inadequate comprehension of, feminist contributions not only undermines specifically 'feminist' objectives. In so far as analytical gender has systemic and epistemological implications, its continued marginalisation is detrimental to advancing political economy knowledge/theory/analysis more generally. In the next section I attempt to substantiate these claims by providing a 'big picture' analysis of GPE that takes both empirical and analytical gender seriously.[20]

Gendered political economy of globalisation

Neoliberal policies guiding contemporary globalisation are promoted primarily by geopolitical elites in the interest of powerful states and the inter- and transnational institutions they effectively control. Deregulation has permitted the hypermobility of ('foot-loose') capital, induced phenomenal growth in crisis-prone financial markets and increased the power of private capital interests. Liberalisation is selectively implemented: powerful states engage in protectionism, less through tariffs than rules, regulations and subsidies,[21] while developing countries have limited control over protecting domestic industries, the goods thereby produced and the jobs provided. Privatisation has entailed loss of nationalised industries in developing economies and a decrease in public sector employment and provision of social services worldwide. The results of restructuring are complex, uneven and controversial. While economic growth is the objective and has been realised in some areas and sectors, evidence increasingly suggests expanding inequalities, indeed a polarisation, of resources within and between countries.

Globalisation is a gendered process that reflects both continuity and change. Men, especially those who are economically, ethnically and racially privileged, continue to dominate institutions of authority and power worldwide. And masculinist thinking continues to dominate economic theorising and policy making: top-down, decontextualised (non-holistic), formulaic and over-reliant on growth and quantifiable indicators (rather than provisioning and measures of human wellbeing and sustainability). But globalisation is also disrupting gendered patterns by altering conventional beliefs, roles, livelihoods and political practices worldwide. While some changes are small and incremental, others challenge our deepest assumptions (e.g. male breadwinner roles) and most established institutions (e.g. patriarchal families). Feminists argue that not only are the benefits and costs of globalisation unevenly distributed between men and women, but that masculinist bias in theory/practice exacerbates structural hierarchies of race/ethnicity, class and nation.

With other critical scholars I argue that dominating accounts of GPE perpetuate economistic, modernist/positivist and masculinist commitments. In particular, these preclude adequate analyses of two central features of global restructuring. First, today's globalisation is distinguished by its dependence on historically contingent and socially embedded information and communication technologies (ICTs) specific to the late twentieth century. Due to the inherently conceptual/cultural nature of information, not only empirical but analytical challenges are posed by the unprecedented fusion of culture and economy – of virtual and material dimensions – afforded by ICTs. In brief, the symbolic/virtual aspects of today's GPE expose – to a unique extent and in new developments – how conventional (positivist) separations of culture from economy are totally indefensible and how poststructuralist lenses are essential for adequately analysing today's GPE. Second, globalisation and its effects are extremely uneven, manifested starkly in global, intersecting stratifications of ethnicity/race, class, gender and nation. To address these conditions adequately requires critical and especially feminist postcolonial lenses.

Moreover, to investigate the interconnections among structural hierarchies I deploy gender analytically, arguing that denigration of the feminine (coded into masculinist/modernist dichotomies as hierarchical) pervades language and culture, with systemic effects on how we 'take for granted' (normalise/ depoliticise) the devaluation of feminised bodies, identities *and* activities. This has particular relevance for economics, where assessments of 'value' are key. I argue that feminisation of identities and practices effectively devalues them in cultural as well as economic terms. Briefly: the taken-for-granted devaluation of 'women's work' is generalised from women to include feminised 'others': migrants, marginalised populations, 'unskilled' workers, the urban underclass and developing countries. Women and feminised others constitute the vast majority of the world's population, as well as the vast majority of poor, less skilled, insecure, informalised and flexibilised workers;

and the global economy absolutely depends on the work that they do. Yet their work is variously unpaid, underpaid, trivialised, denigrated, obscured and uncounted: it is devalorised. This economic devalorisation is either hardly noticed or deemed 'acceptable' because it is consistent with cultural devalorisation of that which is feminised. The key point here is that feminisation devalorises not only women but also racially, culturally and economically marginalised men *and* work that is deemed unskilled, menial and 'merely' reproductive.

Moving beyond a narrow definition of economics, I develop an alternative analytical framing of reproductive, productive and virtual economies that shifts how we see the terrain of globalisation and hence how we might interpret, understand and respond to it. I refer not to conventional but Foucauldian economies: as mutually constituted (therefore coexisting and interactive) systemic sites through and across which power operates. These sites involve familiar exchanges, but also include sociocultural processes of subject formation and cultural socialisation that underpin identities and their political effects. The conceptual and cultural dimensions of these sites are understood as inextricable from (mutually constituted by) material effects, social practices and institutional structures. The objectives are to demonstrate the co-constitution of culture and economy, the interaction of identification processes and their politics, and the value of deploying a critical feminist, poststructuralist lens as a means to exposing the operating codes of neoliberal capitalism. Here I review only major trends in each economy, emphasising how they are gendered.

The productive economy

I begin with the familiar 'productive economy', understood as 'formal' – regularised and regulated – economic activities identified with primary, secondary and tertiary production. Globalisation variously complicates these distinctions, especially as ICTs reconfigure each sector. First, the dramatic decline in world prices of and demand for (non-oil) primary products has been devastating to Third World economies where primary production dominates: unemployment problems are exacerbated, ability to attract foreign investment is reduced, and debt dependency may be increased. One effect is viewing (unregulated) labour as a competitive resource and/or encouraging out-migration in search of work.

Second, 'de-industrialisation' especially affects advanced industrialised countries and major cities, manifested variously through downsizing, 'jobless growth', loss of skilled and often unionised positions, growth in low-wage, semi- and unskilled jobs, and relocation of production to lower wage areas. Job security is additionally eroded for all but elite workers through 'flexibilisation': more temporary, part-time, non-unionised jobs with fewer benefits, and more 'just-in-time', decentralised and subcontracted production processes. These shifts tend to increase un- and underemployment (especially of men) and coupled with erosion of union power translate into a decline in real incomes and household resources.

Flexibilisation tends to increase the power and autonomy of management and be attractive to those with highly valued skills. Some find that flexible arrangements better suit their life conditions. Mothers and single parents may prefer flexible arrangements, although this must be assessed in the context of childcare availability and limited access to better-paying and more secure employment opportunities. Specific trade-offs depend on specific contexts, but a general point remains: in the absence of regulatory frameworks that protect workers' rights and generate living wages, flexibilisation translates into greater insecurity of employment and income for the majority of the world's workers.[22]

Third, employment shifts from manufacturing to information-based services as technologies transform the nature of work worldwide. Income polarisation is exacerbated in so far as service jobs tend to be either skilled and high-waged (professional-managerial jobs; for which read 'masculinised') or semi-, unskilled and poorly paid (personal, cleaning, retail and clerical services; for which read: 'feminised'). Hence, this shift also favours countries with developed technology infrastructures and relatively skilled workers.[23]

The fourth trend is feminisation of employment, understood simultaneously as a material, embodied transformation of labour markets (increasing proportion of women), a conceptual characterisation of deteriorated and devalorised labour conditions (less desirable, meaningful, safe or secure) and a reconfiguration of worker identities (feminised managers, female breadwinners). Women's formal employment has been increasing worldwide, while male participation has been falling (this indicates less an empowerment of women than a deterioration in working conditions for men). As jobs require few skills, and flexibilisation becomes the norm, the most desirable workers are those who are perceived to be undemanding (unorganised), docile but reliable, available for part-time and temporary work, and willing to accept low wages. Gender stereotypes depict women as especially suitable for these jobs and gender inequalities render women especially desperate for access to income. In short, as more jobs become casual, irregular, flexible and precarious, more women – and feminised men – are doing them.

Fifth, globalisation increases flows of people: to urban areas, export-processing zones, seasonal agricultural sites and tourism locales. Migrations are shaped by colonial histories, geopolitics, immigration policies, capital flows, labour markets, cultural stereotypes, skill attributions, kinship networks and identity markers. Given the nature of 'unskilled' jobs most frequently available (cleaning, harvesting, domestic service, sex work), migrant worker populations are especially marked by gender and race/ethnicity. Being on the move – for work, recreation or escape – affects personal and collective identities and cultural reproduction. Not least, traditional family forms and divisions of labour are disrupted, destabilising men's and women's identities and gender relations more generally. Shifting identities have complex effects at numerous 'levels', whether expressed in anti-immigrant racism, nationalist state-building, ethnocultural diasporas, ethnic cleansing or patriarchal religious fundamentalisms.[24]

Sixth, feminists have generated extensive research on structural adjustment policies, documenting not only their gender-differentiated effects but also gender, class and racial/ethnic biases in policy making. Privatisation has patterned effects in so far as reductions in public spending have generalisable consequences. When social services are cut, women are disproportionately affected because they are more likely to depend on secure government jobs and on public resources in support of reproductive labour. When public provisioning declines, women are culturally expected to fill the gap, in spite of fewer available resources, more demands on their time and minimal increases in men's caring labour. Effects include more women working a 'triple shift', the feminisation of poverty worldwide, and both short- and long-term deterioration in female health and human capital development.

Trade liberalisation is associated with increases in women's labour force participation worldwide, with complicated gender effects. In general, elite, educated and highly skilled women benefit from the 'feminisation of employment' and employment in any capacity arguably benefits women in terms of access to income and the personal and economic empowerment this affords.[25] Women, however, continue to earn 30–40 per cent less than men, and the majority of women are entering the workforce under adverse structural conditions. Work in export-processing zones is tedious yet demanding, and sometimes hazardous, with negative effects on women's health and long-term working capacity. When new technologies are implemented it is also typically men – not women – who are retained or rehired as machine operators.[26]

The uneven and gendered effects of these trends are most visible in relation to production processes and working conditions. For the majority of families worldwide, one-third of which are female-headed, restructuring has meant declining household income, reduced access to safe and secure employment, and decreased provision of publicly funded social services. Global poverty is increasingly feminised and is especially stark among female-headed households and elderly women. In developed economies reduction of social services disproportionately hurts women, the urban underclass and immigrant families. Structural adjustment programmes imposed on developing countries exacerbate women's poverty by promoting outward-oriented growth, rather than meeting domestic subsistence needs. They reduce public subsidies that lower prices of basic goods, spur urbanisation and labour migration that increases the number of female-headed households, aggravate un- and underemployment of men that reduces household income, and disrupt traditional social forms of support for women.

These conditions force people to pursue 'survival strategies' and seek income however they can. The global trend is towards the un- and underemployment of men, increasing employment of women as cheaper workers, and a phenomenal growth of 'informal' work in the home, community and shadow economy and in criminal activities. Feminists argue that these trends not only differentially affect women, men and feminised 'others', but they are also shaped by masculinist ways of thinking in regard to how 'work' and 'economics' are defined, who should do what kinds of work, and how different activities are valued.

The reproductive economy

Conventional – and continuing – neglect of the 'reproductive economy' exemplifies masculinist and modernist bias in political economy. This neglect continues due to masculinising the (valorised) public sphere of power and formal (paid) work, and feminising the (marginalised) family/private sphere of emotional maintenance, leisure and caring (unpaid) labour. Here I focus on three reasons for taking the reproductive economy seriously: the signifi-cance of subject formation and socialisation, the devalorisation of 'women's work' and the increasing role of informalisation in the GPE.

Socialisation presumably teaches us how to become individuals/subjects/ agents according to the codes of a particular cultural environment. Subject formation begins in the context of family life, and the language, cultural rules, and ideologies we acritically imbibe in childhood are especially influen-tial. This is where we first observe and internalise gender differences, their respective identities and divisions of labour. Moreover, gender acculturation is inextricable from beliefs about race/ethnicity, age, class, religion and other axes of 'difference'.

Feminists have long argued that subject formation matters structurally for economic relations. It produces individuals who are then able to 'work' and this unpaid reproductive labour saves capital the costs of producing key inputs. It also instils attitudes, identities and belief systems that enable soci-eties to function. Capitalism, for instance, requires not only that 'workers' accept and perform their role in 'production', but that individuals more gen-erally accept hierarchical divisions of labour and their corollary: differential valorisation of who does what kind of work.

Socialisation and the caring labour required to sustain family relations are stereotyped as 'women's work' worldwide. Yet, in spite of romanticised motherhood and a glut of pro-family rhetoric, neoliberal globalisation reduces the emotional, cultural and material resources necessary for the wellbeing of most women and families. Similarly, the ideology of patriarchal states, reli-gions and nuclear families that locates women in the home (as loyal depend-ents and loving service providers) is today contradicted by two realities: many women wish to work outside of the home, whilst for many other women economic realities (and consumerist ideologies) compel them to seek formal employment. As already noted, when household resources decline, masculin-ist ideologies hold women disproportionately responsible for family survival. Women everywhere are increasing the time they spend on reproductive labour, in ensuring food availability and health maintenance for the family, in providing emotional support and taking responsibility for young, ill and elderly dependents. Mothers often curtail their own consumption and health-care in favour of serving family needs, and daughters (more often than sons) forfeit educational opportunities when extra labour is needed at home. The effects are not limited to women because the increased burdens they bear are inevitably translated into costs to their families, and hence to societies more generally.[27] As a survival strategy, women especially rely on informal work to ensure their own and their family's wellbeing.

Informal activities are not unique to, but have nonetheless greatly expanded in, the context of neoliberal restructuring.[28] Increasing un- and under-employment, flexibilisation and erosion or prohibition of union power has meant declining real incomes and decreased job security worldwide. Deregu-lation and privatisation undercut welfare provisioning, state employment and collective supports for family wellbeing. People are thus 'pushed' to engage in informal activities as a strategy for securing income however they can. Infor-malisation has a variety of direct and indirect effects on labour relations. In general, it decreases the structural power of workers, reaps higher profits for capital, depresses formal wages, disciplines all workers and, through the iso-lation of informalised labour, impedes collective resistance. Women, the poor, migrants and recent immigrants are the prototypical (feminised) workers of the informal economy;[29] in the context of increasing flexibilisation, the devalued conditions which informalisation demands are arguably the future for all but elite workers worldwide.

Informalisation tends to be polarised between a small, highly skilled group able to take advantage of and prosper from deregulation and flexibili-sation, and the majority of the world's workers who participate less out of choice than necessity due to worsening conditions in the formal economy. Among those with less choice women are the majority, as informal work constitutes a survival strategy for sustaining households. Insecure and risky work in domestic services and the sex industry are often the primary options. This reflects not only dire economic needs, but also masculinist thinking that identifies domestic labour as women's work and objectifies female bodies as sources of pleasure for men. Masculinist institutions collude in promoting economic policies (tourism as a development plan, remittances as a foreign currency source) that 'push' women into precarious informal work.[30]

Informalisation is heterogeneous and controversial. Some individuals prosper by engaging in entrepreneurial activities afforded by a less regulated environment. This is especially evident in micro-enterprises (favoured by neo-liberals) where innovation may breed success and multiplying effects; in tax evasion and international pricing schemes that favour larger operations; in developing countries where informal activities are crucial for income generation; and in criminal activities that are 'big business' worldwide (for example, traffic in drugs, arms and the bodies of sex workers and illegal immigrants).[31] In sum, informalisation is key to the current GPE, yet is rela-tively undertheorised. Due to its unprecedented and explosive growth, the unregulated and often semi-legal or illegal nature of its activities, its feminisation and effects on conditions of labour, it poses fundamental challenges for adequately analysing the GPE.

The virtual economy

Globalisation is especially visible in flows of symbols, information and communication through electronic and wireless transmissions that defy territorial constraints. It is not only the new scale and velocity of these transmissions but the different (symbolic, non-material, virtual) nature of these processes that we must address, as intangible symbols contravene familiar notions of time and space as well as conventional analyses of material goods. The unprecedented fusion of symbols/culture and commodities/economy in today's GPE requires an understanding of 'culture' and 'economy' as co-constituted. Given the newness of these developments, specifying a 'virtual economy' is a first step. I identify three (interactive) modes of this economy – financial, informational, cultural – and review them briefly here with a focus on how they are gendered.

Since the 1970s floating exchange rates, reduced capital controls, offshore transactions, desegmentation, new financial instruments, securitisation and the rise of institutional investors have interacted to amplify the speed, scale and complexity of global financial transactions. (Male-dominated) powerful states have been complicit in, and (masculinist?) technologies have been decisive for, enabling the mobility of capital and its enhanced power. The key result is an 'enormous mass of "world money" . . . [that] is not being created by economic activity like investment, production, consumption, or trade . . . It is virtual [symbolic] rather than real [commodity] money.'[32] The point is not that this 'delinking' (of symbolic from commodity money) insulates the real economy from global finance; rather, prices 'set' in the virtual economy (e.g. through interest and exchange rates) have decisive (and gendered) effects throughout the socioeconomic order. For example, investment strategies shift toward short-term horizons and away from infrastructural and arguably more socially-beneficial endeavours; production shifts toward flexibilisation, with its problematic job insecurities; and labour markets are polarised between high-tech, highly skilled masculinised jobs and devalorised feminised services. In global financial markets, what does distinguish symbolic from commodity money is the extent to which its symbolic/informational content (e.g. stock market values and forecasts) is a function less of 'objective' indicators than processes of interpretation that involve subjective ideas, identities and expectations. Financial crises and stock market scandals reveal the extent to which (primarily male) agents in this rarefied environment rely on guesswork, trust in their colleagues' opinions, and purely subjective assessments as they 'play' casino capitalism. Moreover, feminists have documented the role of masculine identities among power wielders, as a shift from more state-centric 'Chatham House Man' to market-centred 'Davos Man' and as shaping the subjectivities of financial traders.[33]

Effects of global finance are multiple. The allure of financial trading exacerbates the devalorisation of manufacturing and encourages short-term over long-term investments in industry, infrastructure and human capital. The expansion, complexity and non-transparency of global financial transactions makes money laundering easier, which enhances opportunities for illicit financial trading as well as organised crime (including the gendered practices of trade in women, guns and drugs) and decreases tax contributions that underpin public welfare. Access to credit becomes decisive for individuals and states, and is deeply structured by familiar hierarchies. Increasing urgency in regard to 'managing money' and investment strategies shifts status and decision-making power within households, businesses, governments and global institutions. These changes disrupt conventional identities, functions and sites of authority, especially as pursuit of profits displaces provisioning needs and governments compete for private global capital at the expense of public welfare.

Moreover, the instability of financial markets increases risks that are socialised (hurting public welfare) and, when crises ensue, women suffer disproportionately. Two entwined issues emerge: first, women and gender-sensitive analyses are absent – or at best marginalised – in the decision-making processes and analytical assessments of the financial order. Women are underrepresented in the institutions of global finance, a model of elite agency and (instrumental) economic 'efficiency' is deemed common sense, and the masculinism of financial players and their practices is obscured. Second, these exclusions and blinders filter what elite analysts are able – or willing – to 'see'. In particular, they obscure the gendered costs of crises: loss of secure jobs and earning capacity due to women's concentration in precarious forms of employment; lengthened work hours for women as they 'cushion' the impact of household income; decreased participation of girls in education and deteriorating health conditions for women; increased child labour and women's licit and illicit informal activities; and increased acts of violence against women.[34]

These costs not only disproportionately hurt women in the immediacy and aftermath of crises, but have important long-term effects. On the one hand, girls and women are less able to participate as full members of society and have fewer skills required for safe and secure income-generation, whilst the intensification of women's work with fewer resources imperils social reproduction more generally. On the other hand, entire societies are affected as deteriorating conditions of social reproduction, health and education have long-term consequences for collective wellbeing and national competitiveness in the new world economy.

The informational mode of the virtual economy features the exchange of knowledge, information or 'intellectual capital'. While all processes involve information/knowledge, information here *is* the commodity: ideas, codes, concepts, knowledge are what is being exchanged. This commodification poses questions poorly addressed in conventional analyses. In particular, the informational economy has unique characteristics: its self-transforming feedback loop, the imperative of accelerating innovation, defiance of exclusive possession, capacity to increase in value through use and intrinsic dissolution of cultural-economic distinctions. Hence, the informational economy *necessarily* involves a transformation not only of goods, but also of (gendered) thinking, knowledge and cultural codes.

Computer-based digitisation enables the conversion (reduction) of information, images, literature, music and even human experience into a binary code of 1s and 0s available to anyone with the relevant 'reading' capacity (conceptual and technological, access to which is gendered). These many and diverse phenomena are reduced to a common, universal code and circulated 'virtually' around the world, without the constraints of time and space. Digitisation also effectively 'objectifies' these diverse phenomena, rendering them objects/commodities that are tradeable.

Economic and political developments are simultaneously embedded in, affected by and profoundly shape sociocultural beliefs and practices. Not all information/knowledge is deemed worthy of digitisation or incorporation in networks of communication, and the selection processes at work are pervasively gendered. Media conglomerates – dominated by elite men and the corporate, consumerist interests they serve – determine the content of what is transmitted. The news industry focuses on traditionally male-defined activities: war, power politics, financial markets and 'objective' indicators of economic trends. Women are relatively invisible in these accounts, except as victims or those who deviate from gender expectations. The significance of media domination and its effects cannot be overstated, for it ultimately shapes what most of us know about 'reality' *and* our subjective interpretation of reality is shaped by the cultural codings of global media. News reporters, politicians and advertisers know that the media powerfully shape what we have knowledge of, believe in, hope for and work toward; they create and direct consumer desire, as well as social consciousness and political understanding. More generally, the politics of knowledge/information include whose questions are pursued, whose concerns are silenced, whose health needs are prioritised, whose methods are authorised, whose paradigm is presumed, whose project is funded, whose findings are publicised, whose intellectual property is protected. All of these are deeply structured by gender, as well as racial, economic and national hierarchies.

The conceptual and ideological commitments of digitisation and the informational economy are inextricable from the embodied practices of this economy. Whose history, stories, lives, language, music, dreams, beliefs and culture are documented, much less celebrated? Who is accorded credibility and authority: as religious leader, economic expert, marketing genius, financial guru, scientific expert, objective journalist, leading scholar, technological wizard, 'average American', 'good mother', 'man on the street'? Who is empowered to speak on behalf of their identity group, who on behalf of 'others'? Who benefits and how from English as the global lingua franca? Who determines what information is publicised – witnessed, replicated, published, disseminated, broadcast? Again, gender features prominently in these questions, and the politics they reveal. In sum, like money, information is not neutral. It carries, conveys and confers power in multiple ways, with diverse effects. Adequate analysis of these developments requires taking the politics of cultural coding seriously and taking seriously the gender of cultural coding.

The third mode of the virtual economy features the exchange of aesthetic or cultural symbols, treated here as heightened consumerism. The consumer economy/society involves the creation of a 'social imaginary' of particular tastes and desires, and the extensive commodification of tastes, pleasure and leisure. Aesthetics figure prominently here as, first, the value-added component of goods is less a function of information/knowledge and more a production of ephemeral, ever-changing tastes, desires, fashion and style, and, second, this production is increasingly key to surplus accumulation. In an important sense, capital focuses less on producing consumer goods than on producing both consumer subjectivities and a totalising 'market culture' that sustain consumption. Consumerism also involves a political economy of signs in the explicit sense of the power of symbols, signs and codes to determine meaning and hence value. The basic argument is that commodities do not have value in and of themselves, but only as a function of the social codes/context (including material conditions) within which they have significance. The significance of (gendered) cultural coding is amplified as consumerism deepens the commodification of the lifeworld. For example, adoptable children, sexualised bodies and sensual pleasures are for sale, based on gendered assumptions regarding the 'need to mother', the male 'sex drive', and whose pleasures are prioritised.

Consider how economics and culture are fused through shopping malls, theme parks, marinas, arts centres, museums, sports complexes and entertainment areas that are designed to foster consumption and have us think of it as culture. These 'cultural industries' serve to legitimate consumerism and increase subjective internalisation of capitalist ideology. On the one hand, individuals are encouraged to identify cultural gratification with consumption, rather than other perhaps more meaningful and less profit-oriented activities (e.g. critical reflection, spiritual/moral development, building egalitarian and sustainable communities). On the other hand, even political activities shift to market-based expressions: identity-based groups become particular targets of marketing and use consumption as an identity 'marker', whilst political action is increasingly consumer-based as people 'vote' through what they do or do not buy.

As a status indicator, consumption assumes greater significance as consumer goods are made available, consumption becomes a 'way of life' and market-created codes determine what is 'worth' consuming. The politics of advertising – who decides what we 'want' and with what effects – is explicitly about using cultural codes to manipulate consciousness. Gender and the reproductive economy figure prominently here, as gendered stereotypes and divisions of labour continue to identify women/housewives as the key consumers whose primary motivation for consumption is presumably to please men and improve family life. This raises a number of issues: advertising is disproportionately targeted at women (and tends to depend on and reproduce heterosexist stereotypes); constructions of 'femininity' are arguably more dependent on market/consumer ideologies and the aesthetics they promote than are constructions of 'masculinity';[35] women must learn and use particular (but typically unacknowledged) skills as informed and competent consumers; women/housewives exercise varying forms of power as consumers, especially within the household but also as investment decision makers; masculinist paradigms tend to neglect consumption 'work' (and skills); and masculinist and productivist paradigms have been slow to recognise the economic role of consumption in today's economy.

Similarly, arts and entertainment are increasingly less an expression of local cultures and spontaneous creativity than big business on a global scale where selling sex and sensationalism is a lucrative strategy. Popular music and videos feature perennial themes of love sought, gained and lost, while sexual themes are increasingly more explicit, graphic and violent. Women's bodies continue to be objectified, and their sexual interests either trivialised or exaggerated into causes of male desperation, perversion and destruction. Similarly, women rarely appear as strong, independent or competent, except as adjuncts of male exploits, a challenge to be overcome, or a caution against 'excessive' female power. Feminisms are rarely depicted positively, but denigrated as disruptive, 'anti-family', irrational or, at best, 'too idealistic'. Negative representations in 'popular culture' not only undercut the political efficacy of feminist activism, but also undermine the acceptability and credibility of feminist interventions in all spheres, including the academy and its knowledge production.

While affluent consumption is the privilege of only a small percentage of the world's population, it shapes the desires, choices and valorisation of those without affluence.[36] The political economy of consumption involves consumerism as an ideology (fuelled by pervasive advertising and global media that propel even the poorest to desire consumer goods as an expression of self-worth), as well as the more familiar power-laden practices of consumption. Whose needs, desires, and interests are served? Whose bodies and environments are devalorised in pursuit of consumerism and the neoliberal commitment to growth (rather than redistribution) that fuels it? Finally, consumerism requires purchasing power, increasingly sought through access to credit. As already noted, patterns regarding who has it, how much they have, and how they use it correspond tellingly to class, race/ethnicity, gender and geopolitical stratifications.

Conclusion

My review of feminist political economy positions has indicated the breadth and depth of scholarship in the past decade. The issues that feminists debate reflect differing empirical/substantive priorities, ideological preferences and, especially, epistemological orientations. In particular, feminists are differentiated by how they understand and deploy gender: as an empirical category that tends to become a synonym for 'women' (in relation to 'men') or as an analytical category that pervades meaning systems more generally. The former is an indispensable starting point and continually generates a wealth of research for gendering political economy. In so far as empirical gender is compatible with orthodox methods, it is more acceptable and credible, which affords important strategic advantages.

By comparison, analytical gender entails a theoretical shift toward more constructivist and poststructuralist orientations, which (variously) accord a constitutive (not exclusive!) role to intersubjective meaning systems. This too has generated rich resources for gendering political economy; it expands and deepens our inquiry, but also complicates it. In so far as gender operates as a governing code, criticising it disrupts foundational assumptions, orthodox methodologies and theoretical frameworks. This renders it less accessible and/or acceptable, and fuels resistance to these orientations and what are perceived to be their political implications. I argue, however, that, unless we shift our epistemological orientation, feminism's most trenchant and transformative insights remain effectively invisible: neither accurately understood nor analytically comprehended. 'Adding women/gender' is essential, but an *exclusive* focus on doing so misses too much and denies us crucial – not coincidental – resources for analysing political economy.

My 'rewriting' of neoliberal globalisation provided an example of taking analytical gender seriously, showing how this adds to, reconfigures and transforms a 'big picture' analysis of today's GPE. In abbreviated fashion I attempted to demonstrate the interdependence of the three (Foucauldian) economies: the co-constitution of culture and economy; the interaction of subjectivities, ideologies and practices; and the value of feminist and poststructuralist orientations. The overview also exposed how the cultural code of feminisation naturalises the economic (material) devaluation of feminised work – work that is done both by women *and* men who are culturally, racially and economically marginalised. This advances the project of gendering political economy and improves our analysis of GPE.

Understanding 'feminisation as denigration' exemplifies the transformative potential of studying gender analytically. On the one hand, we are no longer just referring to embodied individuals but to gender coding of constructs, categories, subjectivities, objects, activities and institutionalised practices. Romanticism notwithstanding, the more any one of these is feminised, the more likely that its devaluation is assumed or 'explained'. On the other hand, we are not simply talking about male-female relations or promoting the status of 'women'. We are, first, addressing the exploitation of *all* whose identities, labour and livelihoods are devalued by being feminised and, second, advancing the critical project of theorising how hierarchies of race/ethnicity, gender, class and nation *intersect*. For scholars committed to new political economy and concerned with oppressive structural arrangements, these contributions alone warrant more serious engagement with gender. More generally, then, I argue that feminist work is not a digression from nor supplement to conventional accounts; rather, it is an essential orientation for advancing our theory *and* practice of political economy.

Notes

I am grateful to Georgina Waylen for her generosity in sharing prepublication work with me; and to Drucilla Barker, Jen Cohen, Deb Figart, Ellen Mutari, Julie Nelson, Paulette Olsen and Ara Wilson for conference discussions regarding feminist economics.

1 Torry D. Dickinson and Robert K. Schaeffer, *Fast Forward: Work, Gender, and Protest in a Changing World* (Rowman & Littlefield, 2001), p. 23.
2 Joanne Cook and Jennifer Roberts, 'Towards a gendered political economy', in: Joanne Cook, Jennifer Roberts and Georgina Waylen (eds), *Towards a Gendered Political Economy* (Macmillan, 2000), p. 3.
3 Pertinent clarifications: I view 'feminist political economy' as a blend of feminist work primarily but not exclusively in economics, development studies, political economy, international relations and international political economy. My treatment here of political economy and 'new political economy' is very much shaped by my specialisation in international relations theory, my research on globalisation, and my belief that today's political economy is significantly *global* political economy. References in this article focus on feminist publications since 1995; for earlier work, see 'gender' articles in *New Political Economy*, especially Georgina Waylen, 'Gender, Feminism and Political Economy', *New Political Economy*, Vol. 2, No. 2 (1997), pp. 205–20, and note 8. I prefer 'global political economy' to international political economy in so far as it emphasises transnational dynamics and transdisciplinary analysis. In this study I characterise scholarship on gender as 'feminist' and do not engage recent claims that gender can or should be studied apolitically. I recognise that phenomena characterised as 'economic' are favoured here at the expense of more 'politically' oriented analyses; a substantial and expanding literature – especially in feminist IR – addresses the latter. For accessibility, I deploy conventional (though problematic) references to 'advanced industrialised countries', 'developing countries', 'Third World' and so on. Finally, slashes between words indicate similarity rather than contrast.
4 *Review of Radical Political Economics* has had seven such issues; see especially 'Feminist Political Economy', Vol. 33, No. 4 (2001).
5 V. Spike Peterson, 'On the cut(ting) edge', in: Frank P. Harvey and Michael Brecher (eds), *Critical Perspectives in International Studies: Millennial Reflections on International Studies* (University of Michigan Press, 2002), pp. 148–63; Marianne A. Ferber and Julie A. Nelson (eds), *Beyond Economic Man: Feminist Theory and Economics* (University of Chicago Press, 1993); and, especially, Gabrielle Meagher and Julie A. Nelson, 'Survey Article: Feminism in the Dismal Science', *The Journal of Political Philosophy*, Vol. 12, No. 1 (2004), pp. 102–26,

and Georgina Waylen, 'You Still Don't Understand: Why Troubled Engagements Continue between Feminists and (Critical) IPE', *Review of International Studies* (forthcoming).

6 Feminist interventions raise not only political/public, but personal/private issues that are 'disturbing' (from religious beliefs and sexual relations to who cleans the toilet and how value and power are masculinised). To the considerable extent that the implications are experienced as personally threatening, they generate defensiveness and resistance that shape receptivity to feminist critiques.

7 Important overviews and coverage of early critiques include: Diane Elson (ed.), *Male Bias in the Development Process* (Manchester University Press, 1991); Antonella Picchio, *Social Reproduction* (Cambridge University Press, 1992); Michèle A. Pujol, *Feminism and Anti-feminism in Early Economic Thought* (Edward Elgar, 1992); Ferber and Nelson, *Beyond Economic Man*; Isabella Bakker (ed.), *The Strategic Silence: Gender and Economic Policy* (Zed, 1994); Nancy Folbre, *Who Pays for the Kids?* (Routledge, 1994); Edith Kuiper and Jolande Sap (eds), *Out of the Margin: Feminist Perspectives on Economics* (Routledge, 1995); Julie A. Nelson, *Feminism, Objectivity and Economics* (Routledge, 1996); Ellen Mutari, Heather Boushey and William Fraher IV (eds), *Gender and Political Economy: Incorporating Diversity into Theory and Policy* (M. E. Sharpe, 1997); Jean Gardiner, *Gender, Care and Economics* (Macmillan, 1997); Cook, Roberts and Waylen, *Towards a Gendered Political Economy*; and Lourdes Benería, Maria Floro, Caren Grown and Martha MacDonald (eds), special issue on 'Globalization', *Feminist Economics*, Vol. 6, No. 3 (2000).

8 Post-1995 histories of the women/gender and development literatures include Joya Misra, 'Gender and the world-system: engaging the feminist literature on development', in: Thomas Hall (ed.), *A World-systems Reader: New Perspectives on Gender, Urbanism, Cultures, Indigenous Peoples, and Ecology* (Rowman & Littlefield, 2000), pp. 105–27; Shirin M. Rai, *Gender and the Political Economy of Development* (Polity, 2002); and Lourdes Benería, *Gender, Development and Globalization: Economics as if People Mattered* (Routledge 2003).

9 Esther Boserup, *Women's Role in Economic Development* (St. Martin's Press, 1970); Nilufer Çağatay, Diane Elson and Caren Grown (eds), special issue on 'Gender, Adjustment and Macroeconomics', *World Development*, Vol. 23, No. 11 (1995); Kathleen Cloud and Nancy Garrett, 'A Modest Proposal for Inclusion of Women's Household Human Capital Production in Analysis of Structural Transformation', *Feminist Economics*, Vol. 3, No. 1 (1997), pp. 151–77; Saskia Sassen, *Globalization and its Discontents* (New Press, 1998) and 'Women's Burden: Counter-geographies of Globalization and the Feminization of Survival', *Journal of International Affairs*, Vol. 53, No. 2 (2000), pp. 503–24; Elisabeth Prügl, *The Global Construction of Gender: Home-Based Work in the Political Economy of the 20th Century* (Columbia University Press, 1999); Marilyn Waring, *Counting for Nothing: What Men Value and What Women are Worth*, 2nd edition (University of Toronto Press, 1999); Rhacel Salazar Parreñas, *Servants of Globalization: Women, Migration and Domestic Work* (Stanford University Press, 2001); Deborah M. Figart, Ellen Mutari and Marilyn Power, *Living Wages, Equal Wages: Gender and Labour Market Policies in the United States* (Routledge, 2002); Caren Grown, Diane Elson and Nilufer Çağatay (eds), special issue on 'Growth, Trade, Finance, and Gender Inequality', *World Development*, Vol. 28, No. 7 (2000); Rita Mae Kelly, Jane H. Bayes, Mary E. Hawkesworth and Brigitte Young (eds), *Gender, Globalization, & Democratization* (Rowman & Littlefield, 2001); Susan Himmelweit, 'Making Visible the Hidden Economy: The Case for Gender-impact Analysis of Economic Policy', *Feminist Economics*, Vol. 8, No.1 (2002), pp. 49–70; and Chandra Talpade Mohanty, *Feminism Without Borders: Decolonizing Theory, Practicing Solidarity* (Duke University Press, 2003).

10 For example, in a comprehensive study, Hewitson persuasively argues that 'neoclassical economics produces femininity as that which must be excluded for it to operate'. Gillian J. Hewitson, *Feminist Economics: Interrogating the Masculinity of Rational Economic Man* (Edward Elgar, 1999), p. 22.

11 For recent examples, see Cecile Jackson (ed.), *Men at Work: Labour, Masculinities, Development* (Frank Cass, 2001); Frances Cleaver (ed.), *Masculinities Matter! Men, Gender and Development* (Zed, 2002); Rai, *Gender and the Political Economy of Development*; Benería, *Gender, Development and Globalization*; and Suzanne Bergeron, *Fragments of Development: Nation, Gender and the Space of Modernity* (University of Michigan Press, 2004).

12 Jacqui M. Alexander and Chandra T. Mohanty (eds), *Feminist Genealogies, Colonial Legacies, Democratic Futures* (Routledge, 1997); Uma Narayan and Sandra Harding (eds), *Decentering the Center: Philosophy for a Multicultural, Postcolonial, and Feminist World* (Indiana University Press, 2000); Rose Brewer, Cecilia Conrad and Mary C. King, 'The Complexities and Potential of Theorizing Gender, Caste, Race, and Class', *Feminist Economics*, Vol. 8, No. 2 (2002), pp. 3–17; Geeta Chowdhry and Sheila Nair (eds), *Power, Postcolonialism and International Relations: Reading Race, Gender and Class* (Routledge, 2002); and Mohanty, *Feminism Without Borders*.

13 Çağatay *et al.*, 'Gender, Adjustment and Macroeconomics'; J. K. Gibson-Graham, *The End of Capitalism (As We Knew It): A Feminist Critique of Political Economy* (Blackwell, 1996); Zillah R. Eisenstein, *Global Obscenities: Patriarchy, Capitalism, and the Lure of Cyberfantasy* (New York Press, 1998) and *Against Empire: Feminisms, Racisms, and the West* (Zed, 2004); Grown *et al.*, 'Growth, Trade, Finance, and Gender Inequality'; Marianne H. Marchand and Anne Sisson Runyan (eds), *Gender and Global Restructuring: Sightings, Sites and Resistances* (Routledge, 2000); Veronika Bennholdt-Thomsen, Nicholas G. Faraclas and Claudia von Werlhof (eds), *There is an Alternative: Subsistence and Worldwide Resistance to Corporate Globalization* (Zed, 2001); Dickinson and Schaeffer, *Fast Forward*; Suzanne Bergeron, 'Political Economy Discourses of Globalization and Feminist Politics', *Signs*, Vol. 26, No. 4 (2001), pp. 983–1006; Kelly *et al.*, *Gender, Globalization, & Democratization*; Sheila Rowbotham and Stephanie Linkogle (eds), *Women Resist Globalization: Mobilizing for Livelihood and Rights* (Zed, 2001); Nancy Naples and Manisha Desai (eds), *Women's Activism and Globalization: Linking Local Struggles and Transnational Politics* (Routledge, 2002); Martha Gutierrez (ed.), *Macro-Economics: Making Gender Matter – Concepts, Policies and Institutional Change in Developing Countries* (Zed, 2003); and Valentine M. Moghadam, *Globalizing Women: Transnational Feminist Networks* (Johns Hopkins University Press, 2005).

14 Drucilla K. Barker and Edith Kuiper (eds), *Toward a Feminist Philosophy of Economics* (Routledge, 2003).

15 As it is typically deployed, however, constructivists (on my reading) fail to address adequately the relationship between language, power and knowledge. In particular, they resist poststructuralist claims that the *meaning* of all words, 'things' and subjectivities is produced through/by discursive practices that are embedded in relations of power; that language produces power by constituting the codes of meaning that govern how we think, communicate and generate knowledge claims – indeed, how we understand 'reality'. Operations of power are not extricable from the power coded into our meaning systems and their social, 'material' effects. Hence, knowledge projects that presume analytical adequacy and political relevance must address the power that inheres in governing codes, which requires, I believe, the adoption of poststructuralist/postmodernist insights. For elaboration, see V. Spike Peterson, 'Transgressing Boundaries: Theories of Knowledge, Gender, and International Relations', *Millennium: Journal of International Studies*,

Vol. 21, No. 2 (1992), pp. 183–206, and *A Critical Rewriting of Global Political Economy: Integrating Reproductive, Productive, and Virtual Economies* (Routledge, 2003); for a succinct defence of poststructuralism against its most frequent criticisms, see Hewitson, *Feminist Economics*; and for discussion of poststructuralism/ postmodernism in economics, see Gibson-Graham, *The End of Capitalism*; Carole Biewener, 'A Postmodern Encounter', *Socialist Review*, Vol. 27, Nos. 1 & 2 (1999), pp. 71–96; Stephen Cullenberg, Jack Amariglio and David F. Ruccio (eds), *Postmodernism, Economics and Knowledge* (Routledge, 2001); Nitasha Kaul, 'The anxious identities we inhabit', in: Barker and Kuiper, *Toward a Feminist Philosophy of Economics*, pp. 194–210; and Eiman O. Zein-Elabdin and S. Charusheela (eds), *Postcolonialism Meets Economics* (Routledge, 2004).

16 Ferber and Nelson, *Beyond Economic Man*; Marilyn Power, 'Social Provisioning as a Starting Point for Feminist Economics', *Feminist Economics*, Vol. 10, No. 3 (2004), pp. 3–20; and Drucilla K. Barker and Susan F. Feiner, *Liberating Economics: Feminist Perspectives on Families, Work, and Globalization* (University of Michigan Press, 2004).

17 On sexualities, see M. V. Lee Badgett, 'Gender, Sexuality, and Sexual Orientation: All in the Feminist Family?', *Feminist Economics*, Vol. 1, No. 1 (1995), pp. 121–40; and Rosemary Hennessey, *Profit and Pleasure: Sexual Identities in Late Capitalism* (Routledge, 2000).

18 Poststructuralism is particularly associated with cultural studies, where cultural and literary phenomena are, appropriately, the central focus. Early poststructuralist theory necessarily highlighted discourse and culture to criticise and counteract orthodox understandings of 'reality' as pre-discursive, or independent of intersubjective meaning systems. But poststructuralism/postmodernism explicitly rejects conventional dichotomies and categorical separations in favour of relational/contextual analysis that exposes how cultural codes produce, and are produced by, material 'reality'. Moreover (see note 15), it affords critiques of how power operates that would advance the project of 'not just understanding the world but changing it'.

19 On Sen and economic rights respectively, see Bina Agarwal, Jane Humphries and Ingrid Robeyns (eds), special issue on 'Amartya Sen's Work and Ideas: A Gender Perspective', *Feminist Economics*, Vol. 9, No. 2/3 (2003); and Laura Parisi, *Gendered Disjunctures: Globalization and Women's Rights*, dissertation, University of Arizona, 2004. Microcredit loan programmes get mixed feminist reviews; see, for example, Anne Marie Goetz and Rina Sen Gupta, 'Who Takes the Credit? Gender, Power, and Control over Loan Use in Rural Credit Programs in Bangladesh', *World Development*, Vol. 24, No. 1 (1996), pp. 45–64; S. Charusheela, 'On History, Love, and Politics', *Rethinking Marxism*, Vol. 12, No. 4 (2000), pp. 45–61; Winifred Poster and Zakia Salime, 'The limits of microcredit', in: Nancy A. Naples and Manisha Desai (eds), *Women's Activism and Globalization* (Routledge, 2002), pp. 189–219; and Suzanne Bergeron, 'Challenging the World Bank's narrative of inclusion', in: Amitava Kumar (ed.), *World Bank Literature* (University of Minnesota Press, 2003), pp. 157–71.

20 For reasons of space, in this section I cite only key references not already identified herein; for elaboration of argumentation and extensive citations, see Peterson, *A Critical Rewriting of Global Political Economy*; and 'Getting real: the necessity of critical poststructuralism in Global Political Economy', in: Marieke de Goede (ed.), *International Political Economy and Poststructural Politics* (Palgrave, forthcoming).

21 Peter Drucker, 'Trading Places', *The National Interest* (Spring 2005), p. 103.

22 Guy Standing, *Global Labour Flexibility: Seeking Distributive Justice* (Macmillan, 1999); and Christa Wichterich, *The Globalized Woman: Reports from a Future of Inequality* (Zed, 2000).

23 Manuel Castells, *The Information Age, Volume 1, The Rise of the Network Society*, 2nd edition (Blackwell, 2000).

24 Avtar Brah, *Cartographies of Diaspora: Contested Identities* (Routledge, 1996); Manuel Castells, *The Information Age, Volume 2, The Power of Identity* (Blackwell, 1997); and Sassen, *Globalization and its Discontents* and 'Women's Burden'.

25 See, respectively, S. Charusheela, 'Empowering work? Bargaining models reconsidered', in: Barker and Kuiper, *Toward a Feminist Philosophy of Economics*, pp. 287–303; and Naila Kabeer, 'Globalization, Labor Standards, and Women's Rights: Dilemmas of Collective (In)action in an Independent World', *Feminist Economics*, Vol. 10, No. 1 (2004), pp. 3–36, for problematising 'Western' claims that 'work is empowering' or that enforcing global labour standards serves the interests of export workers in poor countries.

26 Wichterich, *The Globalized Woman*.

27 On erosion of women's wellbeing and social capital through 'overworking' women, see David H. Ciscel and Julia A. Heath, 'To Market, To Market: Imperial Capitalism's Destruction of Social Capital and the Family', *Review of Radical Political Economics*, Vol. 33, No. 4 (2001), pp. 401–14; and Martha MacDonald, Shelley Phipps and Lynn Lethbridge, 'Mothers' Milk and Measures of Economic Output', *Feminist Economics*, Vol. 11, No. 1 (2005), pp. 63–94. For the most comprehensive analysis of the crisis of social reproduction, see Isabella Bakker and Stephen Gill (eds), *Power, Production and Social Reproduction: Human In/security in the Global Political Economy* (Palgrave, 2003).

28 Debates on how to theorise, define, measure and evaluate informalisation are addressed in Peterson, *A Critical Rewriting of Global Political Economy*, ch. 4. The underground economy has been estimated to be worth US$9 trillion (*The Economist*, 28 August 1999, p. 59); the value of 'housework' to be US$10–15 trillion (Mary Ann Tetreault and Ronnie D. Lipschutz, *Global Politics as if People Mattered* (Rowman & Littlefield, 2005), p. 25).

29 *The World's Women 2000: Trends and Statistics* (United Nations, 2000), pp. 120–7.

30 Jean Pyle, 'Critical globalization studies and gender', in: Richard P. Appelbaum and William I. Robinson (eds), *Critical Globalization Studies* (Routledge, 2005), pp. 249–58.

31 A variety of sources provide the following estimates (in US dollars, per year) – of 'white collar crime' in the US: $200 billion; of profits from trafficking migrants: $3.5 billion; of money laundering: as much as $2.8 trillion; of tax revenue lost to the US by hiding assets offshore: $70 billion; of tax evasion costs to the US government: $195 billion. See Peterson, *A Critical Rewriting of Global Political Economy*, pp. 196, 201.

32 Peter Drucker, 'The Global Economy and the Nation-State', *Foreign Affairs*, Vol. 76, No. 5 (1997), p. 162.

33 Lourdes Benería, 'Globalization, Gender and the Davos Man', *Feminist Economics*, Vol. 5, No. 3 (1999), pp. 61–83; Charlotte Hooper, *Manly States: Masculinities, International Relations, and Gender Politics* (Columbia University Press, 2001); and Stacey Mayhall, *Riding the Bull/Wrestling the Bear*, dissertation, York University, 2002.

34 These claims are variously documented in Nahid Aslanbeigui and Gale Summerfield, 'The Asian Crisis, Gender, and the International Financial Architecture', *Feminist Economics*, Vol. 6, No. 3 (2000), pp. 81–104; Nahid Aslanbeigui and Gale Summerfield, 'Risk, Gender and the International Financial Architecture', *International Journal of Politics, Culture and Society*, Vol. 15, No. 1 (2001), pp. 7–26; Grown *et al.*, 'Growth, Trade, Finance, and Gender Inequality'; Thanh-Dam Truong, 'The Underbelly of the Tiger: Gender and the Demystification of the Asian Miracle', *Review of International Political Economy*, Vol. 6, No. 2 (1999), pp. 133–65; Robert O'Brien, Anne Marie Goetz, Jan Aart Scholte and

Marc Williams, *Contesting Global Governance: Multilateral Economic Institutions and Global Social Movements* (Cambridge University Press, 2000); Ajit Singh and Ann Zammit, 'International Capital Flows: Identifying the Gender Dimension', *World Development*, Vol. 28, No. 7 (2000), pp. 1249–68; Mario Floro and Gary Dymski, 'Financial Crisis, Gender, and Power: An Analytical Framework', *World Development*, Vol. 28, No. 7 (2000), pp. 1269–83; and Irene Van Staveren, 'Global finance and gender', in: Jan Aart Scholte and Albrecht Schnabel (eds), *Civil Society and Global Finance* (Routledge, 2002), pp. 228–46.

35 Women are the primary consumers of goods and services designed to 'improve' individual appearance: from cosmetics, hairstyles and clothes to dieting programmes and surgical procedures. This reflects the tremendous pressure on girls and women to appear aesthetically and sexually attractive as a measure of their social/economic value, and subjects them disproportionately to the disciplining effects of marketisation and resource depletion on 'unnecessary' expenditures.

36 For example, consumerism's commodification of culture has effects worldwide on how people think (due to the global, though always locally-mediated, exposure to advertising and marketing messages), what resources they have (due to naturalising the ideology of elite consumption), and what work they do (due to production processes driven by Northern consumption).

6 When national territory is home to the global

Old borders to novel borderings

Saskia Sassen

One angle into the question of national territory, at a time of global and digital capabilities, is the border. It is one of the critical national institutions that those capabilities can unsettle and even neutralise. Borders, in turn, bring up the national state as the key historic actor shaped partly by the struggle about and institutionalising of territorial borders. The globalisation of a broad range of processes is producing ruptures in the mosaic of border regimes underlying the international system of exclusive territorial demarcations. There is much disagreement about the effect of these global and digital capabilities on state territorial jurisdictions, with some seeing much and others little real change.[1] But both sides of the debate tend to share one assumption, often implicit: the territorial exclusivity of the nation-state which makes of the border a line that divides the national and the global into two mutually exclusive domains.

And yet, the changes under way are shifting the meaning of borders, even when the actual geographic lines that demarcate territories have not been altered. Perhaps more importantly, these changes are contributing to the formation of new types of borders. Such changed meanings and new types of borders make legible the fact that bordering takes place in far more sites than geographic border-lines and their linked institutions, such as consulates and airport immigration controls. And they make legible the extent of state capture in the historiography and geography covering the geopolitics of the last two centuries, an issue that has received considerable attention in the last few years.[2]

The organising argument in this chapter is that we are seeing the incipient formation of a type of bordering capability and state practice regarding its territory that entails a partial denationalising of what has been constructed historically as national and hence an unsettling of the meaning of geographic borders. Critical to this argument is the thesis that global processes also take place at subnational levels,[3] hereby disrupting the notion of mutually exclusive domains for the national and the global. Much attention in the scholarship has gone to the loss of functions by states to supranational, global and private entities.[4] Much less attention has gone to the thesis that state territorial authority is being affected by the proliferation of subnational scalings of global processes and institutions. When we conceive of globalisation as partly enacted at various subnational scales and institutional domains we can posit the possibility of a proliferation of borderings inside national territories. The thesis organising this chapter is that economic globalisation is in fact a politico-economic system partly located inside national states; as a result, we see: a) a partial, often highly specialised and hence obscure, denationalising of specific components of state work, the economy, society and the polity; and b) that the specialised transnational regimes being implemented to govern global processes also enter national institutional space and geographic territory,[5] and that both of these dynamics (a and b) produce a variety of novel borderings inside national territory which often can function in ways unaffected by the continuing geographic demarcation of state territories.[6] A focus on such bordering capabilities allows us to see something about territory and space that is easily obscured in the more prevalent analyses which assume the mutual exclusivity of the national and the global.

First, I will examine the main lines of the debate about the state and the question of borders and exclusive territorial authority. Next, I will examine the question of global processes at the subnational level to get at the thesis that concerns me here: the partial unbundling of traditional territorial national borders and the formation of new bordering capabilities.[7] Finally, I will discuss borders and new bordering capabilities and the kinds of theoretical and research issues they bring to the scholarly agenda.

National territories and global processes

There have been many epochs when territories were subject to several systems of rule. In this regard the current condition we see developing with globalisation is probably by far the more common one and the more exceptional period is the one that has seen the strengthening of the national state. The gradual institutional tightening of the national state's exclusive authority over its territory took off particularly after the First World War in most of the developed countries. So did the elaboration of the categories for analysis, research techniques and data-sets in the social sciences that refined the national state perspective. Accommodating the possibility of multiple relations between territory and institutional encasement, rather than the singular one of national territory and sovereign rule, requires theoretical and empirical specifications – a collective task well under way.

The multiple regimes that constitute the border as an institution can be grouped into a formalised apparatus that is part of the interstate system. The first has at its core the body of regulations covering a variety of international flows – flows of different types of commodities, capital, people, services and information. No matter their variety, these multiple regimes tend to cohere around: a) the state's unilateral authority to define and enforce regulations, and b) the state's obligation to respect and uphold the regulations coming out of the international treaty system or out of bilateral arrangements.[8] While never fully effective, today this formalised apparatus is not only partly being unbundled, but also confronts an emerging, still far less formalised, array of novel types of borderings lying largely outside the framing of the interstate system. Further, this emergent array of borderings does not necessarily entail a self-evident crossing of borders; it includes a range of dynamics arising out of specific contemporary developments, notably emergent global law systems and a growing range of globally networked digital interactive domains.

The national state capture in these modes of analysis has had the effect of simplifying the question of the border: the border is largely reduced to a geographic event and the immediate institutional apparatus through which it is controlled, protected and generally governed. What globalisation brings to this condition is the actual and heuristic disaggregating of 'the border' typically represented as a unitary condition in policy discourse and making legible its multiple components. The globalisation of a broad range of processes shows us that the 'border' can extend deep into national territory and is constituted through many more institutions and has many more locations than is suggested by standard representations. These globalising processes also help make legible the features and the conditionalities of what has been the dominant border regime, associated with the nation-state, which though still the prevalent border regime of our times is now less so than it was even 15 years ago.

Globalisation thus engages the territory of the state, and thereby inevitably the question of state borders. One of the critical literatures for these issues and the main lines of debate, even when not directly addressed, is that of the state and globalisation. In many ways the issues that concern me here are addressed indirectly or obliquely, because the framing in the literature is rather more like a tug of war given assumptions of mutual exclusivity – what one wins, the other loses. For the purposes of this chapter it is worth examining the assumptions that are made on each side of the debate, even when the actual question of the border is often not central. To repeat, most marked is the fact that both sides basically take for given the fact of the border as demarcating mutual exclusivity.

This scholarship is large and growing, and by now increasingly familiar. Very briefly, and simplifying, we can identify two major strands. For some, states remain as the key actors and hence not much has changed for states and the inter-state system, each state enjoying mutually recognised territorial borders.[9] For others, even if states remain important there are today other key actors who are accumulating rights and powers to cross those borders.[10] Some see these as new actors; others do not and rather emphasise the weakening of their powers alongside the strengthening of national states over the last 100 years.[11] Even if we accept that the present era is, at a very general level, a continuation of a long history of changes that have not altered the fundamental fact of state primacy, it still demands detailed research about the specificities of the current changes.

Focusing on the formation of novel bordering capabilities brings to the fore particular aspects of territory and space that are easily overlooked.[12] Unlike analyses of private authority which emphasise the shift out of the public domain and into the private domain,[13] no doubt a critical dimension,[14] here I seek to detect the presence of private agendas and authority inside the public domain of the state.[15] This can go further to an emphasis on the privatisation of norm-making capacities: these capacities were once in the public domain, but today they have become private and use the public domain to enact private norms.[16] This perspective thus also differs from a literature that emphasises the decline and obsolescence of the state.[17] It comes close to the scholarship that emphasises state transformations,[18] even though this literature tends to discard the specificity of the current phase of globalisation.[19]

One of my efforts here is, then, to blur some longstanding dualities in state scholarship, notably, those concerning the distinctive spheres of influence of respectively the national and the global, of state and non-state actors, and of the private and the public.[20] While it may indeed be the case that mostly the two sides of the duality are separate and mutually exclusive, I argue for the critical importance of recognising and deciphering conditions or components that do not fit in this dual structure. Borders and novel bordering capacities then function as a heuristic device to detect deeper transformations.[21] An important methodological assumption here is that focusing on economic globalisation can help us disentangle some of these issues precisely because, in strengthening the legitimacy of claims by foreign investors and firms and the legitimate authority of international regimes inside the country, it renders visible the work of accommodating these rights and authorities in what remain basically national economies and national polities.[22]

The embeddedness of the global requires at least a partial lifting of national encasements and hence signals a necessary participation by the state, even when it concerns the state's own withdrawal from regulating the economy. Does the weight of private, often foreign, interests in this specific work of the state become constitutive of a particular form of state authority that does not replace but works alongside older well-established forms of state authority?[23] My argument is that the mix of processes we describe as globalisation is indeed producing, deep inside the national state, a very partial but significant form of authority, a hybrid that is neither fully private nor fully public, neither fully national nor fully global.[24]

As states participate in the implementation of cross border regimes, whether the global economic system or the international human rights regime, they have undergone at times significant transformations because this accommodation entails a negotiation. In the case of the global economy, this negotiation entails the development inside national states – through legislative acts, court rulings, executive orders, policy – of the mechanisms necessary for the reconstitution of certain components of national capital into 'global capital', and necessary to develop and ensure new types of rights/entitlements for foreign capital[25] in what are still national territories that in principle remain under the exclusive authority of their states.[26]

National borders and subnational scalings of the global

As particular components of national states become the institutional home for the operation of some of the dynamics that are central to globalisation, they undergo change that is difficult to register or name. This is one instantiation of what I call a process of incipient denationalisation. This partial, often highly specialised or at least particularised, denationalisation can also take place in domains other than that of economic globalisation, notably, the more recent developments in the human rights regime which increasingly make it possible for a plaintiff in a given country to sue a firm[27] (and even a dictator) in that country's courts. Another instance is the use of human rights instruments to grant undocumented immigrants certain rights. Denationalisation is, thus, multivalent: it endogenises global agendas of many different types of actors, not only corporate firms and financial markets, but also human rights objectives.

The question for research then becomes: what is actually 'national' in some of the institutional components of states linked to the implementation and regulation of economic globalisation? The hypothesis here would be that some components of national institutions, even though formally national, are not national in the sense in which we have constructed the meaning of that term over the last hundred years. One of the roles of the state vis-à-vis today's global economy has been to negotiate the intersection of national law and foreign actors – whether firms, markets or supranational organisations. This raises a question as to whether there are particular conditions that make execution of this role in the current phase distinctive and unlike what it may have been in earlier phases of the world economy.

We need to understand more about the nature of this engagement than is represented by concepts such as deregulation. It is becoming clear that the role of the state in the process of deregulation involves the production of a series of instruments that grant foreign actors and international regimes rights to the territory of the state in a way that represents a rupture with the history of the last hundred years. This is also evident in the proliferation of specialised, often semi-autonomous regulatory agencies and the specialised crossborder networks they are forming which are taking over functions once enclosed in national legal frameworks.[28] One way of conceptualising this is to posit that these instruments produce new types of borders deep inside the territory of the national state. They do not shift the geographic line that demarcates the 'border' recognised in international treaties. But they do produce new borders and they do change the institutional apparatus that gives meaning to the geographic border.

Critical here is that processes that do not necessarily scale at the global level as such can be part of globalisation. These processes take place deep inside territories and institutional domains that have largely been constructed in national terms in much, though by no means all, of the world. What makes these processes part of globalisation, even though localised in national, indeed subnational settings, is that they involve transboundary networks and formations connecting or articulating multiple local or 'national' processes and actors.[29] Among these processes I include particular aspects of the work of states, such as specific monetary and fiscal policies critical to the constitution of global markets – which are thus being implemented in a growing number of countries as these become integrated into global markets.[30] Other instances are crossborder networks of activists engaged in specific localised struggles with an explicit or implicit global agenda, as is the case with many human rights and environmental organisations; non-cosmopolitan forms of global politics and imaginaries that remain deeply attached or focused on localised issues and struggles and yet are also part of global lateral networks containing multiple other such localised efforts. A particular challenge in the work of identifying these types of processes and actors as part of globalisation is the need to decode at least some of what continues to be experienced and represented as national.

Important to the argument in this chapter is the thesis that these types of nation-based practices and dynamics can be conceptualised as constitutive of global scalings we do not usually recognise as such. This brings to the fore internal and novel borderings produced in the encounter between a global process – whether economic, cultural, political or subjective – and existing thick national environments. This encounter can assume many different shapes and contents. It can be a highly charged event with multiple individual, institutional and/or structural contestations, victories and retreats on each side. Or it can be a highly specialised insertion noticeable directly only within that specialised domain, as might be the case with some of the new standards in finance and accounting.

The research needed to get at these types of issues can vary enormously depending on the content (political, economic, cultural or subjective) and on location (institutional, structural, demographic, subjective, and so on). Yet cutting across this variability is the need to distinguish: a) the various scales constituted through global processes, ranging from supranational and global to subnational and translocal;[31] and b) the specific sites of a given object of study in this multi-scalar globalisation.[32] Geography more than any other of the social sciences today has contributed to a critical stance toward scale, recognising the historicity of scales and resisting the reification of the national scale so present in most of social science.

This in turn brings up a critical conceptual task: the need to decode particular aspects of what is still represented or experienced as 'national' which may in fact have shifted away from what had historically been considered or constituted as national. This is in many ways a research and theorisation logic that is the same as that developed in the economics of global city studies. But, while a growing number of scholars today have come around to recognise and code global city functions as part of the global, this cannot be said for a range of other subnational instances of the global still coded and represented as local and national.

Three types of cases serve to illustrate some of the conceptual, methodological and empirical issues in these types of studies aimed at detecting the global inside the national, signalling the existence of novel types of borderings. One of these concerns the role of place in many of the circuits constitutive of economic and political globalisation. A focus on places allows us to unbundle globalisation in terms of the multiple specialised crossborder circuits on which different types of places are located.[33] Yet another example is that of global cities as subnational places where multiple global circuits intersect and thereby position these cities on several structured crossborder geographies, each typically with distinct scopes and constituted in terms of distinct practices and actors.[34] This type of analysis produces a different picture of globalisation from one centred on global firms and markets, international trade, or the pertinent supranational institutions. It is not that one type of focus is better than the other, but rather that the latter focus, the most common focus by far, is not enough.

A second type of case, partly involved in that described above, is the role of the new interactive technologies in repositioning the local, thereby inviting us to a critical examination of how we conceptualise the local. Through these new technologies a financial services firm becomes a micro-environment with continuous global span. But so do resource-poor organisations or households; they can also become micro-environments with global span, as might be the case with activist organisations. These micro-environments can be oriented to other such micro-environments located far away, thereby destabilising both the notion of context which is often imbricated with that of the local and the notion that physical proximity is one of the attributes or markers of the local. A critical reconceptualisation of the local along these lines entails at least a partial rejection of the notion that local scales are inevitably part of nested hierarchies of scale running from the local to the regional, the national and the international.[35]

A third type of case concerns a specific set of interactions between global dynamics and particular components of national states. The crucial conditionality here is the partial embeddedness of the global in the national, of which the global city is perhaps emblematic. My main argument here is that, in so far as specific structurations of the global inhabit what has historically been constructed and institutionalised as national territory, this engenders a variety of negotiations. One set of outcomes evident today is what I describe as an incipient, highly specialised and partial denationalisation of specific components of national states.

In all three instances the question of scaling takes on very specific contents in that these are practices and dynamics that pertain to the constituting of the global, yet are taking place at what has been historically constructed as the scale of the national. With few exceptions, most prominently among which is a growing scholarship in geography, the social sciences have not had critical distance, that is, historicised the scale of the national. The consequence has been a tendency to take it as a fixed scale, reifying it, and, more generally, to neutralise the question of scaling, or at best to reduce scaling to a hierarchy of size. Associated with this tendency is also the often uncritical assumption that these scales are mutually exclusive, most pertinently for my argument here, that the scale of the national is mutually exclusive with that of the global. A qualifying variant which allows for mutual imbrications, though of a very limited sort, can be seen when scaling is conceived of as a nested hierarchy.[36]

National borders and subnational borderings

The three cases described above go against those assumptions and propositions that are now often captured through the concept of methodological nationalism. But they do so in a distinct way. Crucial to the existing body of work representing a critique of methodological nationalism is the need for transnationalism: the nation as container category is inadequate given the proliferation of dynamics and formations that go beyond the nation-state.[37] What I am focusing on here is a set of reasons other than transnationalism for supporting the critique of methodological nationalism: the fact of multiple and specific structurations of the global inside what has historically been constructed as national. In many ways I focus on the other end of the transnationalism dynamic: I look inside the national. Along these lines, I find that Xiangming Chen's recent work also captures this particular combination.[38] Further, I posit that, because the national is highly institutionalised and thick, structurations of the global inside the national entail a partial, typically highly specialised and specific denationalisation of particular components of the national. This approach, then, is a critique of methodological nationalism, but its starting point is not exclusively predicated on the fact of transnationalism, rather bringing in the possibility of internal denationalisation.

One analytic pathway into this bundle of empirical and conceptual issues is to disaggregate state-centred border regimes and to locate a given site in a global web of bordered spaces. One of the key analytic distinctions to be made is that between the ongoing presence of border regimes centred in the state and the interstate system and the emergence of the types of novel borderings associated with the multiplication of subnational global scalings discussed above.

State-centred border regimes have also undergone significant change even as they remain part of older formalisations, such as international treaties. Globalisation, neoliberal supranational regimes and new forms of private authority have all affected old border regimes.[39] The outcome is that we see a great diversity of institutional locations even among state-centred regimes. For instance, crossborder flows of capital will require a sequence of interventions that move deep inside the national institutional apparatus, and also differ in character from that of traded goods, for example. The actual geographic border crossing is part of the crossborder flow of goods, but not necessarily of capital, except if actual cash is being transported. Each border-control intervention point can be conceived of as one site in a chain of locations. In the case of traded goods these might involve a pre-border inspection or certification site. In the case of capital flows the chain of locations will involve banks, stock markets and electronic networks. The financial and the trade bordering functions each contain specific institutional and geographic locations, increasingly including some internal to the nation-state. The geographic borderline is but one point in the chain; institutional points of border control intervention can form long chains inside the country.

One image we might use to capture this notion of multiple locations is that the sites for the enforcement of border regimes range from banks to bodies. When a bank executes the most elementary money transfer to another country, the bank is one of the sites for border-regime enforcement. A certified good represents a case where the object itself crossing the border is one of the sites for enforcement: the emblematic case is a certified agricultural product. But it also encompasses the case of the tourist carrying a tourist visa and the immigrant carrying the requisite certification. Indeed, in the case of immigration, it is the body of the immigrant herself which is both the carrier of much of the regime and the crucial site for enforcement; and in the case of an unauthorised immigrant, it is, again, the body of the immigrant that is the carrier of the violation of the law and of the corresponding punishment (such as detention or expulsion).

A direct effect of globalisation, especially corporate economic globalisation, has been to create increasing divergence among different border regimes. In some cases these divergences are the effect of enormous specialisation and remain rather obscure; in other cases they are quite elementary. One familiar instance that captures some of this is the lifting of border controls on a growing variety of capital, services and information flows alongside ongoing and even strengthened closure in other border regimes, for example the migration of low-wage workers. We are also seeing the construction of specific 'borderings' to contain and govern emerging, often strategic or specialised, flows that cut across traditional national borders, as is the case, for instance, with the new regimes in the North American Free Trade Association and the General Agreement on Tariffs and Trade (GATT) for the crossborder circulation of high-level professionals.[40] Where in the past these professionals may have been part of a country's general immigration regime, now we have an increasing divergence between the latter and the specialised regime governing professionals.

In what follows I examine briefly some of the key analytic distinctions we might use in researching these emergent questions about national territory, old borders and novel types of borderings inside national territory. First, I discuss what it might mean to study a subnational site as part of global processes and hence to recognise the formation of novel types of bordering. Next, and to conclude, I focus on the larger issues of territory and state authority raised at the beginning of this chapter by examining some novel types of bordering dynamics as these intersect with the national territorial authority of the state, particularly the destabilised meaning of conventional borders under the impact of multiple forms of globalisation.

Positioning a site in a global web of borders

If we were to consider what might be involved in locating an economic site in a global web of 'borders' a first step in my research practice is to conceive of the global economy as constituted through: a) a set of specialised/partial circuits, and b) multiple, often overlapping, space economies. The question then becomes how a given area is articulated with various circuits and space economies.

The articulation of a site with global circuits can be direct or indirect, and part of long or short chains. An instance of a direct articulation would be a site located on a specialised global circuit, as might be the case with export forestry, a mine, offshore manufacturing or offshore banking. An instance of an indirect articulation might be a site located on national economic circuits, such as a site for the production of processed consumer goods where exports happen through multiple complex national and foreign urban markets. The chains of transactions involved in these different types of products are likely to be shorter in the case of extractive industries than in manufacturing, especially in consumer goods where export/import handlers and multiple distributors are likely to be part of the chain.

As for the second element, the space economies involved, a first critical issue is that a given site can be constituted through one or more space economies. A forestry site or an agricultural site is likely to be constituted through fewer space economies than a financial centre or a manufacturing complex. Secondly, none, only one, or several might be global space economies. It seems to me crucial to disaggregate a site along these lines, and not reify an area. For instance, the space economy even of a sparsely populated area, such as a forestry site, can be far more complex than common sense might suggest: even if it is located on only one global circuit, such as an international logging company that has contracted for all the wood produced in the site. That logging multinational's acquisition of the wood requires it also to satisfy a great mix of requirements typically executed via specialised corporate services, notably accounting and law, and it is likely to require financing, in turn subject to national regulations.

We might then say that the forestry site is actually constituted through several space economies, and at the least two: logging and specialised corporate services. But it is likely to be part of a third space economy, that of global financial markets. For instance, if the logging company is part of a stock exchange listing, it may well have 'liquefied' the logs by converting them into derivatives that can then circulate as financial instruments in the global capital market.[41] This insertion in global financial markets is to be distinguished from the financing of, in this case, the actual work of logging; it has, rather, to do with the capabilities of global finance today to liquefy even the most immobile material good, such as real estate, so it may circulate as a profit-making financial instrument in the global capital market, in addition to the profit-making potential of the material good itself.

There is a kind of analytics that emerges out of the particularity of this discussion of state-centred border regimes and the empirical work of locating a site that is part of a global web of such state-centred border regimes. These are analytics that aim at disaggregating the border function into the character, locations and sites for enforcement of a given border regime. The effect is to make legible the multiple territorial, spatial and institutional dimensions of 'the border'.

Disembedding the border from its national encasements

A critical and growing component of the broader field of forces within which states operate today is the proliferation of specialised types of private authority. These include the expansion of older systems, such as commercial arbitration, into new economic sectors, and they include new forms of private authority that are highly specialised and oriented towards specific economic sectors, such as the system of rules governing the international operations of large construction and engineering firms.

One outcome of key aspects of these various trends is the emergence of a strategic field of operations that represents a partial disembedding of specific bordering operations from the broader institutional world of the state geared to national agendas. It is a fairly rarefied field of crossborder transactions aimed at addressing the new conditions produced and demanded by economic globalisation. The transactions are strategic, cut across borders, and entail specific interactions among private actors and, sometimes, government agencies or officials. They do not entail the state as such, as in international treaties, for these transactions consist of the operations and aims of private actors – in this case, mostly firms and markets aiming at globalising their operations. These are transactions that cut across borders in that they concern the standards and regulations imposed on firms and markets operating globally; in so doing, these transactions push towards convergence at the level of national regulations and law aimed at creating the requisite conditions for globalisation.

There are two distinct features about this field of transactions that lead me to posit that we can conceive of it as a disembedded space that is in the process of getting structured. One of these features is that, while operating in familiar settings – the state and interstate system for officials and agencies of governments and the supranational system and the 'private sector' for non-state economic actors – the practices of these agents are constituting a distinct field that assembles bits of territory, authority and rights into new types of specialised and typically highly particularised structures. The field of practices getting constituted cannot be confined to the institutional world of the interstate system. The second feature is the proliferation of rules that begin to assemble into partial, specialised systems of law. Here we enter a whole new domain of private authorities – fragmented, specialised, increasingly formalised, but not running through national law *per se*. The implications of this proliferation of specialised, mostly private or supranational systems of law, is that they signal the destabilising of conventional understandings of national borders.

One perhaps extreme instance that captures current processes that disembed the national border from its national encasements is the formation of multiple, albeit very partial, global law systems.[42] Over the last two decades we have seen a multiplication of crossborder systems of rule that evince variable autonomy from national law. At one end are systems clearly centred in what is emerging as a transnational public domain and, at the other, systems that are completely autonomous and are largely private. Some scholars see in this development an emergent global law. We might conceive of it as a type of law that is disembedded from national law systems. At the heart of the notion of something akin to global law lies the possibility of a law that, firstly, is not centred in national law, unlike international law today, and, secondly, that goes beyond the project of harmonising the different national laws, which is the case with much of the supranational system developed to address economic globalisation, environmental issues and human rights. There is, in fact, a rapid growth over the last decades of such autonomous, highly differentiated systems of rules, some connected to the supranational system but not centred in national law, and others privatised and autonomous.

There is disagreement as to the notion itself of global law. Some scholars have long argued that there is no such entity as global law, though the specifics of their analysis[43] might accommodate its presence if they were writing today.[44] Whatever the approach, these scholars prefer to conceive of 'global law' as a site where multiple competing national systems interact. For instance, Dezalay and Garth note that the 'international' is itself constituted largely out of a competition among national approaches.[45] Thus the international emerges as a site for regulatory competition among essentially national approaches, whatever the issue whether it be environmental protection, constitutionalism or human rights.[46] The project *vis-à-vis* the global corporate economy, for example, is then one of harmonising differences through the specialised branch of law called conflicts law or through force. Much of the scholarship on global governance comes from this type of perspective.

For other scholars,[47] there is an emerging global law centred in the development of autonomous partial regimes. The project on 'International Courts and Tribunals' has identified approximately 125 international institutions, in which independent authorities reach final legal decisions.[48] These range from those in the public domain, such as human rights courts, to those in the private sector. They function through courts, quasi-courts and other mechanisms for settling disputes, such as international commercial arbitration.[49] They include the international maritime court, various tribunals for reparations, international criminal courts, hybrid international-national tribunal instances, trade and investment judicial bodies, regional human rights tribunals and convention-derived institutions, as well as other regional courts, such as the European Court of Justice, the European Free Trade Association Court and the Benelux Court.[50] The number of private systems has grown sharply in the last decade.

The formation of these novel global regimes is not premised on the integration, harmonisation or convergence of national legal orders. They also produce, in this process, novel types of borderings, notably through the juridification of the regime; this, then, often entails an insertion of a distinctly bordered space into a national territory marked by its own specific bordering – the conventional border. In this sense, then, these new regimes go beyond the type of international economic law, such as those arising out of the Trade-related Intellectual Property Rights agreements of the World Trade Organization involving the community of member states, which requires states to institute particular regulations in their national legal systems. Most prominently, Teubner sees a multiplication of sectoral regimes that is an overlay on national legal systems.[51] The outcome is a foundational transformation of the criteria for differentiating law; not the law of nations, nor the distinction between private and public, but rather the recognition of multiple specialised segmented processes of juridification, which today are largely private. As he put it, 'societal fragmentation impacts upon law in a manner such that the political regulation of differentiated societal spheres requires the parcelling out of issue-specific policy-arenas, which, for their part, juridify themselves'.[52] In this perspective, global law is segmented into transnational legal regimes which define the 'external reach of their jurisdiction along issue-specific rather than territorial lines, and which claim a global validity for themselves'.[53]

To take a concrete case, a type of private authority that illustrates some – though by no means all – of these issues can be seen in the so-called *lex constructionis*. This case combines: a) the notion of an autonomous global system of rules internal to an economic sector with b) the fact of a few large firms having disproportionate control over a sector which thereby facilitates the making of such private systems of rules. It is a combination of rules and standard contracts for crossborder construction projects. The sector is dominated by a small number of well organised private associations: the International Federation of Consulting Engineers, the International European Construction Federation, the British Institution of Civil Engineers, the Engineering Advancement Association of Japan and the American Institute of Architects. In addition, the World Bank, the United Nations Commission on International Trade Law, the International Institute for the Unification of

Private Law and certain international law firms also contribute to developing legal norms for how the sector is meant to function. Because of the nature of large construction and engineering projects, this case also illuminates the ways in which an autonomous system of rules and the type of power possessed by large global firms does not mean that these firms can escape all outside constraints. Indeed, these firms increasingly 'need' to address environmental protection. The way this issue gets handled in the *lex construc-tionis* is also emblematic of other such autonomously governed sectors; largely a strategy of deference that aims at externalising the responsibility for regulating the environmental issues arising out of large-scale construction projects. The externalising is to the 'extra-contractual' realm of the law of the host-state, using 'compliance' provisions that are today part of the standard contract.

These and other such transnational institutions and regimes do signal a shift in authority from the public to the private when it comes to governing the global economy. They also contain a shift in the capacity for norm-making and, in that regard, raise questions about changes in the relation between state sovereignty and the governance of global economic processes. International commercial arbitration is basically a private justice system, credit rating agencies are private gate-keeping systems, and the *lex construc-tionis* is a self-regulatory regime in a major economic sector dominated by a limited number of large firms. Along with other such institutions, they have emerged as important governance mechanisms whose authority is not centred in the state. Each is a bordered system – a key conditionality for its effectiveness and validity. But the bordering capability is not part of national state borders.

Conclusions

State sovereignty is usually conceived of as a monopoly of authority over a particular territory. Today, it is becoming evident that national territories may remain demarcated along the same old geographic borderlines, but that novel types of borderings resulting from globalisation are increasingly present inside national territory. Sovereignty remains as a systemic property, yet its institutional insertion and its capacity to legitimate and absorb all legitimating power have become unstable. The politics of contemporary sovereignties is far more complex than notions of mutually exclusive territories can capture.

The question of a bordered exclusive territory as a parameter for authority and rights has today entered a new phase. While the exclusive territorial authority of the state remains prevalent, the constitutive regimes are today less absolute than they were once meant to be. In this sense, then, state-centred border regimes – whether open or closed – remain foundational elements in our geopolity, but they coexist with a variety of other bordering dynamics and capabilities.

This does not mean that states are simply losing some putative battle against global forces. In so far as the state has historically had the capability to encase its territory through administrative and legal instruments, it also has the capability to change that encasement – for instance, deregulate its borders and open up to foreign firms and investment. But, I argued here, this comes with some foundational changes, particularly the partial denationalising of what was once national. This in turn points to the formation of novel types of bordering in the encounter of the global and the national inside national territory.

One critical aspect of this emergent research agenda is to study the global not only in terms of that which is explicitly global in scale, but also in terms of practices and institutions that scale at subnational levels. Further, it entails recognising that many of the globally scaled dynamics, such as the global capital market, actually are partly embedded in subnational sites and move between these differently scaled practices and organisational forms. For instance, the global capital market is constituted both through electronic markets with global span and through locally embedded conditions, such as financial centres and all they entail, from infrastructure to systems of trust.

A focus on such subnationally based processes and dynamics of globalisation requires methodologies and theorisations that engage not only global scalings but also subnational scalings *as* components of *global* processes, thereby destabilising older hierarchies of scale and conceptions of nested scalings. Studying global processes and conditions that get constituted subnationally has some advantages over studies of globally scaled dynamics; but it also poses specific challenges. It does make possible the use of longstanding research techniques, from quantitative to qualitative, in the study of globalisation. It also gives us a bridge for using the wealth of national and subnational data-sets, as well as specialised scholarships such as area studies. Both types of studies, however, need to be situated in conceptual architectures that are not quite those held by the researchers who originally generated these research techniques and data-sets, since their efforts have mostly had little to do with globalisation.

Notes

1 For a summary and attempted synthesis of these viewpoints, see John M. Hobson and M. Ramesh, 'Globalisation Makes of States What States Make of It: Between Agency and Structure in the State/Globalisation Debate', *New Political Economy*, Vol. 7, No. 1 (2002), pp. 5–22.
2 For example, Peter Taylor, 'World Cities and Territorial States under Conditions of Contemporary Globalisation (1999 Annual Political Geography Lecture)', *Political Geography*, Vol. 19, No. 1 (2000), pp. 5–32; Robert Jessop, 'Reflections on globalization and its illogics', in: Kris Olds *et al.* (eds), *Globalization and the Asian Pacific: Contested Territories* (Routledge, 1999), pp. 19–38; Ulrich Beck, *What is Globalization?* (Polity, 2000); and Neil Brenner, *State Spaces* (Oxford University Press, 2003).

3 For a series of articles with examples of varying theses, see *New Political Economy*, Vol. 5, No. 3 (2000).

4 For a typical example, see Isidro Morales, 'Mexico's Post-NAFTA Privatisation Policies: The Case of the Petrochemical Sector', *New Political Economy*, Vol. 2, No. 3 (1997), pp. 427–51.

5 For example, Linda Weiss, 'The State-augmenting Effects of Globalisation', *New Political Economy*, Vol. 10, No. 3 (2005), pp. 345–53.

6 Saskia Sassen, *Losing Control? Sovereignty in an Age of Globalization*, The 1995 Columbia University Leonard Hastings Schoff Memorial Lecture (Columbia University Press, 1996), chs 1 and 2; and Saskia Sassen, *Territory, Authority, Rights: From Medieval to Global Assemblages* (Princeton University Press, forthcoming 2006).

7 See also Sassen, *Territory, Authority, Rights*.

8 For an example, see Martin Lodge and Lindsay Stirton, 'Regulatory Reform in Small Developing States: Globalisation, Regulatory Autonomy and Jamaican Telecommunications', *New Political Economy*, Vol. 7, No. 3 (2002), pp. 415–22.

9 For example, Stephen Krasner, 'Globalisation and the state', in: Paul Edwards and Keith Sisson (eds), *Contemporary Debates in International Relations* (Ohio University Press, 2004), pp. 60–82; Louis Pauly, 'Global finance, political authority, and the problem of legitimation,' in: Thomas J. Biersteker and Rodney Bruce Hall (eds), *The Emergence of Private Authority and Global Governance* (Cambridge University Press, 2002), pp. 67–90; Eric Helleiner, 'Sovereignty, territoriality and the globalisation of finance', in: D. Smith, D. Solinger and S. Topik (eds), *States and Sovereignty in the Global Economy* (Routledge, 1999), pp. 158–67; Paul Hirst and Grahame Thompson, *Globalization in Question: The International Economy and the Possibilities of Governance* (Polity, 1996); and Christian Joppke (ed.), *Challenge to the Nation-State* (Oxford University Press, 1998).

10 For example, Philip G. Cerny, *The Changing Architecture of Politics* (Sage, 1990); Philip G. Cerny, 'Structuring the political arena: public goods, states and governance in a globalizing world', in: Ronen Palan (ed.), *Global Political Economy: Contemporary Theories* (Routledge, 2000), pp. 21–35; Susan Strange, *The Retreat of the State: The Diffusion of Power in the World Economy* (Cambridge University Press, 1996); Claire A. Cutler, Virginia Haufler and Tony Porter (eds), *Private Authority in International Affairs* (SUNY Press, 1999); Yale H. Ferguson and R. J. Barry Jones (eds), *Political Space: Frontiers of Change and Governance in a Globalising World* (SUNY Press, 2002); Ken Dark, 'The informational reconfiguring of global geopolitics', in: Ferguson and Jones, *Political Space*, pp. 61–86; and Ronen Palan, 'Offshore and the institutional environment of globalization', in: Ferguson and Jones, *Political Space*, pp. 211–24.

11 For what is probably the most comprehensive mapping of the main strands in the scholarship on globalisation and the state, see David Held, Anthony McGrew, David Goldblatt and Jonathan Perraton, *Global Transformations: Politics, Economics and Culture* (Polity, 1999), who categorise the two major emerging strands as 'hyperglobalists', who posit that national states are becoming weak and are on their way out, and 'transformationalists', who contend that globalisation has brought about significant changes in state authority and the work of states.

12 Beyond issues pertaining to the global economy, the question of state participation is also at the heart of a far broader debate about globalisation and the state. There is an older scholarship on world-order systems, such as Richard Falk, *Explorations at the Edge of Time: The Prospects for World Order* (Temple University Press, 1992), and 'The making of global citizenship', in: J. Brecher and T. Costello (eds), *Global Visions: Beyond the New World Order* (South End Press, 1993), recently invigorated by debates about cosmopolitanism (see David Held, *Democracy and the Global Order: From the Modern State to Cosmopolitan Governance* (Stanford

University Press, 1995); and Held *et al.*, *Global Transformations*). It examines and theorises the possibilities of transcending nationally oriented state authority and instituting world-level institutional orders. This literature often includes partial world-level orders such as the international human rights regime (see Alison Brysk (ed.), *Globalization and Human Rights* (University of Berkeley Press, 2002)), or certain features of international environmental treaties (see Ronnie Lipschutz and Judith Meyer, *Global Civil Society and Global Environmental Governance: The Politics of Nature from Place to Planet* (SUNY Press, 1996)), and, quite prominently, discussions about the possibility of a global civil society (see Held *et al.*, *Global Transformations*; and A. Annheur, M. Glasius and M. Kaldor (eds), *Global Civil Society Yearbook 2002* (Oxford University Press, 2002)). See also note 19 below.

13 A growing literature that often overlaps with particular parts of the above cited strands in the scholarship emphasises the relocation of national public government functions to private actors both within national and transnational domains (see Cutler *et al.*, *Private Authority in International Affairs*; and Alfred C. Aman Jr, 'The Globalising State: A Future-Oriented Perspective on the Public/Private Distinction, Federalism, and Democracy', *Vanderbilt Journal of Transnational Law*, Vol. 31, No. 4 (1998), pp. 769–870). For a state of the art elaboration on the rise of private authority, see generally Thomas J. Biersteker, Rodney Bruce Hall and Craig N. Murphy (eds), *Private Authority and Global Governance* (Cambridge University Press, 2000). For the emergence of crossborder governance mechanisms, see generally Ferguson and Jones, *Political Space*.

14 Sassen, *Territory, Authority, Rights*, ch. 4.

15 A good examination of these issues as they materialise in specific institutional settings can be found in Aman, 'The Globalising State'. An excellent collection of essays that seeks to capture these types of dynamics can be found in Michael Likosky (ed.), *Transnational Legal Processes* (Butterworth's LexisNexis Group, 2002).

16 Sassen, *Territory, Authority, Rights*, chs 4 and 5.

17 Perhaps the best known, though not necessarily the most precise, authors here are Kenichi Ohmae, *The End of the Nation-State: The Rise of Regional Economies* (Free Press, 1995); Walter B. Wriston, *The Twilight of Sovereignty: How the Information Revolution is Transforming Our World* (Scribner 1992); Stephen J. Kobrin, 'The MAI and the Clash of Globalizations', *Foreign Policy*, No. 112 (1998), pp. 97–109; and Benjamin J. Cohen, 'Electronic Money: New Day or False Dawn?', *Review of International Political Economy*, Vol. 8, No. 2 (2001), pp. 197–225.

18 There is today a growing literature that interprets deregulation and privatisation as the incorporation by the state of its own shrinking role; in its most formalised version this position emphasises the state's constitutionalising of its own diminished role. See Kevin R. Cox (ed.), *Spaces of Globalization: Reasserting the Power of the Local* (Guilford, 1997); Leo Panitch, 'Rethinking the role of the state in an era of globalization', in: James H. Mittelman (ed.), *Globalization: Critical Reflections* (Lynne Rienner, 1996), pp. 83–116; James H. Mittelman, *The Globalization Syndrome: Transformation and Resistance* (Princeton University Press, 2000); and Stephen Gill, 'Globalization, democratization, and the politics of indifference', in: Mittelman, *Globalization*, pp. 205–28.

19 Perhaps the best example is Helleiner, 'Sovereignty, territoriality and the globalisation of finance', who examines the regulatory changes brought on by the emergence of global financial systems and shows how states remain as key actors. See also note 12 above.

20 A good source in this regard is Edward D. Mansfield and Richard Sisson, *The Evolution of Political Knowledge* (Ohio State University Press 2003), which contains

papers by major scholars in international relations addressing key issues about the state and the current features of the interstate system, with responses by critics from other disciplines.

21 For a development of some of these issues, see Saskia Sassen, 'Territory and Territoriality in the Global Economy', *International Sociology*, Vol. 15, No. 2 (2000), pp. 372–93. In this context, I find interesting parallels in a specific type of legal scholarship focused on the construction of jurisdictions and the location of particular issues in jurisdictions that may today be less and less adequate. See, for instance, George A. Bermann, 'International regulatory cooperation and US federalism', in: G. A. Bermann, M. Herdegen and P. L. Lindseth (eds), *Transatlantic Regulatory Cooperation: Legal Problems and Political Prospects* (Oxford University Press, 2002), pp. 373–84; see also the extraordinary analysis in Judith Resnik, 'Categorical Federalism: Jurisdiction, Gender, and the Globe', *The Yale Law Journal*, Vol. 111, No. 3 (2001), pp. 619–80.

22 However, these dynamics can also be present when privatisation and deregulation concern native firms and investors – *pace* the fact that, in much of the world, privatisation and deregulation have been constituted through the entry of foreign investors and firms.

23 Several scholars have focused on the nature of this engagement: see Strange, *The Retreat of the State*; Cerny, 'Structuring the political arena'; Dark, 'The informational reconfiguring'; Jan Aart Scholte, 'Global Capitalism and the State', *International Affairs*, Vol. 73, No. 3 (1997), pp. 427–52; Leo Panitch and Colin Leys (eds), *Global Capitalism Versus Democracy* (Merlin Press & Monthly Review Press, 1999); Paul N. Doremus, William W. Keller, Louis W. Pauly and Simon Reich, *The Myth of the Global Corporation* (Princeton University Press, 1999); and Boris Kagarlitsky, 'The challenge for the left: reclaiming the state', in: Panitch and Leys, *Global Capitalism Versus Democracy*, pp. 294–313. One way of organising the major issues is to ask whether the role of the state is simply one of reducing its authority – for example, as suggested with terms such as deregulation and privatisation, and generally 'less government' – or whether it also requires the production of new types of regulations, legislative items, court decisions; in brief, the production of a whole series of new 'legalities'. I use this term to distinguish this production from 'law' or 'jurisprudence'. See Sassen, *Losing Control?*, ch. 1.

24 Among the issues raised by this type of analysis are the increased autonomy and influence of a whole variety of types of processes and actors, including non-state actors. The literature on non-governmental organisations, including transnational ones, and the associated forms of activism, has also generated a series of interesting insights into the changed position of states in a context of multiple globalisation. See, for example, Margaret Keck and Kathryn Sikkink, *Activists Beyond Borders: Advocacy Networks in International Politics* (Cornell University Press, 1998); Robert O'Brien, Anne Marie Goetz, Jan Aart Scholte and Marc Williams, *Contesting Global Governance: Multilateral Economic Institutions and Global Social Movements* (Cambridge University Press, 2000); and David Bollier, 'Reinventing Democratic Culture in the Age of Electronic Networks', available at http://www.netaction.org/bollier. For a critical account that partly rejects the notion that these non-state actors actually represent a politics that undermines existing forms of authority, including that of the state, see André Drainville, 'Left internationalism and the politics of resistance in the New World Order', in: David A. Smith and Josef Borocs (eds), *A New World Order: Global Transformation in the Late Twentieth Century* (Greenwood Press, 1995), pp. 217–38. I would also include here a variety of emergent global networks that are fighting equally emergent global agents such as trafficking gangs. See Global Survival Network, 'Crime and Servitude: An Exposé of the Traffic in Women for Prostitution from the Newly Independent States', available at http://www.witness.org; and Coalition to Abolish

Slavery and Trafficking, 'Resources: Factsheet', available at http://www.castla.org/news/resources.htm. For a general review of these types of organisations, see Sassen, 'Territory in the Global Economy'. Along these lines a new set of concrete instances has come about with the 11 September 2001 attack on the World Trade Center, that is, the use by international organised terrorism of the global financial system and the international immigration regime. See, for a variety of analyses, Craig J. Calhoun, Paul Price and Ashley S. Timmer, *Understanding September 11* (New Press 2002); and Saskia Sassen, 'Spatialities and Temporalities of the Global', *Public Culture* (Millennium Issue on Globalization), Vol. 12, No. 1 (2000), pp. 215–32.

25 Seen from the perspective of firms and investors operating transnationally, the objective is to enjoy the protections traditionally exercised by the state in the national realm of the economy for national firms, notably guaranteeing property rights and contracts. How this gets done may involve a range of options. See Cutler *et al.*, *Private Authority in International Affairs*; and Biersteker and Hall, *The Emergence of Private Authority and Global Governance*.

26 Two very different bodies of scholarship which develop lines of analysis that can help in capturing some of these conditions are represented by the work of James Rosenau, particularly his examination of the domestic 'frontier' inside the national state (James N. Rosenau, *Along the Domestic-Foreign Frontier: Exploring Governance in a Troubled World* (Cambridge University Press, 1997)), and by the work of R. B. J. Walker problematising the distinction inside/outside in international relations theory (R. B. J. Walker, *Inside/Outside: International Relations as Political Theory* (Cambridge University Press, 1993)). An interesting variant on this subject is Thomas Callaghy, Ronald Kassimir and Robert Latham (eds), *Intervention and Transnationalism in Africa: Global-Local Networks of Power* (Cambridge University Press, 2001), who examine the proliferation of global non-state-centred networks in the case of Africa.

27 See Beth Stephens, 'Corporate Liability: Enforcing Human Rights through Domestic Litigation', *Hastings International & Comparative Law Review*, Vol. 24, No. 3 (2002), pp. 401–15.

28 We can see this in particular features of a variety of domains; for instance, competition policy (Edward O. Graham and J. D. Richardson, *Global Competition Policy* (Institute for International Economics, 1997); Brian Portnoy, *Constructing Competition: The Political Foundations of Alliance Capitalism*, unpublished Ph.D. dissertation, University of Chicago, Chicago, Illinois, 2000)); specific aspects of international business collaboration (John Dunning, *Alliance Capitalism and Global Business* (Routledge, 1997); Indiana Journal of Global Legal Studies, *Symposium: The Internet and the Sovereign State: The Role and Impact of Cyberspace on National and Global Governance*, Vol. 5, No. 2 (1998)); in networks among members of the judiciary (Anne-Marie Slaughter, *A New World Order* (Princeton University Press, 2004)); and, in a very different domain, the new opening among the top leadership in a growing number of unions to organising immigrants (Leah Haus, *Unions, Immigration, and Internationalization: New Challenges and Changing Conditions in the United States and France* (Palgrave, 2002)).

29 For example, Shaun Breslin, 'Decentralisation, Globalisation and China's Partial Re-engagement with the Global Economy', *New Political Economy*, Vol. 5, No. 2 (2000), pp. 205–26.

30 For more on states and global markets, see the collection of articles in *New Political Economy*, Vol. 8, No. 1 (2003).

31 For example, Taylor, 'World Cities and Territorial States'; Erik Swyngedouw, 'Neither global nor local: "globalization", and the politics of scale', in: Cox, *Spaces of Globalization*, pp. 137–66; Ash Amin and Nigel Thrift, *Globalization, Institutions and Regional Development in Europe* (Oxford University Press, 1994);

M. Peter Smith and Luis E. Guarnizo, *Transnationalism from Below* (Transaction, 1998); Sanjeev Khagram, *Dams and Development: Transnational Struggles for Water and Power* (Cornell University Press, 2004); and Robert C. Smith, *Mexican New York: Transnational Lives of New Immigrants* (University of California Press, 2005).

32 For example, Doreen Massey, 'Politics and space/time', in: M. Keith and S. Pile (eds), *Place and the Politics of Identity* (Routledge, 1993), pp. 141–61; Richard Howitt, 'A World in a Grain of Sand: Towards a Reconceptualisation of Geographical Scale', *Australian Geographer*, Vol. 24, No. 1 (1993), pp. 33–44; and Andrew Jonas, 'The Scale Politics of Spatiality', *Environment and Planning D: Society and Space*, Vol. 12, No. 3 (1994), pp. 257–64.

33 Elsewhere I examine the emergence of forms of globality centred on localised struggles and actors that are part of crossborder networks; this is a form of global politics that runs not through global institutions but through local ones. See Saskia Sassen, 'Electronic markets and activist networks: the weight of social logics in digital formations', in: Robert Latham and Saskia Sassen (eds), *Digital Formations: IT and New Architectures in the Global Realm* (Princeton University Press, 2005). For a full development of this thesis, see Sassen, *Losing Control?*, chs 4 and 5.

34 For instance, at least some of the circuits connecting São Paulo to global dynamics are different from those of Frankfurt, Johannesburg or Bombay. Further, distinct sets of overlapping circuits contribute to the constitution of distinctly structured crossborder geographies. We are, for instance, seeing the intensifying of older hegemonic geographies, such as the increase in transactions among New York, Miami, Mexico City and São Paulo. See, for example, Sueli Schiffer Ramos, 'São Paulo: articulating a cross-border regional economy', in: Saskia Sassen (ed.), *Global Networks/Linked Cities* (Routledge, 2002), pp. 209–36; Christoff Parnreiter, 'The making of a global city: Mexico City', in: Sassen, *Global Network/Linked Cities*, pp. 145–82, as well as newly constituted geographies, such as the articulation of Shanghai with a rapidly growing number of crossborder circuits. See Felicity Rose Gu and Zilia Tang, 'Shanghai: reconnecting to the global economy', in: Sassen, *Global Networks/Linked Cities*, pp. 273–308.

35 For a critical examination along these lines, see Benedicte Bull and Morten Boas, 'Multilateral Development Banks as Regionalising Actors: The Asian Development Bank and the Inter-American Development Bank', *New Political Economy*, Vol. 8, No. 2 (2003), pp. 245–61.

36 In my early research on the global city I began to understand some of these questions of reified scales. Much of the literature on global and world cities has a critical appraisal of questions of scaling, but, with important exceptions (Peter J. Taylor, 'World cities and territorial states: the rise and fall of their mutuality', in: P. J. Taylor and P. L. Knox (eds), *World Cities in a World-System* (Cambridge University Press, 1995), pp. 48–62; Neil Brenner, 'Global Cities, Global States: Global City Formation and State Territorial Restructuring in Contemporary Europe', *Review of International Political Economy*, Vol. 5, No. 2 (1998), pp. 1–37), this appraisal tends to be in embryo, undertheorised and not quite explicated. On the other hand, the scholarship on 'glocalisation' recognises and theorises questions of scale but often remains attached to a notion of nested scalings (for example, Swyngedouw, 'Neither global nor local'). I find that among the literatures in geography that come closest in their conceptualisation, albeit focused on very different issues, to what I develop in this chapter are those on first-nation peoples' rights claiming. See Howitt, 'A World in a Grain of Sand'; Steven E. Silvern, 'Scales of Justice: Law, American Indian Treaty Rights and Political Construction of Scale', *Political Geography*, No. 18 (1999), pp. 639–68; and Claudia Notzke, 'A New Perspective in Aboriginal Nature Resource Management:

Co-Management', *Geoforum*, Vol. 26, No. 2 (1995), pp. 187–209. Clearly, there is a particularly illuminating positioning of the issues in this case because from the outset there is: a) the coexistence of two exclusive claims over a single territory; and b) the endogeneity of both types of claims – that of the modern sovereign and that of the indigenous nation. In my case here, it is the coexistence of the claim of the historical sovereign and the claim of the global as endogenised in the reconstituted sovereign. For a full development of this somewhat abstract statement, see Sassen, *Territory, Authority, Rights*.

37 For example, Taylor, 'World cities and territorial states'; and Beck, *What is Globalization?*.

38 Xiangming Chen, *As Borders Bend: Transnational Spaces on the Pacific Rim* (Rowman & Littlefield, 2005).

39 For example, Paul Williams and Ian Taylor, 'Neoliberalism and the Political Economy of the "New" South Africa', *New Political Economy*, Vol. 5, No. 1 (2000), pp. 21–41.

40 Sassen, *Losing Control?*, ch. 3; and Saskia Sassen, *Globalization and its Discontents* (New Press, 1998), ch. 4.

41 Finally, and I cannot resist, we might want to say that a spent, used-up, sparsely populated area – for instance, a completely logged forest, where the forest ceases to exist – represents an instance of 'dead land' on what may well continue to be very dynamic global circuits, such as the logging multinationals now operating in other sites, in the same or other countries. The point here is that one of the key articulations of that site remains that global logging circuit, and to keep a dead site on the circuits that caused its death is part of a critical social science. Why render it invisible?

42 For a fuller development, see Sassen, *Territory, Authority, Rights*, ch. 5.

43 For example, see Martin Shapiro, 'The Globalization of Law', *Indiana Journal of Global Legal Studies*, No. 1 (1993), pp. 37–64.

44 Shapiro in *ibid.* notes that there is not much of a regime of international law, either through the establishment of a single global lawgiver and enforcer or through a nation-state consensus. He also posits that, if there was, we would be dealing with an international rather than a global law. Nor is it certain that law has become universal – that is, that human relations anywhere in the world will be governed by some law, even if not by a law that is the same everywhere. Globalisation of law refers to a very limited, specialised set of legal phenomena, and Shapiro argues that it will almost always refer to North America and Europe, only sometimes to Japan and to some other Asian countries. There have been a few particular common developments and many particular parallel developments in law across the world. Thus, as a concomitant of the globalisation of markets and the organisation of transnational corporations, there has been a move towards a relatively uniform global contract and commercial law. This can be seen as a private law-making system where the two or more parties create a set of rules to govern their future relations. Such a system of private law-making can exist transnationally even when there is no transnational court.

45 Yves Dezalay and Garth Bryant, *Dealing in Virtue: International Commercial Arbitration and the Construction of a Transnational Legal Order* (University of Chicago Press, 1996).

46 David Charny, 'Competition among Jurisdictions in Formulating Corporate Law Rules: An American Perspective on the "Race to the Bottom" in the European Communities', *Harvard International Law Journal*, Vol. 32, No. 2 (1991), pp. 423–56; and Joel Trachtman, 'International Regulatory Competition, Externalization, and Juridiction', *Harvard International Law Journal*, Vol. 34, No. 1 (1993), pp. 47–104. There are two other categories that may partly overlap with internationalisation as Americanisation, but are important to distinguish, at

least analytically. One is multilateralism and the other is what John Ruggie has called multiperspectival institutions. See J. G. Ruggie, *Constructing the World Polity* (Routledge, 2000).

47 For example, Gunther Teubner, 'Societal constitutionalism: alternatives to state-centered constitutional theory', in: Christian Joerges, Inger-Johanne Sand and Gunther Teubner (eds), *Transnational Governance and Constitutionalism* (Hartford Publishing, 2004), pp. 3–29.

48 The Project on 'International Courts and Tribunals' (PICT) was founded in 1997 by the Center on International Cooperation (CIC), New York University, and the Foundation for International Environmental Law and Development. From 2002 onwards, PICT has been a common project of the CIC and the Centre for International Courts and Tribunals, University College London. See http://www.pict-pcti.org

49 For example, see Roger P. Alford, 'The American Influence on International Arbitration', *Ohio State Journal on Dispute Resolution*, Vol. 19, No. 1 (2003), pp. 69–88.

50 PICT (Notation 4) has gathered good documentation on legal frameworks and explicatory literature; see, further, Diana Shelton, *Remedies in International Human Rights Law* (Oxford University Press, 1999); and on 'hybrid courts', see Laura Dickinson, 'The Promise of Hybrid Courts', *American Journal of International Law*, Vol. 97, No. 2 (2003), pp. 295ff.

51 Teubner, 'Societal constitutionalism'.

52 *Ibid.*

53 See Dirk Lehmkuhl, 'The Resolution of Domain Names vs. Trademark Conflicts: A Case Study on Regulation Beyond the Nation-State and Related Problems', *Zeitschrift für Rechtssoziologie*, Vol. 23, No. 1 (2003), pp. 61–78.

7 Beyond the 'new' regionalism

Björn Hettne

Over the last decade regionalism, or what has become known as 'new regionalism', has become a prominent issue in a number of social science specialisations: European studies, comparative politics, international economics, international relations and international political economy. The approach of these different academic specialisations varies considerably, which means that regionalism means different things to different people.[1] In fact, we are facing an intriguing ontological problem. There has been little agreement about what we study when we study regionalism. This implies that there also is a lack of agreement about how we should study it; in other words, we are facing an epistemological problem as well. The great divide, albeit an exaggerated one, is between what has been termed 'old' and 'new' regionalism. Whatever the merits of this distinction, I shall use it in this chapter as a pedagogical device to underline the shifting terrain and the instruments to explore it. Yet I shall also propose its dissolution, and a move beyond new regionalism, in looking more generally for the role of the regional factor in global transformation. It is in any case awkward to call something 'new' that now is already more than two decades old. But the search for continuities does not mean that regionalism constitutes exactly the same phenomenon across time. On the contrary. The competing approaches (as well as the earlier approaches here called 'old') in no way lack merits; it is my ambition to do justice to what durable contributions they have provided.

Part 1 thus describes the first generation of regionalism studies, focused on regional integration in Europe, and the subsequent 'big leap' from the 'old' to the 'new' regionalism, which really was the study of regionalisms in the context of globalisation. The 'old' regionalism has been well documented before, so my purpose is rather to look for continuities.[2] The discontinuities are of course also acknowledged.[3] Part 2 goes into the various dimensions of the more recent regionalism, the actors driving it and the societal levels at which it manifests itself. Besides the globalised context, this multidimensional, multiactor and multilevel character – or, in short, complexity – was what distinguished the 'new' regionalism. Part 3 moves from regionalism as such to regionalism as a dimension of the changing international political economy and world order. I shall suggest that regionalism might actually shape world order. In a concluding section the achievements as well as the remaining gaps and unresolved issues of this fascinating field are discussed.

Generations of regionalisms: continuities and discontinuities

As suggested, regionalism is one of those contested concepts that has continued to baffle social scientists for years. I have therefore to start with the problem of definition, even if this often has proved to be somewhat of a dead end, due to the fact that region, regional cooperation, regional integration, regionalism, regionalisation and region building are moving targets. The overproduction of concepts signals a certain disarray. Thus we have to come back to the problem of definition when dealing with different approaches to the elusive phenomenon of regionalism.

Conceptualisation

The concept of region is used differently in different disciplines: in the field of geography, regions are usually seen as subnational entities, either historical provinces (which could have become nation-states) or more recently created units. In IR, regions are often treated as supranational subsystems of the international system. It is of some importance whether regions are seen as subsystems of the international system or as emerging regional formations with their own dynamics. Even so, such macroregions can be defined in different ways: as continents or as supranational formations of countries sharing a common political and economic project and having a certain degree of common identity. The minimum definition of a world region is typically a limited number of states linked together by a geographical relationship and a degree of mutual interdependence.[4] According to a more comprehensive view, a region consists of 'states which have some common ethnic, linguistic, cultural, social, and historical bonds'.[5] Even more comprehensively, regions can be differentiated in terms of social cohesiveness (ethnicity, race, language, religion, culture, history, consciousness of a common heritage), economic cohesiveness (trade patterns, economic complementarity), political cohesiveness (regime type, ideology) and organisational cohesiveness (existence of formal regional institutions).[6] Such parsimonious attempts at definition seem to have come to an end. Today, researchers acknowledge the fact that there are no 'natural' regions: definitions of a 'region' vary according to the particular problem or question under investigation. Moreover, it is widely accepted that it is how political actors perceive and interpret the idea of a region and notions of 'regionness' that is critical: all regions are socially constructed and hence politically contested.[7]

But there are other pitfalls. Often a region is simplistically mixed up with a particular regional organisation. The organisation tries to shape what it defines as 'its' region by promoting cooperation among states and other actors, which is possible to the extent that a genuine experience of shared interests in a shared political community exists – that the region is 'real' and not only 'formal'. Regional integration belongs to an earlier discourse, primarily related to a spiralling translocal market integration (thus including the building of national markets as well). Regional integration as a translocal process, simply defined in terms of market factors, has occurred over a long period of time.[8] The concept of integration can also be made more or less complex. According to Joseph Nye, the concept of integration groups too many disparate phenomena to be helpful, and should therefore be broken down into economic integration (the formation of a transnational economy), social integration (the formation of a transnational society) and political integration (the formation of a transnational political system).[9] Regional cooperation is somewhat less complex and normally refers to joint efforts by states to solve specific problems. Ernst B. Haas defined the concept as follows: 'regional cooperation is a vague term covering any interstate activity with less than universal participation designed to meet commonly experienced need'.[10] Andrew Axline asserted that 'regional cooperation can only be understood from the perspective of the national interests of the individual member states, and that the politics of regional negotiations will involve accommodating these interests for all partners'.[11] Regional integration is, in contrast, normally taken to imply some change in terms of sovereignty. According to Haas, 'the study of regional integration is concerned with explaining how and why states cease to be wholly sovereign'.[12]

Regionalism and regionalisation are two more recent concepts, and much effort has been devoted to the distinction between them. Regionalism refers to a tendency and a political commitment to organise the world in terms of regions; more narrowly, the concept refers to a specific regional project. In some definitions the actors behind this political commitment are states; in other definitions the actors are not confined to states. According to Anthony Payne and Andrew Gamble, 'regionalism is a state-led or states-led project designed to reorganize a particular regional space along defined economic and political lines'.[13] They go on in their pioneering book to say that 'regionalism is seen as something that is being constructed, and constantly reconstructed, by collective human action',[14] which sounds like a more comprehensive view as far as agency is concerned.[15] Other authors find it difficult to confine the regionalism project to states. Helge Hveem also makes a firm distinction between regionalism and regionalisation, but talks about 'an identifiable group of actors' trying to realise the project.[16] Andrew Hurrell lets the concept of regionalism contain five varieties: regionalisation (informal integration), identity, interstate cooperation, state-led integration and cohesion.[17] Sometimes, particularly in a neoliberal discourse, regionalism is identified with protectionism, normally with (worried) reference to the rise of economic nationalism in secluded regional markets in the interwar period.

Regionalisation refers to the more complex processes of forming regions; whether these are consciously planned or caused by spontaneous processes is not agreed upon by all authors. In my view, they can emerge by either means.

More recently, the concept of region building (in analogy with nation building) has been employed to signify 'the ideas, dynamics and means that contribute to changing a geographical area into a politically-constructed community'.[18] Iver B. Neumann in particular has developed a region-building approach, which he himself terms 'post-structural' and which sees the region as born in discourse on 'inside and outside'.[19] The enlargement of Europe, particularly the current debate on Turkey's inclusion or exclusion, provides a rich source for this kind of analysis.

The early debate

Today the concept of regionalism has become the most common, and it has also become commonplace to distinguish between an older wave or generation of regionalism (then often referred to as regional integration) in the 1950s and 1960s and a more recent new 'wave' or 'generation' of regionalism (the new regionalism) starting in the latter half of the 1980s and today being a prevalent phenomenon throughout the world.[20] 'Old' theories or approaches to regionalism were all concerned with peace, and tended to see the nation-state as the problem rather than the solution.[21] The relevant theories were federalism, functionalism and neofunctionalism. Federalism, which inspired the pioneers of European integration, was not really a theory but rather a political programme; it was sceptical of the nation-state, although what was to be created was in fact a new kind of state. There was no obvious theorist associated with federalism. In contrast, functionalism has been much identified with one particular name, that of David Mitrany. This was also an approach to peace building rather than a theory. The question for functionalists was on which political level various human needs (often defined in a rather technical way) could best be met. Usually, the best way was found to be going beyond the nation-state, but not necessarily going regional.[22] Thus both federalism and functionalism wanted the nation-state to go, but through different routes and by different means. International organisations should be established in the promotion of cooperation and transnational activities around basic functional needs, such as transportation, trade, production and welfare. Economics was seen as more important than politics. Functionalism was rather technocratic and therefore unrealistic. Form, in the functionalist view, was supposed to follow function, whereas for federalists it was really form that mattered. Mitrany criticised both federalism and regional integration in general because both were primarily based on territory rather than function. For functional solutions there should be no territorial boundaries. Territoriality was seen as part of the Westphalian logic and Westphalia implied conflict and war. However, in contrast to the European Community (EC), which was a political community, the European Coal and Steel Community was, according to Mitrany, a functional and therefore acceptable organisation (for here the technical question was: how can coal and steel production best be organised?).

One early approach that to a larger extent had theoretical ambitions was neofunctionalism: the theory (but also strategy) of European integration. The central figure here was Ernst Haas. He challenged the functionalist assumption of the separability of politics, claiming that the technical realm was in fact made technical by a prior political decision. Neofunctionalists argued that raising levels of interdependence would set in motion a process eventually leading to political integration. The emphasis was on process and purposeful actors, far away from functional automaticity. Haas in fact theorised the 'community method' of Jean Monnet. Even if the outcome of this method could be a federation, the way of building it was not by constitutional design. The basic mechanism was 'spillover', this key concept being defined as 'the way in which the creation and deepening of integration in one economic sector would create pressures for further economic integration within and beyond that sector, and greater authoritative capacity at the European level'.[23] Bela Balassa applied a similar logic to economic integration. A free trade area would lead to a customs union and further to a common market, economic union and political union.[24]

Europe was the centre of the debate about old regionalism. In the 1960s the fit between the neofunctional description (and prescription) and the empirical world, now dominated by de Gaulle's nationalism, disappeared. Stanley Hoffman asserted that integration could not spread from low politics (economics) to the sphere of high politics (security).[25] Integration happened only as long as it coincided with the national interest. The image of the EC began to diverge. According to Alan Milward, the EC should be seen as a 'rescue of the nation-state'.[26] The EC could furthermore be understood as a confederation rather than a federation, according to the intergovernmentalist turn in the study of European integration. The ontological shift thus implied an epistemological shift towards a more state-centric, realist analysis.

Haas responded to his critics by calling the study of integration 'pre-theory' (since there was no clear idea about dependent and independent variables), then spoke about the field in terms of obsolescence, and ended up suggesting that the study of regional integration should cease to be a subject in its own right. Rather, it should be seen as an aspect of the study of interdependence (a concept then popularised by Robert Keohane and Joseph Nye).[27] This was again a new turn. The global context was not really considered by old regionalism theory, concerned as it was with regional integration as a planned merger of national economies through cooperation among a group of nation-states. Comparative studies were for obvious reasons rare. Haas listed a number of background factors for successful integration and Philippe Schmitter focused particularly on Latin America.[28] Axline criticised neofunctionalism for being Eurocentric: 'The goal of integration and the dependent variable of the theory used to understand integration remained a higher degree of political unification from the neo-functionalist perspective. Yet the goal of regional integration in the Third World was not political unification.'[29]

The recent debate

In the real world the 1970s was a period of 'Eurosclerosis' within the EC. Elsewhere, those attempts to create regional organisations that had been made were failing and most of these organisations fell into dormancy. However, the 1985 white paper on the internal market started a new dynamic process of European integration. This was also the start of the 'new regionalism' elsewhere; after some time, everywhere. Naturally, this attracted a lot of interest in the late 1980s and early 1990s. What was striking, though, was the lack of correspondence in this respect between economics and political science. At that time few introductions to IR, IPE or development studies contained sections on regionalism. Today, this is commonplace.

The studies of the new regionalism considered new aspects, particularly those focused on conditions related to what increasingly came to be called globalisation, a phenomenon which was to give rise to another academic growth industry.[30] Regionalism is strongly related to globalisation, but there are, as we shall see, different views on the nature of this relationship. Is regionalisation an integral part of globalisation, or is it a political reaction against that process? In fact, it can be both.

Regionalisation and globalisation represent related but different aspects of the contemporary transformation of world order; globalist and regionalist political projects may have different impacts at different points in time. Contemporary globalisation can, in accordance with the classical theory of Karl Polanyi, be seen as a 'second great transformation', a 'double movement', where an expansion and deepening of the market is followed by a political intervention in defence of societal cohesion – the expansion of market constituting the first movement and the societal response the second.[31] The 'second movement' contains counter-movements caused by the dislocations associated with market penetration into new areas. Regionalism is thus part of both the first and second movement, with a neoliberal face in the first, and a more interventionist orientation in the second. There is thus a transnational struggle over the political content of regionalisation, as well as over that of globalisation.

However, regions must at the same time be understood as endogenous processes, emerging from within the geographical area in question. They are not simply geographical or administrative objects, but subjects in the making (or un-making); their boundaries are shifting, and so are their capacities as actors, which can be referred to as their level of regionness.[32] Regionness defines the position of a particular region in terms of regional cohesion, which can be seen as a long-term historical process, changing over time from coercion, the building of empires and nations, to voluntary cooperation. In general terms one can speak of five levels of regionness: a regional space, a translocal social system, an international society, a regional community and a regionally institutionalised polity. The regional space is a geographic area, delimited by more or less natural physical barriers. In social terms the region is organised by human inhabitants, at first in relatively isolated communities, but more and more creating some kind of translocal relationship. The region as a social system implies ever widening translocal relations, in which the constituent units are dependent on each other, as well as on the overall stability of the system. The region as international society is characterised by norms and rules which increase the level of predictability in the system. The region as community takes shape when an enduring organisational framework facilitates and promotes social communication and convergence of values and behaviour throughout the region. Finally, the region as institutionalised polity has a more fixed structure of decision making and stronger actor capability. The five levels must not be interpreted in a deterministic fashion as a necessary sequence. Since regionalism is a political project, created by human actors, it may, just like a nation-state project, fail. In this perspective, decline could mean decreasing regionness; ultimately a dissolution of the region itself.[33]

Thus endogenous (levels of regionness) and exogenous (the challenges of globalisation) factors must both be considered. Globalism and regionalism became competing ways of understanding the world, and much analytical work was devoted (or wasted?) in trying to clarify how the two processes were related. Since the impact of globalisation differs in various parts of the world, the actual process of regionalisation also differs between the emerging world-regions, thus giving shape to many regionalisms. Globalisation and regionalisation processes interact under different conditions of regionness, creating a variety of pathways of regionalisation. This also meant that many different understandings of regionalism coincided, resulting in great confusion. Let us try to clarify some of them.

With regard to old and new regionalism, the former was a Cold War phenomenon. It was specific with regard to its objectives (some organisations being primarily security-motivated, others more economically oriented), whereas the latter resulted from a more comprehensive, multidimensional societal process. The new regionalism took shape in a multipolar world order and in a context of globalisation. It formed part of a global structural transformation. In this transformation a variety of non-state actors were to be found operating at several levels of the global system.

The new regionalism as studied in IPE can also be contrasted both to what is better termed 'the new protectionism', which was basically an early interpretation of the new wave of regionalism by neoliberal economists who feared that the sudden interest in regionalism heralded a new protectionism.[34] The difference lay very much in the ontological and epistemological perspectives. Neoliberals conceived the new regionalism as a trade promotion policy, building on regional arrangements rather than a multilateral framework; by contrast, for IPE, regionalism was a comprehensive multidimensional programme, including economic, security, environmental and many other issues. To neoliberals, regionalism could only be a second-best contribution to the task of increasing the amount of world trade and global welfare, and at worst a threat against the multilateral order. The IPE perspective, on the other hand, held that free trade was not the main issue and that regionalism could contribute to solving many problems, from security to environment, that were not efficiently tackled on the national level and to which there were no market solutions. Thus, for the neoliberals, regionalism was 'new' only in the sense that it represented a revival of protectionism or neomercantilism, whereas IPE saw the current wave of regionalism as qualitatively new, in the sense that it could only be understood in relation to the transformation of the world economy. This also implied that the closure of regions was not on the agenda; rather, the new regionalism was 'open regionalism', which emphasised that the integration project should be market-driven and outward-looking, should avoid high levels of protection and should form part of the ongoing globalisation and internationalisation process of the world political economy.[35] Cable and Henderson defined 'open regionalism' as a 'negotiating framework consistent with and complementary to GATT'.[36] For Gamble and Payne, 'one of the most striking characteristics common to all the regionalist projects is their commitment to open regionalism'.[37]

Another important issue discussed in the context of more recent regionalism has been that it is a worldwide phenomenon, covering both more and less developed countries and, in some cases, combining both in the same regional organisation. Regions can thus be ordered in the world system hierarchy. Three structurally different types of regions can be distinguished: core regions, peripheral regions and, between them, intermediate regions. The regions are distinguished, first, by their relative degree of economic dynamism and, second, by their relative political stability, and the dividing line may run through existing states. The borderlines are impermanent. Rather, one could think of the hierarchical structure as consisting of zones which the regions enter or leave depending on their economic position and political stability, as well as their level of regionness. This means that the regions may be differently situated and defined at different occasions, or at different times in world history. The level of regionness can purposively be changed. For instance, security cooperation within a region would lead to improved stability, making the region more attractive for international investment and trade, and development cooperation would mean a more efficient use of available resources.

The 'blind man metaphor' is relevant also for the recent debate. It contains a number of different theoretical approaches, from a revival of neofunctionalism to social constructivism, and with neorealism, neoliberal institutionalism and liberal intergovernmentalism in between. There are quite a few interesting theoretical explanations of specified aspects of regionalism. The problem with rigid theorising is that it must delimit the object for study, even while the object refuses too much reductionism.[38] An empirical case can (and perhaps should) be approached from different theoretical angles. Different theories illuminate different dimensions of a multidimensional phenomenon. Therefore I will not propose any preferred theory in this overview.

Dimensions, actors and levels

In contrast with the time in which Haas was writing there are today many regionalisms and thus a very different base for comparative studies.[39] Different kinds of regions in interaction have appeared on different levels of the global system. Old regional organisations continued but with new functions, while new regional organisations were formed to meet new challenges. At the same time various actors began to operate in these regional arenas, dealing with regional and global problems and providing regional and global public goods. In view of all of this, it is rather obvious that neither the object for study (ontology) nor the way of studying it (epistemology) will have been likely to have remained the same. The new regionalism must be seen as a new political landscape in the making, characterised by several interrelated dimensions, many actors (including the region itself) and several interacting levels of society.

The second part of this chapter deals with this regional complexity, a complexity not minimised by the difficulty of clarifying what is influencing what in this triangle and the fact that the three issues overlap, particularly level and actor. An important point here is that the idea of levels is a gross simplification. It is better probably to talk about scales of regionalism in various regional formations, which overlap and interact in different issue areas. This complexity is a major challenge for social science, particularly IR and IPE.

Dimensions

The central issue on which studies of both old and new regionalism focused was trade. Regional formations were seen as more or less synonymous with trade blocs. Indeed, as noted above, some were afraid that these trade blocs represented a step backwards towards protectionism; others saw them as a good substitute to a badly functioning multilateralism; others again saw them as a step towards global free trade. Monetary issues are of course inseparable from trade. However, other dimensions were soon added to the regional complexity. There was, first of all, the problem of development, which, albeit often related to trade, is quite distinct and has generally been discussed in terms of developmental regionalism. Security also emerged as a regional issue, thus creating an interest in so-called security regionalism.[40]

Trade blocs

As already indicated, regional trading arrangements are often seen as a 'second-best' and therefore judged according to whether they contribute to a more closed or more open multilateral trading system, embodied in the so-called 'stumbling block vs. stepping stone' dichotomy. Many of the regional trading arrangements that existed during the era of the old regionalism in the 1950s and 1960s were inward-looking and protectionist, and were often regarded by contemporary economists as failures. At the time, however, they were widely considered to be instruments for enhancing industrial production, as in the strand of development thinking associated with the United Nations Economic Commission for Latin America and the even more ambitious strategy of the United Nations Conference on Trade and Development, both led by Raúl Prebisch. The culmination of this process was the demand for a New International Economic Order. Regionalism developed into a form of global mobilisation against an unequal world order, but lost some of its strength in the process. As suggested by Percy Mistry, the World Trade Organization has been 'hijacked' by the governments of the OECD countries to protect their interests in a world where power is challenged by developing counties.[41] It should thus be recognised that much of today's regionalism, especially but not only in the South, has often developed in response to the dominance of the WTO and globalisation. As Mistry again put it, 'new regionalism is being embraced because old multilateralism no longer works'.[42]

Furthermore, members of regional trading arrangements are increasingly likely to demand new services from the WTO, so that its discipline serves to 'police' regional relations and contribute to their health. This need is a severely understated demonstration of 'how regionalism is providing a substance to multilateralism'.[43] In other words, regionalism can be seen as a prerequisite for reconstructing multilateralism on a more equal basis.

Monetary regionalism

The monetary issue has been neglected due to the heavy concentration on trade in the regionalist discourse. Monetary regionalism may have many objectives, the most important of which is likely to be financial stability, which means the absence of excess mobility. Since financial crisis has the potential to spread across countries, it requires a collective response, the main question in this context being at what level. The exit of international investors from one particular 'emerging market' transforms a national public 'bad' into a regional and eventually global public 'bad'.[44] Like the trading system of the world, the financial system is asymmetric. Financial stability is a global issue, but the global instruments show a bias against the weak, which has raised the issue of building regional institutions for protection against excess volatility.

The 'Asian financial crisis' of 1997 underlined the degree of interdependence within the larger region of Southeast and East Asia and 'exposed the weakness of existing regional institutional economic arrangements', causing crises for both the Association of Southeast Asian Nations (ASEAN) and Asia–Pacific Economic Cooperation (APEC), the two competing regional organisations.[45] The affected countries were frustrated over the lack of remedies offered on the global level. In the West the opportunity was taken to impose neoliberal policies in a region known (and criticised) for its interventionism.

Before the Asian crisis there was little discussion about regional approaches to the management of financial stability outside Europe. Monetary regionalism in Europe is itself not a complete success story, but it shows the importance of institutional backing as well as of political commitment and a common approach to economic policy. This discovery was later made in East Asia. A regional approach in the form of an Asian Monetary Fund was proposed by Japan, but received little support and was resisted by the International Monetary Fund (IMF), the United States and the EU. This underscored the need for deeper institutionalisation and stronger commitments from the countries in the region. In May 2002 there was a meeting of the ASEAN Plus Three (APT) countries in Chiang Mai about the ways that regional cooperation could combat financial crises on the regional level. This meeting may prove to have been a breakthrough for monetary regionalism, but it is too early to tell what the result will be. Looking at the dynamics of the crisis, it is obvious that ASEAN (which is a sophisticated regional organisation) is too small, whereas APEC (being transregional) is too big and contains too many contradictory interests. An appropriate organisation, the APT, is now emerging, which underlines the fact that the nature of the regional problem impacts directly on the organisational development of regionalism.

Developmental regionalism

By developmental regionalism is meant concerted efforts from a group of countries within a geographical region to enhance the economic complementarity of the constituent political units and capacity of the total regional economy. This can be pursued via trade agreements or through more comprehensive regional development strategies. Development is a multidimensional phenomenon which depends on positive spillover and linkages between different sectors of an economy and society; it can be said to require a regional approach, whereby trade integration is coupled with other forms of economic and factor market integration (for example, investment, payments, monetary integration and harmonisation), as well as various types of economic cooperation in specified sectors (such as transport and communications).[46] This approach is both fairer and more politically feasible as it is easier to liberalise with regard to neighbours than on a multilateral basis; it is also easier to handle distributional issues in a regional context. Furthermore still, regional trade clubs can deal more effectively with non-trade economic and political challenges, such as environmental protection and migration.[47]

This line of thinking can be said to be part of the EU model and has started to have effect in different versions in other parts of the world (in ASEAN in Southeast Asia, in the Andean Community and Southern Common Market (Mercosur) in Latin America, and in the Southern African Development Community (SADC) in Africa). The strategy is only manageable within multidimensional and comprehensive regional organisations, such as those mentioned, since these can exploit spillover effects and linkages between trade and non-trade and economic and political sectors/benefits. By contrast, the North American Free Trade Agreement is mainly a trade agreement and will find it more difficult to exploit such linkages. What this highlights is the general trend towards more multidimensional forms of regional cooperation and towards regional organisations with a higher degree of 'actorness' – a concept to which we will return shortly.

Security regionalism

We have already noted that the first generation of regional integration was concerned initially with economics but ultimately with peace and security. In more recent theorising, security concerns are seen as causal factors that force countries to cooperate because of the risk of the regionalisation of conflict. By this I mean both the outward spread or spillover of a local conflict into neighbouring countries, and the inward impact from the region in the form of diplomatic interference, military intervention and, preferably, conflict resolution carried out by some kind of regional body. Security regionalism has now become a genre in its own right.[48]

Regionalism and conflict can be related in many different ways. One has to do with the choice of unit for investigation, such as a 'regional security complex', defined by Barry Buzan as 'a group of states whose primary security concerns link together sufficiently closely that their national security cannot realistically be considered apart from one another'.[49] Buzan goes on to note that 'the task of identifying a security complex involves making judgements about the relative strengths of security interdependencies among different countries'.[50] The concept has later been rethought in a multisectoral and social constructivist direction,[51] making the actual delimitation of the unit more nuanced, but not necessarily easier to utilise since different security sectors (economic, environmental, societal) may define different regions. The region is thus primarily understood as a level of analysis and is not seen to possess actor capacity.[52] This is different from the approach applied here in which region is both level of analysis and actor.

A second link between regionalism and conflict concerns the regional implications of a local conflict, which depends on the nature of the security complex and the way various security problems are linked. A third has to do with the conflict management role of the organised region (if there is one) for internal regional security, or 'regional order',[53] for the immediate environment (e.g. the neigbourhood policy of Europe) of the region, and for world order as a whole (to the extent that there is actorness enough to influence the shape of world order). Conflict management with regard to the immediate environment (but outside the region) can refer to an acute conflict or aim at preventively transforming the situation by stabilisation or integration. No clear-cut distinctions can really be made.

By security regionalism is thus meant attempts by states and other actors in a particular geographical area – a region in the making – to transform a security complex with conflict-generating inter-state and intra-state relations in the direction of a security community with cooperative external (inter-regional) relations and domestic (intra-regional) peace. The routes may differ and pass through several stages. The concept also includes more acute interventions in crises, but the long-term implications should always be kept in mind. The region can be cause (the regional complex), means (regional intervention) and solution (regional development). Indeed, in discussing regional crisis management in the longer perspective beyond intervention, it is important to link security regionalism and development regionalism. Ultimately, these two dimensions are complementary and mutually supportive. This is implied in the concept of security communities, which Karl W. Deutsch famously defined as 'the attainment of institutions and practices strong enough and widespread enough to assure, for a long time, dependable expectations of peaceful change among its population'.[54]

Actors

Much of current mainstream regionalism theory continues to be dominated by state-centric perspectives. In summing up the body of research on regionalism produced by the United Nations University/World Institute for Development Economics Research (UNU/WIDER), the editors admitted that 'our project, in spite of good intentions to the contrary, has been too state-centric and too focused on formal organisations rather than pinpointing the processes of more informal regionalisation that take place on the ground'.[55] This is by no means equivalent to rejecting the state. States and intergovernmental organisations are often crucial actors and objects of analysis in the process of regionalisation. The state, as well as the forces of state making and state destruction, are all at the core of understanding today's political economy of regionalism. However, there is a need to understand how this so-called national/state interest is formed in the first place. Neither states nor regions can be taken for granted. The 'national interest' is often simply a group-specific interest or even the personal interest of certain political leaders, rather than the public good or national security and development understood in a more comprehensive sense. The UNU/WIDER project suggested that, in the context of globalisation, the state was being 'unbundled', with the result that actors other than the state were gaining strength. By implication, the focus of analysis should not only be on state actors and formal interstate frameworks, but also on non-state actors and what is sometimes referred to broadly as non-state regionalism.[56] A prominent non-state-centric contribution is Etel Solingen's coalitional approach, in which regional orders are deemed to be shaped by domestic coalitions.[57] In this approach the region is defined by the 'grand strategies' of relevant coalitions. Other authors treat the region itself as an actor.[58] Accordingly, I have distinguished below between actors in the regional arena, and regions as actors in their own right.

Actors in the regional arena

In his book on the political economy of regionalism in Southern Africa, Fredrik Söderbaum 'unpacks' the state and addresses the question for whom and for what purpose regionalisation is being pursued.[59] He shows how ruling political leaders engage in a rather intense diplomatic game, whereby they praise regionalism and sign treaties, such as free trade agreements and water protocols. In so doing, they can be perceived as promoters of the goals and values of regionalism, which enables them to raise the profile and status of their authoritarian regimes. Often, the 'state' is not much more than a (neopatrimonial) interest group. Furthermore, although the rhetoric and ritual of regional diplomacy serves the goal of the reproduction and legitimisation of the state, it can also be a means to create a facade that enables certain regime actors to engage in other more informal modes of regionalism, such as trans-state regionalism or networks of plunder.[60] This has also been referred to as 'shadow regionalism'.

Business interests are often supposed to be globalist in their orientation. However, this seems to be a myth. Globalisation strategies tend actually to end up creating more regionalised patterns of economic activity.[61] According to Robert Wade, one should talk about the regionalisation rather than the globalisation of business.[62] For example, the larger European business interests were very much behind the EU's 1992 project, led by Jacques Delors.[63] For their part, civil societies are still generally neglected in the description and explanation of new regionalism. This is an important gap. Similarly, even if the external environment and globalisation are often readily called into account, extra-regional actors themselves are also generally weakly described and conceptualised within the study of regionalism. This is somewhat surprising, given the considerable attention which 'external' actors – such as foreign powers, donors, international financial institutions, non-governmental organisations, transnational corporations and so on – receive in the study of national and local transformation processes, especially in the South. In the final analysis, it is not really a question of state-led regionalism versus non-state-led regionalism. On the contrary, 'state, market, civil society and external actors often come together in a variety of mixed-actor collectivities, networks and modes of regional governance'.[64]

The region as actor

As indicated, the region is not only an arena, but can also be seen as an actor, simply through the regional organisation that represents it.[65] It can be conceptualised in effect as a system of intentional acts, which would include numerous actors operating in some way in concert. From this perspective, the difference from a state is one of degree.[66] Furthermore, the capacity of a regional organisation to act changes over time. There is a link between the organisational capacity and the cohesiveness of the region as such. When different processes of regionalisation in various fields and at various levels of society intensify and converge within the same geographical area, the distinctiveness of the emerging region increases. This process of regionalisation was described earlier in relation to the notion of increasing regionness, which implies that a geographical area is transformed from a passive object (an arena) to an active subject (an actor) that is increasingly capable of articulating the transnational interests of the emerging region.[67]

Actorness, usually referring to external behaviour, implies a larger scope of action and room for manoeuvre, in some cases even a legal personality. The concept of actorness (with respect to the EU's external policies) was developed by Charlotte Bretherton and John Vogler.[68] Capacity to act is of course relevant internally as well, for instance in the cases of security, development and environmental regionalism – three areas where increased regional cooperation may make a difference within the region itself.

Actorness is a phenomenon closely related to regionness, the latter implying an endogenous process of increasing cohesiveness, the former a growing capacity to act that follows from the strengthened 'presence' of the regional unit in different contexts, as well as the actions that follow from the interaction between the actor and its external environment. Actorness with reference to the outside world is thus not only a simple function of regionness, but also an outcome of a dialectical process between endogenous and exogenous forces. The unique feature of regional (as compared to national great power) actorness is that this has to be created by voluntary processes and therefore depends more on dialogue and consensus building than coercion. This way of operating is the model that Europe holds out as a preferred world order, since this is the way the 'new Europe' (organised by the EU) has developed in its recent peaceful evolution.

Actorness defines the capability to influence the external environment. Regionness defines the position of a particular region in terms of its cohesion. The political ambition of establishing regional cohesion, a sense of community and identity has been of primary importance in the ideology of the regionalist project. A convergence of values may take place even if this is not the explicit purpose of the project. The approach of 'seeing region as process' implies an evolution of deepening regionalism, not necessarily following the idealised stagist model presented here, for that mainly serves a heuristic purpose. Since regionalism is always a political project, created by human actors, it may, assuming that it gets off the ground in the first place, not only move in different directions, but also, just like a nation-state project, fail. In this perspective, decline would mean decreasing regionness. Enlargement, or 'widening', also implies decreasing regionness. Generally in the history of the EU, this trend has been countered by reforms aimed at 'deepening'. Widening and deepening can thus be seen as a dialectic of loss and gain with regard to actorness. To the extent that an enlarged region can retain the same level of actorness, its presence will increase because of sheer size. The original European Economic Community contained 185 million people, compared to today's EU with 450 million. European integration has in fact become the unification and even extension of Europe. But, in terms of actorness, this has not, judging from the current crisis, increased actor capacity.

Levels

In spite of the enormous literature to date, there is little consensus on the appropriate terminology of regionalism when it appears on different levels or scales, constituting a multitude of forms in complex interrelationship to each other. Macroregions or world-regions are supranational. Subregions are more or less distinct parts of large macroregions, such as the new Europe, and often represent more dense supranational cooperation. If by region we mean instrumental regions with some actor capacity, we can also make a distinction between intra-continental and inter-continental transregionalism. Intra-continental regional organisations, such as the African Union (AU) and the Organization of American States (OAS), are usually weak paper organisations without much actor capacity, and therefore also lack inter-continental relations of any importance. Regional organisations of a more substantive kind below the continental level, which then develop relations between continents, have more actor capacity, and their mutual relations therefore gain a certain significance for the organisation of world order. In what follows I will focus on 'lower' and 'higher' levels of regionalism as being thus far undertheorised in the literature. As 'higher' levels (interregionalism and multiregionalism) link up to the discussion on world order in the next part of the chapter, I will start with the former.

Lower level regionalisms

As indicated, in the terminology employed here subregions are smaller parts of macroregions. Glenn Hook and Ian Kearns defined subregionalism as a regionalist project promoted by weaker states in contradistinction to the 'Triad' or the 'Core'.[69] This corresponds to what I referred to earlier as inter-mediate and peripheral regions. In my understanding, regions can be weak or strong, but, as long as they display internally some degree of regionness, cohesion and actorness, they are to be seen as distinct regional formations. The Economic Community of West African States (ECOWAS) is in this view a region, but it is doubtful whether APEC is a region. Rather, it is a transregional organisation.

Microregions exist between the 'national' and the 'local' level, because they consist of 'subnational' territories rather than whole countries.[70] Historically, microregions have been seen as subnational regions within the territorial boundaries of particular nation-states (or before that empires). Microregions may or may not fall within the borders of a particular nation-state. Increasingly, they are constituted by a network of transactions and collaboration across national boundaries, which may very well emerge as an alternative or in opposition to the challenged state, and sometimes also in competition with states-led regionalism.[71] However, as illustrated by the various concepts of growth polygons, growth triangles, development corridors and spatial development initiatives, microregionalism is often created by networks of state and non-state actors, and even interpersonal transnational networks (ethnic or family networks, religious ties and so on).[72] Thus conventional distinctions between international and domestic, as well as between states and non-state actors, are being diluted. The so-called growth triangles are particularly interesting from the perspective of the micro-macro relationship, not the least since there exist a series of interpretations of the nature of these linkages. Joakim Öjendal points out that the growth triangle strategy has been described in a multitude of ways in the literature – for instance, as a response to global political transformation, as a complement to macroregional economic integration, as paving the way for macroregionalism, and as a means to achieve regional integration while avoiding the creation of a time-consuming macroregional political bureaucracy.[73] Growth triangles are certainly one of the most important forms of microregionalism in Southeast Asia, being frequently considered as driving forces behind economic growth. They utilise the different endowments of the various countries, exploiting cooperative trade for production and development opportunities. The initiatives are generally constructed around partnerships between the private sector and the state, which explains why they have been referred to as a form of 'trans-state development'.[74] In such partnerships the private sector provides capital for investment, whereas the public sector provides infrastructure, fiscal incentives and the administrative framework to attract industry and investment.

Still, it is evident that micro-level forms of regionalism may sometimes be less formal and inter-state than formal macroregions; they may ultimately be more reflective of private sector interests than those of either states or civil societies. However, at the same time there is increasing evidence also that macroregions and subregions are themselves increasingly influenced by non-state actors. So, if regions are made up by actors other than states alone, and if state boundaries are becoming more fluid, then it also becomes more difficult to uphold old distinctions between microregionalism and macroregionalism.

Higher level regionalisms

Regionalisation has structural consequences beyond and 'above' the particular region. Transregionalism refers to actors and structures mediating between regions. To the extent that this takes place in a formal way between the regions as legal personalities one can use the word interregionalism. If the pattern of interregional relations becomes more predominant, constituting a new regionalised form of multilateral world order, we speak of multiregionalism. This is of course a very distant and highly uncertain prospect (to the extent indeed that it is seen as a prospect at all). Like new regionalisms operating on the regional level, all transregional arrangements are voluntary and cooperative, but can become more or less institutionalised and formalised, thus forming the structure of a multiregional world order.

Interregionalism is the latest step in the theorising of regionalism. The phenomenon is very much a consequence of the EU policy of creating and relating to regions as preferred counterparts in the international system. From this perspective, interregionalism simply constitutes a part of the foreign policy of the EU, being the hub of a global pattern of interregional relations. On the other hand, if regionalism is a global phenomenon, and there are different regionalisms in different parts of the world, it is reasonable to expect that many of these emerging regions, to the extent that they develop actorship (with varying degrees of actorness), will establish some kind of links with each other. Thus interregionalism can also be explained in relation to the global system.

This point is reinforced by the fact that other regions (ASEAN, Mercosur, SADC) also now establish interregional relations. Of course, these regions, albeit harbouring potential structural changes in world governance, are still embryonic; it is possible therefore to read different trends of theoretical significance into them. In other words, the problem lies in the ontological status of what we call interregionalism. The problem, again, is that there is a lack of consensus regarding that phenomenon as well.

The existing definitions to date are *ad hoc* and rather provisional, rather than based on a systematic overview of the phenomenon to be conceptualised and theorised. To my mind, it is important that the concept of interregionalism is reserved for formal relations between regions as juridical or at least quasi-juridical entities, since this is a new political phenomenon, possibly signifying a new post-Westphalian era. It does not imply 'post-sovereignty' since the regions get their actorness from the pooling of national sovereignties. Maybe one should talk instead about the emergence of a putative neo-Westphalian phenomenon?

Interregionalism can also be seen as one of the more regulated forms that globalisation may be taking. As compared to market-led globalisation in a Westphalian world of nation-states, it is more rooted in territory; and, in contrast to traditional multilateralism, it is a more exclusive relationship, since access to regional formations is limited by the principle of geographical proximity. Nevertheless, interregionalism, not to speak of multiregionalism, is a long-term, non-linear and uncertain trend which certainly will include setbacks, the final outcome of which we cannot yet expect to know.

In sum, looking at the existing patchwork of transregional and interregional agreements there is, in terms of structural outcome, presently no clear picture on the horizon. Transregional arrangements are voluntary and cooperative. They are also very diverse and difficult to categorise. Few are interregional in the proper sense of the word; some relations are trans-regional, some bilateral (for example, hybrid relations between a regional organisation and a great power). The fact that the EU constitutes the hub of these arrangements is in full accordance with its regionalist ideology, which, as is well known, encompasses not only trade and foreign investment but also political dialogue and cultural relations between regions. We shall come back to this in the third part below.

Regionalism and world order

To go beyond the new regionalism, which was the expressed purpose of this overview, implies to my mind looking at the context in which regionalisation occurs, as well as the interrelationships between regions and the larger context, not least other regions. It is significant that the pioneering works in exploring the new regionalism referred even in their titles to 'world order' (Gamble and Payne) or 'international order' (Fawcett and Hurrell).[75] In the third and final part of this chapter I will therefore discuss ways in which regionalism may affect the future world order, defined in terms of governance, structure and legitimisation. I will investigate alternative models derived from this somewhat formalistic definition of world order. The recent coercive trend towards Pax Americana, where regionalism only serves a unilateral purpose, is contrasted with what I regard as the more deliberative European model, according to which institutionalised regionalism, inter-regionalism and ultimately multiregionalism, to different degrees, will gradually shape a post-Westphalian world order. In view of decreasing actorness in the wake of the current constitutional crisis in the EU, I will also raise the question of whether interregional relations will be promoted by other regions as well.

Conceptualising world order

The concept of world order is rarely defined. In recent books the concept often occurs in the text (sometimes even in the title), but is absent in the index, which means that it is given a common sense meaning seemingly in no need of being defined, or used as an attractive slogan, but apparently not really meant to be thought of as an analytical concept. Hedley Bull focused on international order, which meant the system of states, and saw world order as both a more general and a more normative concept, but he left it at that.[76] According to Robert Cox, who is one of the few to have used the concept in a conscious way for analytical purposes, it is genuinely transhistorical (there is always a world order of some sort, but not necessarily an orderly one). However, this order is seen as an outcome of underlying factors – social forces and political units – which then gain more analytical importance for understanding world order.[77] The concept is, furthermore, commonly used normatively in a more political sense, which is to say it describes not primarily the actually existing order (or historical orders) but models and/or utopian projects. It has even been used as a political slogan.[78]

In order to be able to compare alternative models, I propose a non-normative and mainly political definition of world order as constituted by three dimensions: structure, mode of governance and form of legitimisation. Structure is the way the units of the system are related, that is, different forms of polarity determined by the distribution of power and resources; mode of governance refers to avenues of influence on decision making and policy making; legitimisation is the basis on which the system is made acceptable to the constituent units. On the structural dimension, I make a further distinction between the unipolar, the bipolar and the multipolar. Polarity can define relations between regions as well as great powers and these relations are not necessarily hostile (as postulated in realist theory). In the area of governance, the distinction I draw is between the unilateral, the plurilateral and the multilateral. The difference between plurilateral and multilateral is especially important. A plurilateral grouping of actors is exclusive, whereas multilateral by definition implies inclusion, provided the rules of the game are accepted by all parties. Multilateralism is therefore often seen as preferable, but, for many purposes, regionalism, as a form of plurilateralism defined by geographical proximity, is just as useful. By contrast, unilateralism undermines collective arrangements and may even be a path towards imperialism. By relying on unilateral decision making, which means prioritising the national interest over collective security, structural anarchy is promoted for as long as no single power is able to impose its will on the whole of international society. In that eventuality the structural result, to the extent that such a policy ultimately succeeds, will be unipolarity (or imperialism). Needless to say, a well functioning multilateral world order requires a certain degree of institutionalisation that counters unilateral action, limited bilateral solutions, or ill-considered political or military reactions which aggravate sensitive security situations. Finally, in terms of legitimisation, I discern a declining scale from the universally accepted rule of international law, through hegemony exercised by one great power (which means 'acceptable dominance'), to pure dominance, legitimised only by the national interest of the dominant power and relying on coercion and pre-emption. The dividing line between hegemony and dominance is not a very sharp one, but trends in one direction or the other can easily be established within the general diplomatic/political international debate. For example, the preparedness to accept dominance increases after crises such as 9/11.

With the help of this framework a comparative analysis can be made between alternative models, as well as of changes in and of world orders over time. The concepts of international order and world order are often used as pseudonyms. Here international order connotes a more state-centric conception, whereas world order connotes a more complex multidimensional and post-sovereign order. An international system can furthermore be less than globally encompassing, for instance Europe as a regional international system in the 19th century. World order of course implies a system including all of the world and all human beings. The degree of order within a region or in the international system can vary; thus different security theories speak of regional security complexes, anarchies, anarchic societies, regional security communities and so on. The security agenda is broadened, which makes regional approaches to security more relevant.

Identifying world orders

Theoretically, there are various options of world order. After the First World War, Europe believed in the power of collective security through the League of Nations. After its collapse, the United Nations (UN) constituted mankind's new hope for a stable and just world order based on multilateralism and international law (and the fiction of an international community of equal states). As we saw, the early theorising on regional integration was, above all, concerned with international order. Later, in the 1970s, there was discussion of a New International Economic Order and thus the issue of order *and* justice was raised on a global plane. More recently, after the first Gulf war in 1991, President George H. W. Bush coined the concept 'a new world order', based on multilateralism and international law and upheld via US hegemony. Significantly, George Bush Senior did not seek to change the regime in Baghdad after this war. This gives an indication of his enduring respect for the multilateral world order, since then demolished by the neoconservative movement and its influence on the present US administration. In short, the old multilateral world order, based on US hegemony, is being transformed. The question is: in what direction?

The liberal view of globalisation (globalism), which still enjoys a hegemonic position, stresses the homogenising impact of market forces on the creation of an open society. Liberals take a minimalist view on political authority and are sceptical of regionalism. To interventionist thinkers on the left, who want to politicise the global, this liberal project is not realistic; these critics tend to see the unregulated market system as analogous to political anarchy and demand political control of the market. The return of the 'political' may appear in various forms of governance. One possible form, assuming a continuous role for state authority, is a reformed 'neo-Westphalian order' (another 'rescue of the nation-state'), governed either by a reconstituted UN system that can be called 'assertive multilateralism', or by a more loosely organised 'concert' of dominant powers, assuming the exclusive privilege of governance (including intervention) by reference to a shared value system grounded in stability and order rather than justice. This we can call 'militant plurilateralism'. The first is preferable in terms of legitimacy, but, judging from several unsuccessful attempts at reform, hard to achieve; the second is more realistic but dangerously similar to old balance-of-power politics (the Concert of Europe of the 19th century). The multilateral model in a more 'assertive' form would be based on radical reforms designed to upgrade the UN into a world order model. Instead, the UN has lately entered its worst crisis ever, after the unilateral attack on Iraq in 2003 and the corruption scandal relating to the Iraq 'Oil for Food Programme' in 2005.

A more appropriate form for the return of 'the political' in today's globalised world would be a post-Westphalian order, where the locus of power moves up the ladder to the transnational level by means of the voluntary pooling of state sovereignties. The state can be replaced or complemented by a regionalised order, or by a strengthened global civil society supported by a new 'normative architecture' of world order values.[79] 'Global cosmopolitanism' thus emphasises the role of community at the global level, as well as the formation of global norms. The most likely candidate for such a role, although it does not appear to be imminent, is the interregional network pursued by the EU, facilitating multiregional governance as the major alternative to unilateralism. There is also the possibility of moving down the ladder, which implies a decentralised, 'neomediaeval' world, whether constituted by self-reliant communities ('stable chaos') suggested by 'green' political theory[80] or something more Hobbesian ('durable disorder'), which at present seems more likely.[81] Transnational forms of government on the regional and global level are meant to prevent such a 'decline of world order' and 'pathological anarchy'.[82]

After 11 September 2001 there existed initially, to a greater degree even than in connection with the first Gulf war, the possibility of forging an institutionalised multilateralism, an international regime based on the premises of an extended scope for international law and extensive participation by states and other transnational actors. Of course, there was never such a thing as fully-fledged multilateralism. By 'false multilateralism' is meant political and military actions that take place in the guise of multilateralism, but which in reality are expressions of more limited interests: plurilateralism, if it is a matter of a group of major powers; regionalism, if it is a geographically united bloc; or unilateralism, if a superpower or regional major power is, to all intents and purposes, acting alone. Unilateralism globally obviously encourages unilateralism at the regional level. A certain kind of regionalism (interregionalism) may, however, be supportive of multilateral principles (regional multilateralism, or multiregionalism). But this is a long-term perspective and will depend on the strength of the political project of taking regionalism as the crucial element in reorganising world order. At present, this project is represented principally by the EU.

A European world order: Pax Europaea?

What impact will or could Europe – or rather the EU – have on the future world order? The alternative world orders discussed above will of course not appear in their pure 'ideal' form, but rather in various hybrid forms of combination within which the influence of regionalism differs. From a moderately conservative perspective, one form of world order could be the notion of a 'neo-Westphalian order', governed either by a reconstituted UN system, in which preferably the major regions or, perhaps more likely, the major powers of the world have a strong influence; another alternative would be a more loosely organised global 'concert' of great powers and the marginalisation of the UN. The relevant powers in both models will be the regional powers of the world. In the former case, the UN will make use of the old idea of complementary 'regional arrangements'.[83] In the latter case, regionalism will suffer from imposed or hegemonic regionalism, and the regions as such will be far from the ideal of security communities. It will thus be a multipolar and plurilateral world, but the concert model will be lacking in legitimacy.

Regionalism would, however, put its mark on a future post-Westphalian governance pattern. In such a world order, the locus of power would move irreversibly to the transnational level. The states system would be replaced or complemented by a regionalised world order and a strengthened global civil society, supported by a 'normative architecture' of world order values, such as multiculturalism and multilateralism. The EU's recent emphasis on inter-regionalism may in the longer run prove to be important in the reconstruction of a multilateral world order in a regionalised form, here called multiregional-ism, meaning a horizontalised, institutionalised structure formed by organised regions, linked to each other through multidimensional partnership agree-ments. The EU's ambition is to formalise these as relations between regional bodies rather than as bilateral contacts between countries; but, for the moment for pragmatic reasons, the forms of agreement show a bewildering variety. The EU's relations with the various geographical areas are furthermore influ-enced by the 'pillared approach' in its own internal decision making, creating artificial divisions between, for instance, foreign and development policy.[84] The development of the pattern has also been influenced over time by shifting bilateral concerns among additional members: for example, the United Kingdom and South Asia, Iberia and Latin America.

Even so, a multipolar system in which the EU constitutes the hub and driving actor does already exist in an embryonic form. The core of the global interregional complex contains triangular relations within the Triad. East Asia is dominated by the two great powers, China and Japan, with which both the US and the EU have bilateral relations as well. Transregional links within the Triad are constituted by APEC and by the Asia-Europe Meeting (ASEM), as well as various transatlantic agreements linking the US and Europe. The partnership between the EU and ASEAN is a prominent example of a formal interregional relationship, but the relevant region here (albeit still very informal) is, as argued earlier, the APT, which is becoming increasingly important not only in the context of ASEM relations but also for internal purposes. Indeed, the APT may soon become an East Asian Community.[85] Relations between the EU and Mercosur and between the EU and the group-ing of African, Caribbean and Pacific countries further extend the global web that has the EU at its centre.

There is thus a clear pattern in the EU's external policy, namely, to shape the world order in accordance with Europe's (more recent) experience of solving conflicts through respect for 'the other', dialogue, multilateralism based on international law, and institutionalised relations. This can be called 'soft imperialism', based on 'soft power', since, despite fine diplomacy, it is often felt as an imposition in other parts of the world. The policy varies along widening circles from integration (making certain neighbours EU members), to stabilisation (by entering privileged partnerships with the 'near abroad'), to partnership agreements with other regions and important great or middle powers.

Imperialism as world order: Pax Americana?

Yet regionalism, implying the institutionalised multipolar world order structure preferred by the EU, is unacceptable to the United States, which, furthermore, has made it very clear that multilateralism, although desirable, also has its limitations as set by US security interests. This is wholly in line with traditional realist security doctrine and therefore not new. Yet the current policy of the US goes beyond classical realism (*à la* Kissinger or Brzezinski) towards reinforcing what the neoconservative think tank, the Project for the New American Century, describes as 'a policy of military strength and moral clarity'. This formulation captures the essence of neoconservatism: military strength and an obligation to use it in a moral mission to change the world in accordance with American values, first amongst which is liberty. The opportunity, 'the unipolar moment', came after the end of the Cold War, which means that this thinking is thus older than 9/11.[86] To my mind, it is wrong to call the present world order 'unipolar', since the remaining superpower has to fill the power vacuum created by the collapse of the other. As shown in Iraq, there is no automaticity involved.

To dub this ideological structure 'neoconservatism' is hardly an appropriate description of what seems rather to be a militant revolutionary doctrine, rejecting the multilateral world order model and the role of the UN as the protector of this order. Neoconservatism, or 'militant libertarianism', and isolationism, however different these typically American doctrines may seem, are both sceptical about subsuming national interests to international cooperation and collective security and constitute different expressions of the specificity (the 'exceptionalism') of the US as the home of a 'chosen people'.

The current US policy (but to a lesser extent also that of the administration of Bill Clinton) is increasingly discussed in terms of 'imperialism', a concept that is used academically, pejoratively and positively by different people.[87] A minimum academic definition of imperialism should surely contain a unilateralist, exploitative, coercive and systematic (the sustainability problem) relationship with the external world, seen as an object for political and military action by a great power (designed by its political class). Yet most analysts in the new literature on imperialism question the dimension of sustainability and point to the problem of exhaustion or overstretch.[88]

Before 9/11 the unipolar moment was just one ideological current within the US. From the US point of view, the question of multilateralism revolved around a realistic balancing between legality and effectiveness, and priority was always given to the latter. Unilateralism maintained the upper hand. This has also marked the US approach to regionalism, which always has been subordinated to the national interest. This is clear, for instance in the cases of NAFTA and APEC and the latter's support for regional cooperation in Southeast Asia. All can be explained by specific, perceived national interests: NAFTA was a globalist policy, APEC an instrument for hegemonic control in the Asia–Pacific region, and support for regional cooperation in Southeast Asia a part of the anti-terrorist struggle.

Conclusion

The first part of this chapter discussed the transition from old to new regionalism, and the continuities and discontinuities involved. Since the new regionalism now has two decades behind it, this may be the time to bury this distinction and recognise the study of regionalism as a search for a moving target, even if this leaves us with a complicated ontological problem. We are not quite sure about or agreed upon the object of study. The very concept of region remains extremely vague and evasive, and makes sense only when associated with the Westphalian logic of bounded, politically controlled territories and the question of what happens to this logic in the context of globalisation and regionalisation. The early theorists looked for post-Westphalian trends, but the global dynamics were then stifled by the bipolar structure.

One discontinuity that emerges in retrospect is thus the stronger normative and prescriptive nature of the early debate, whether the point of departure was federalism, functionalism or neofunctionalism. The idea was to achieve peace by moving beyond the Westphalian logic to find institutionalised forms of permanent international cooperation. The more recent debate is generated much more by the erosion of national borders and the urgent question of how to find an alternative order beyond Westphalia. Neofunctionalism, the only one of the three early approaches with theoretical ambitions, was dismissed before regionalism (or regional integration which was the preferred concept) had shown its real face. There was a lively debate without much happening on the ground, or perhaps it is more correct to say that whatever happened in the field of regional integration was distorted and finally stifled by the Cold War and the bipolar world order. Based on this poor showing in the real, empirical world, the critics, mostly realists, had a fairly easy task in questioning the viability of and the case for regional integration. The new wave of interest in regionalism should thus be seen in the context of the ending of the Cold War and the beginning of globalisation. The challenge now, in other words, is to theorise a fast emerging empirical phenomenon without much theory to work from.

The way the European case relates to the general phenomenon of regionalism is an important field of research. Unfortunately, I myself once called Europe 'the paradigm' for which, although I did not mean a model to apply, I have been criticised. A contrary view was expressed by Shaun Breslin and Richard Higgott, who argued that, 'ironically, the EU as an exercise in regional integration is one of the major obstacles to the development of analytical and theoretical comparative studies of regional integration'.[89] Andrew Axline has also complained about the Eurocentric view of regionalisation and the lack of comparative examples.[90] Today, this is no longer the case, but there is still the need for a conceptual and theoretical framework that can address the complexity of the field. Andrew Hurrell insists that, rather than try to understand other regions through the distorting mirror of Europe, it is better to think in general theoretical terms and in ways that draw both on traditional IR theory and on other areas of social thought.[91]

Identity is constructed, but also inherent in history. Many regions coincide with distinct civilisations. The concept of civilisation is, however, controversial. By civilisation (in its plural meaning) one can quite simply mean the supreme level of aggregation for a complex but nonetheless uniform cultural identity. In Europe it was possible to combine this macrocultural complex with a decentralised political order, but elsewhere it was normally an integrated part of empire building. It lost importance during the nation-state era when the nation became the most important carrier of identity. It is interesting that even writers within the Marxist tradition find it difficult to renounce the concept.[92]

Continental regions can certainly coincide with civilisations; they are often understood in a simple geographic sense. However, there are continental organisations such as the AU and the OAS which may move from paper existence to 'real' regions to the extent that this level becomes functional and operational. It is nevertheless misleading to see more operational regions on a particular continent, for instance Africa, as 'subregions'. Thus ECOWAS and SADC are regions, not subregions, but depending on the strength of the AU they may become subregions in the future.

In the second part of the chapter an attempt was made to show the complexity of more recent regionalisation initiatives and processes in terms of dimensions, actors and levels of action. Regionalism was first interpreted mainly as a trading arrangement, but it soon became clear that this new trend went beyond trade and into monetary policy, development strategy, security and environmental protection, to mention just the most important fields of cooperation or provision of regional public goods. The region thereby became an arena for many actors apart from governments, and, through the increasing cohesion of the region (regionness) as well as through its increasing capacity to act (actorness), the region itself is becoming an important actor, ultimately with the potential of shaping world order. In particular, the phenomenon of interregionalism has to be further theorised. We need to know if it is a general trend in world society or only a projection of the EU view of the world.

Even in the absence of a thoroughly regionalised world (multiregionalism), the process of regionalisation is, in one way or the other, bound to have an impact on the future world order. The current ideology of globalism argues in favour of a particular form of globalisation, namely, neoliberal economic globalisation. Yet it is a simplification to identify globalisation with neoliberalism. Other political contents should in principle be possible and indeed there is emerging a struggle about the shape of the political content of globalisation. Regionalism can unquestionably influence the nature of globalisation. Stronger regions would, for example, shape the form and content of the global order in different ways, depending on political trends in the respective regions, trends that may shift direction, thus altering the preconditions for constructing world order. As discussed in the third section, the future of regionalism, interregionalism and ultimately multiregionalism depends very much on the outcome of the struggle between the two contrasting world order models, represented by the EU and the US. There is a role for regionalism in both, but of very different kinds: neo-Westphalian in the US model, post-Westphalian in the EU case. Because of these differences we can assume that the European vision of world order is different from that of the US and that a European world order would be different. Europe has in effect been given a second chance to influence world order.

The EU also applies its own experiences in conflict resolution and development on neighbourhood relations, as well as on the world as a whole. And so of course does the US. Two different kinds of power, hard and civil, thus face each other. Coercion may be replaced by influence, imposition by dialogue. What has worked in Europe may ultimately prove to have wider relevance. Indeed, the European model may have relevance even if, judging from the debate on the new constitution, Europe no longer seems to believe in it. It is important to note that the differences do not express varieties of national mentality – Europe versus America – but constitute contrasting world order principles held by political groupings in both areas. It is therefore reasonable to expect coexistence, whether uneasy or not, and the emergence of hybrids formed somewhere between these competing world order models. Even so, changes in the US are much the more important. Notwithstanding the election of the second George W. Bush administration, there exists in the US now a call for a return to multilateralism: the 'US and its main regional partners must begin to prepare for life after Pax Americana'.[93] Such a shift would bring Europe and the US closer, but it will not eliminate the difference between the models of multiregionalism and a global concert of regional powers; between a post-Westphalian and a neo-Westphalian world order.

Notes

Much of my recent work in this field has been carried out jointly with Fredrik Söderbaum, and his help in writing this chapter has also been invaluable. Tony Payne's generous support and enthusiasm was also of great importance, now as earlier.

1 Donald Puchala once compared this predicament with the blind man's unsuccessful attempts to define an elephant. See the discussion in Ben Rosamond, *Theories of European Integration* (Palgrave, 2000), p. 12.

2 For introductions to the earlier debate focusing on Europe, see R. J. Harrison, *Europe in Question* (Allen & Unwin, 1974); Rosamond, *Theories of European Integration*; and Dimitris N. Cryssochoou, *Theorizing European Integration* (Sage, 2001).

3 Previous overviews of the recent debate include Björn Hettne, Andras Inotai and Osvaldo Sunkel (eds), *Studies in the New Regionalism*, Vols I–V (Macmillan, 1999/2001); Mario Telò (ed.), *European Union and New Regionalism: Regional Actors and Global Governance in a Post-hegemonic Era* (Ashgate, 2001); and Fredrik Söderbaum and Timothy M. Shaw (eds), *Theories of New Regionalism: A Palgrave Reader* (Palgrave 2003). The most recent addition is Mary Farrell, Björn Hettne and Luk Van Langenhove, *Global Politics of Regionalism* (Polity, 2005), in which theories, key issues and case studies are presented.

4 See Joseph Nye, *Peace in Parts: Integration and Conflict in Regional Organization* (Little, Brown & Co., 1971 and 1987).

5 L. J. Cantori and S. L. Spiegel, *The International Politics of Regions: A Comparative Approach* (Prentice Hall, 1970).

6 Andrew Hurrell, 'Regionalism in theoretical perspective', in: Louise Fawcett and Andrew Hurrell (eds), *Regionalism in World Politics: Regional Organization and International Order* (Oxford University Press, 1995), p. 38.

7 *Ibid.*, pp. 38–9.

8 Walter Mattli, *The Logic of Regional Integration: Europe and Beyond* (Cambridge University Press, 1999).

9 Nye, *Peace in Parts*, pp. 26–7.

10 Ernst B. Haas, *The Uniting of Europe: Political, Social and Economic Forces* (Stanford University Press, 1958), p. 16.

11 W. Andrew Axline (ed.), 'Cross-regional comparisons and the theory of regional cooperation: lessons from Latin America, the Caribbean, South East Asia and the South Pacific', in: W. Andrew Axline (ed.), *The Political Economy of Regional Cooperation: Comparative Case Studies* (Pinter, 1994), p. 217.

12 Ernst B. Haas, 'The Study of Regional Integration: Reflections on the Joy and Anguish of Pretheorizing', *International Organization*, Vol. 24, No. 4 (1970), p. 610.

13 Anthony Payne and Andrew Gamble, 'Introduction: the political economy of regionalism and world order', in: Andrew Gamble and Anthony Payne (eds), *Regionalism and World Order* (Macmillan, 1996), p. 2.

14 *Ibid.*, p. 17.

15 The first mentioned definition is called 'deliberately straightforward' in Anthony Payne, 'Rethinking development inside international political economy', in: Anthony Payne (ed.), *The New Regional Politics of Development* (Palgrave, 2004), p. 16.

16 Helge Hveem, 'The regional project in global governance', in: Söderbaum and Shaw, *Theories of New Regionalism*, p. 83.

17 Hurrell, 'Regionalism in theoretical perspective', p. 39.

18 Sophie Boisseau du Rocher and Bertrand Fort, *Paths to Regionalisation: Comparing Experiences in East Asia and Europe* (Marshall Cavendish, 2005), p. xi.

19 Iver. B. Neumann, 'A region-building approach', in: Söderbaum and Shaw, *Theories of New Regionalism*, pp. 160–78.

20 Sometimes the economic nationalism in the interwar period is referred to as the first wave or generation. Luk Van Langenhove and Ana-Cristina Costea speak of three generations of regionalism, referring to: a first generation of economic integration, a second generation of internal political integration and a third emerging generation of external political integration. Speaking in terms of generations also allows the authors to avoid the dichotomy between 'old' and 'new' regionalism. They believe that a 'neo' new regionalism is shaping up, with greater ambitions in global governance in general and the United Nations institutions in particular. See Luk Van Langenhove and Ana-Cristina Costea, 'Third generation regional integration: the transmutation of multilateralism into multiregionalism?', unpublished manuscript, United Nations University/Comparative Regional Integration Studies (UNU/CRIS), 2005.

21 This section draws on Rosamond, *Theories of European Integration*.

22 David Mitrany, 'The Prospect of Integration: Federal or Functional', *Journal of Common Market Studies*, Vol. 4, No. 1 (1965), pp. 119–49; and David Mitrany, *A Working Peace System* (Quadrangle Books, 1943, 1966).

23 Rosamond, *Theories of European Integration*, p. 60.

24 Bela Balassa, *The Theory of Economic Integration* (Allen & Unwin, 1961).

25 Stanley Hoffman, 'Obstinate or Obsolete? The Fate of the Nation State and the Case of Western Europe', *Daedalus*, No. 95 (1966), pp. 865–85.

26 Alan S. Milward, *The European Rescue of the Nation State* (Routledge, 1992).

27 Robert O. Keohane and Joseph S. Nye (eds), *Transnational Relations and World Politics* (Harvard University Press, 1972); also *Power and Interdependence* (Little, Brown & Co., 1977).

28 Ernst B. Haas, 'International Integration: The European and the Universal Process', *International Organization*, Vol. 15, No. 4 (1961), pp. 366–92; and Ernst B. Haas and Phillipe Schmitter, 'Economics and Differential Patterns of Integration: Projections about Unity in Latin America', *International Organization*, Vol. 18, No. 4 (1964), pp. 259–99.

29 Axline, 'Cross-regional comparisons and the theory of regional cooperation', p. 180.

30 Björn Hettne and Andras Inotai, *The New Regionalism: Implications for Global Development and International Security* (UNU/WIDER, 1994); William D. Coleman and Geoffrey R. D. Underhill (eds), *Regionalism and Global Economic Integration: Europe, Asia and the Americas* (Routledge, 1998); Telò, *European Union and New Regionalism*; Sheila Page, *Regionalism in the Developing Countries* (Palgrave, 2000); Fawcett and Hurrell, *Regionalism in World Politics*; Gamble and Payne, *Regionalism and World Order*; Edward D. Mansfield and Helen V. Milner (eds), *The Political Economy of Regionalism* (Colombia University Press, 1997); and Michael Schulz, Fredrik Söderbaum and Joakim Öjendal (eds), *Regionalization in a Globalizing World: A Comparative Perspective on Actors, Forms and Processes* (Zed, 2001).

31 Karl Polanyi, *The Great Transformation: The Political and Economic Origins of Our Time* (Beacon Press, 1957). There are now three editions of this book: by Farrar and Rinehart in 1944 and by Beacon Press in 1957 and 2001. In the 1957 edition R. M. MacIver stressed the lessons for 'the coming international organization'. The 2001 edition has a foreword by Joseph E. Stiglitz, former chief economist of the World Bank, who makes the very apt remark that 'it often seems as if Polanyi is speaking directly to present-day issues'. Polanyi was also early in analysing regionalism and world order: see Karl Polanyi, 'Universal Capitalism or Regional Planning', *The London Quarterly of World Affairs*, January 1945.

32 Björn Hettne, 'Neo-Mercantilism: The Pursuit of Regionness', *Cooperation & Conflict*, Vol. 28, No. 3 (1993), pp. 211–32; and Björn Hettne and Fredrik Söderbaum, 'Theorising the Rise of Regionness', *New Political Economy*, Vol. 5, No. 3 (2000), pp. 457–74.

33 Europe's contemporary crisis can be compared to that of a 'failed state', based on too fragmented a demos or several demoi, which have no feeling of belonging to the same polity.

34 Others identify new regionalism with one of its aspects, that of 'open regionalism'. See the special issue of *Third World Quarterly*, Vol. 24, No. 2 (2003) on 'Governing the Asia Pacific – Beyond the New Regionalism'.

35 Kym Anderson and Richard Blackhurst (eds), *Regional Integration and the Global Trading System* (Harvester Wheatsheaf, 1993); Jaime de Melo and Arvind Panagariya (eds), *New Dimensions in Regional Integration* (Cambridge University Press, 1993); and Vincent Cable and David Henderson (eds), *Trade Blocs? The Future of Regional Integration* (Royal Institute of International Affairs, 1994).

36 Cable and Henderson, *Trade Blocs?*, p. 8.

37 Andrew Gamble and Anthony Payne, 'Conclusion: the new regionalism', in: Gamble and Payne, *Regionalism and World Order*, p. 251.

38 For surveys of theoretical approaches, see Söderbaum and Shaw, *Theories of New Regionalism*; and Finn Laursen, *Comparative Regional Integration: Theoretical Perspectives* (Ashgate, 2003). The former focuses on theoretical approaches, the latter makes a conscious selection of both theoretical approaches and empirical cases to illuminate them. Two more focused theoretical explorations are Mattli, *The Logic of Regional Integration*; and Stefan A. Schirm, *Globalization and the New Regionalism: Global Markets, Domestic Politics and Regional Cooperation* (Polity, 2002).

39 See the special issue of *Third World Quarterly*, Vol. 20, No. 5 (1999) on 'New Regionalisms in the New Millennium'.

40 The discussion on these issues draws on Björn Hettne and Fredrik Söderbaum, 'Regional cooperation: a tool for addressing regional and global challenges', in: Ministry of Foreign Affairs, *International Task Force on Global Public Goods*, Stockholm, 2004, available at http://www.gpgtaskforce.org/bazment.aspx

41 Percy S. Mistry, 'New regionalism and economic development', in: Söderbaum and Shaw, *Theories of New Regionalism*, pp. 117–39.

42 *Ibid.*, p. 136.

43 Diana Tussie, 'Regionalism: providing a substance to multilateralism?', in: Söderbaum and Shaw, *Theories of New Regionalism*, pp. 99–116.

44 Stephany Griffith-Jones, 'International financial stability and market efficiency as a global public good', in: Inge Kaul, Pedro Conceicao, Katell Le Goulven and Ronald Mendoza (eds), *Providing Global Public Goods: Managing Globalization* (Oxford University Press for United Nations Development Programme, 2003), pp. 435–54.

45 Richard Higgott, 'From Trade-Led to Monetary-Led Regionalism: Why Asia in the 21st Century will be Different to Europe in the 20th Century', UNU/CRIS e-Working Papers No. 1, Bruges, 2002.

46 Peter Robson, 'The New Regionalism and Developing Countries', *Journal of Common Market Studies*, Vol. 31, No. 3 (1993), pp. 329–48.

47 Nancy Birdsall and Robert Z. Lawrence, 'Deep integration and trade agreements: good for developing countries?', in: Inge Kaul, Isabelle Grunberg and Marc A. Stern (eds), *Global Public Goods: International Cooperation in the 21st Century* (Oxford University Press for United Nations Development Programme, 1999), pp. 128–51.

48 Relevant generalising contributions include: David A. Lake and Patrick Morgan, *Regional Orders: Building Security in a New World* (Pennsylvania State University

158   *Björn Hettne*

Press, 1997); Emanuel Adler and Michael Barnett (eds.), *Security Communities* (Cambridge University Press, 1998); and Barry Buzan and Ole Wæver, *Regions and Powers: The Structure of International Security* (Cambridge University Press, 2003).

49 Barry Buzan, *People, States and Fear: An Agenda for International Security Studies in the Post-Cold War Era* (Harvester Wheatsheaf, 1991), p. 190.

50 *Ibid.*, p. 192.

51 Barry Buzan, 'Regional security complex theory in the post-Cold War world', in: Söderbaum and Shaw, *Theories of New Regionalism*, pp. 140–59.

52 See Buzan and Wæver, *Regions and Powers*.

53 See Lake and Morgan, *Regional Orders*.

54 Karl Deutsch, *The Analysis of International Relations* (Prentice Hall, 1968), p. 194.

55 Björn Hettne, Andras Inotai and Osvaldo Sunkel (eds), *Comparing Regionalisms: Implications for Global Development* (Macmillan, 2001), p. xxxii.

56 A large number of labels have been used in the debate for capturing these two similar (but not always identical) phenomena, such as 'top-down' and 'bottom-up' regionalisation; *de jure* and *de facto* regionalisation; states-led regionalism and market and society-induced regionalisation; and formal/informal regionalism.

57 Etel Solingen, *Regional Orders at Century's Dawn: Global and Domestic Influences on Grand Strategy* (Princeton University Press, 1998).

58 See, for instance, Luk Van Langenhove, 'Theorising Regionhood', UNU/CRIS Working Papers No. 1, Bruges, 2003.

59 Fredrik Söderbaum, *The Political Economy of Regionalism: The Case of Southern Africa* (Palgrave, 2003).

60 Morten Bøås, Marianne H. Marchand and Timothy M. Shaw, 'The weave-world: the regional interweaving of economies, ideas and identities', in: Söderbaum and Shaw, *Theories of New Regionalism*, pp. 192–210.

61 Winfried Ruigrok and Rob van Tulder, *The Logic of International Restructuring* (Routledge, 1995).

62 Robert Wade, 'The disturbing rise in poverty and inequality', in: David Held and Mathias Koenig-Archibugi (eds), *Taming Globalization* (Polity, 2003), p. 34.

63 Roland Axtman, *Globalization and Europe* (Pinter, 1998), p 173.

64 Fredrik Söderbaum and Timothy M. Shaw, 'Conclusion: what futures for new regionalism?', in: Söderbaum and Shaw, *Theories of New Regionalism*, p. 222.

65 Theorising actorship has so far been focused on the EU. A pioneering study is that of Gunnar Sjöstedt, *The External Role of the European Community* (Saxon House, 1977).

66 Van Langenhove, 'Theorising Regionhood'.

67 Hettne, 'Neo-Mercantilism'.

68 Charlotte Bretherton and John Vogler, *The European Union as a Global Actor* (Routledge, 1999), p. 38.

69 Glenn Hook and Ian Kearns (eds), *Subregionalism and World Order* (Macmillan, 1999), p. 1.

70 Kenichi Ohmae, who observed the phenomenon at an early stage, referred to these formations as 'region states', which is somewhat misleading. He also saw them as emerging out of globalisation which is a simplification. See Kenichi Ohmae, 'The Rise of the Region-State', *Foreign Affairs*, Vol. 72, No. 1 (1993), pp. 78–87.

71 Bob Jessop, 'The political economy of scale and the construction of cross-border microregionalism', in: Söderbaum and Shaw, *Theories of New Regionalism*, pp. 179–98.

72 James H. Mittelman, *The Globalization Syndrome: Transformation and Resistance* (Princeton University Press, 2000); and Markus Perkmann and Ngai-Ling Sum

(eds), *Globalization, Regionalization and the Building of Cross-Border Regions* (Palgrave, 2002).

73 Joakim Öjendal, 'South East Asia at a constant crossroads: an ambiguous new region', in: Schultz *et al.*, *Regionalization in a Globalising World*, p. 160.

74 James Parsonage, 'South East Asia's "Growth Triangle": A Subregional Response to Global Transformation', *International Journal of Urban and Regional Studies*, Vol. 16, No. 3 (1997), pp. 307–17.

75 Gamble and Payne, *Regionalism and World Order* and the various follow-up studies from the project have even been referred to as 'the world order approach'. See, for instance, Fredrik Söderbaum, 'Introduction: theories of new regionalism', in: Söderbaum and Shaw, *Theories of New Regionalism*, p. 11.

76 Hedley Bull, *The Anarchical Society: A Study of Order in World Politics* (Macmillan, 1995), p. 21.

77 Robert Cox, with Timothy J. Sinclair, *Approaches to World Order* (Cambridge University Press, 1996).

78 President George H. W. Bush's 'new world order' is the obvious example. Cox comments that the concept should not become reduced to 'one specific and political manipulative use of the term': see Cox, *Approaches to World Order*, p. 169.

79 Richard Falk, 'The post-Westphalian enigma', in: Björn Hettne and Bertil Odén (eds), *Global Governance in the 21st Century: Alternative Perspectives on World Order* (Expert Group on Development Issues, Ministry of Foreign Affairs, Sweden, 2002), pp. 147–83; and Richard Falk, *The Great War on Global Terror* (Interlink, 2003).

80 R. R. Goodin, *Green Political Theory* (Polity, 1992).

81 Mark Duffield, 'Reprising durable disorder: network war and the securitization of aid', in: Hettne and Odén, *Global Governance in the 21st Century*, pp 74–105.

82 Richard Falk, 'Regionalism and world order: the changing global setting', in: Söderbaum and Shaw, *Theories of New Regionalism*, pp. 63–80.

83 Alan K. Henrikson, 'The growth of regional organizations and the role of the United Nations', in: Fawcett and Hurrell, *Regionalism in World Politics*, pp. 122–68.

84 Martin Holland, *The European Union and the Third World* (Palgrave, 2002), p. 7.

85 Julie Gilson, *Asia Meets Europe* (Edward Elgar, 2002).

86 The concept has been coined by the American publicist Charles Krauthammer, and stands for the US policy of taking advantage of its military superiority by shaping the world order in accordance with the US national interest (identified with a general interest). This is a project rather than an established fact. See Charles Krauthammer, 'The Unipolar Moment', *Foreign Affairs*, Vol. 70, No. 1 (1991–1992), pp. 23–33; and 'Unilateralism is the key to our success', *Guardian Weekly*, 22 December 2001.

87 Roger Burbach and Jim Tarbell, *Imperial Overstretch: George W. Bush and the Hubris of Empire* (Zed, 2004); Richard Falk, *The Declining World Order: America's Imperial Geopolities* (Routledge, 2004); James J. Hentz (ed.), *The Obligation of Empire: United States' Grand Strategy for a New Century* (University Press of Kentucky, 2004); and Chalmers Johnson, *The Sorrows of Empire: Militarism, Secrecy and the End of the Republic* (Metropolitan Books, 2004).

88 Paul Kennedy, *The Rise and Fall of Great Powers: Economic Change and Military Conflict from 1500 to 2000* (Random House, 1987). Eric Hobsbawm made the following observation regarding old and new imperialism, further underlining the problem of sustainability: 'The present world situation is quite unprecedented. The great global empires that we have seen before . . . bear little comparison with what we see today in the United States empire . . . A key novelty of the US imperial project is that all other great powers and empires knew that they were not

the only ones, and none aimed at global domination. None believed themselves invulnerable, even if they believed themselves to be central to the world – as China did, or the Roman Empire at its peak' (cited in Burbach and Tarbell, *Imperial Overstretch*, p. 179).

89 Shaun Breslin *et al.* (eds), *New Regionalisms in the Global Political Economy* (Routledge, 2002), p. 11.

90 W. Andrew Axline, 'Comparative case studies of regional cooperation among developing countries', in: Axline, *The Political Economy of Regional Cooperation*, p. 11.

91 Andrew Hurrell, 'The regional dimension in international relations theory' in: Farrell *et al.*, *Global Politics of Regionalism*, pp. 38–53.

92 Immanuel Wallerstein makes an interesting distinction between civilisation and the empirical historical system, the empire. 'A civilization refers to a contemporary claim about the past in terms of its use in the present to justify heritage, separateness, rights.' See Immanuel Wallerstein, *Geopolitics and Geoculture: Essays on the Changing World-system* (Cambridge University Press, 1991). Another materialist approach is to be found in Robert Cox, 'Civilisations in World Political Economy', *New Political Economy*, Vol. 1, No. 2 (1996), pp. 141–56. In the globalised condition, civilisations are de-territorialised and constitute 'communities of thought', global projects in conflict and dialogue. The interplay implies a 'supra-intersubjectivity' and, if it takes the form of dialogue rather than conflict, one can speak of a 'new multilateralism'. This concept is developed in Robert W. Cox, *The New Realism: Perspectives on Multilateralism and World Order* (Macmillan, 1997).

93 Charles A. Kupchan, 'After Pax Americana: benign power, regional integration and the sources of stable multipolarity', in: Birthe Hansen and Bertel Heurlin (eds), *The New World Order: Contrasting Theories* (Palgrave, 2000), pp. 134–66.

8 Politics in command

Development studies and the rediscovery of social science

Adrian Leftwich

Power, like wealth, has to exist before it can be distributed.[1]

Rule of thumb economics, which has long dominated thinking on growth policies, can safely be discarded.[2]

From the early 1980s, a good 15 years before *New Political Economy* first saw the light of day, the obituaries for development studies were already being written. Although some celebrated its demise and others mourned its passing, it is the central thrust of this chapter that announcements of its death have been premature. Moreover, if development studies are dead, then so too is social science.

I shall argue from the premise that the most influential and perceptive social scientists, from Adam Smith onwards, have always sought to explore, explain and, sometimes, seek directly to promote the processes by which human welfare has been, and can be, progressively enhanced. Crucially, they have not sought to do so in terms of a single disciplinary framework, but through analysing the complex relations between social, political and economic institutions, within and between societies. As the distinguished American anthropologist, Marvin Harris, observed many years ago: 'My excuse for venturing across disciplines, continents, and centuries is that the world extends across disciplines. Nothing in nature is quite so separate as two mounds of expertise.'[3] Just so: the same is true for 'development' – its analysis and promotion extends across disciplines.

At the core of these concerns has, naturally, been how 'the wealth of nations', understood essentially as economic growth and development, is best achieved. Accordingly, the economy – that is, the character, organisation and control of the system of material production and distribution – has normally been the central focus. Yet many of those working in mainstream economics itself, or in the sometimes narrowly conceived economics of development, drifted into their own and somewhat detached domains, evacuated from interdisciplinary and institutional contexts. To the extent that they did, they lost contact with these essentially society-wide interactions and relations, internal and external, that we now know to have been historically crucial in either promoting or restraining development in all societies, past and present and, especially, in the more recently postcolonial countries of the developing world.[4]

But the best and most challenging social science has always sought to explore the ways in which economic, political and social institutions have interacted over time,[5] and all the big debates in the analysis and promotion of development have, sooner or later, had to engage with the inescapable reality of these interactions. When, by the early 1980s, it had become clear that much of the planned development effort of the postwar years had failed, or faltered, to differing degrees in many (but by no means all) parts of the world, or at least that the initial optimism had been tempered, the most plausible explanations came neither from within development economics nor from the reviving neoclassical orthodoxies, but from the recognition that non-economic factors – primarily political, but also social and cultural – needed to be much more fully comprehended. The strange, if not tragic, aspect of the history of development studies is that, just as this was being recognised, in the early 1980s, that very recognition was eclipsed by the rise and hegemony – but not for long – of the neoclassical orthodoxy which claimed to dispense with both development economics and the wider analysis of growth in a social and political context. Yet, as I shall argue later, the subsequent very mixed record of neoliberal reform, the continuing scandal of global poverty and the deepening differentials within and between many countries of the North and the South[6] (not to mention the political and security angles of this) has led to a healthy recognition of the centrality of institutions and governance for developmental purposes, and the beginning of a realisation that politics is fundamental in shaping both.

Thus, although there were some very important contributions in the 1980s and early 1990s which stressed the salience of politics and the state in achieving successful policy reform and structural adjustment,[7] the general picture was one in which the political and social contexts and conditions of development were sidelined. So it is fascinating to see that the importance of this wider institutional and historical context (as urged in the first editorial of *New Political Economy* in 1996[8]) has again, in the first decade of the twenty-first century, come to be recognised as absolutely central. And not before time. It is also worth noting that this renewed institutional interest has come from scholars (often working within, with or parallel to, development agencies, such as the World Bank) who might be thought to have been least sympathetic to such a wider social scientific approach to the problems of development and most sympathetic to what Albert Hirschman referred to as a 'mono-economics' or 'the orthodox position'.[9] This mono-economics has been based on what Kenny and Williams have recently described, appropriately, as an epistemological and ontological universalism which holds that 'all economies are in some way the same, and hence that economies and economic processes are comparable', thus giving rise to the presumption of laws that operate across all economies in space and time, irrespective of the wider sociopolitical context.[10] Better still is the description of that approach as a kind of 'property rights reductionism – one that views the formal institutions of property rights protection as the end-all of development policy'.[11]

I shall argue, however, that not only does the study and explicit promotion of development remain as important as it has always been, but that it needs to be understood essentially and explicitly as a political process, embedded in, and mutually interacting with, a network of socioeconomic relationships.[12] Hence the title of the chapter. I shall therefore, first, revisit the key milestones in the study, theory and policy practices of 'development' in the postwar era; second, identify some of the key implications and outcomes of these theories and practices; third, suggest that the contemporary priorities of development all presage a rediscovery of social science as development studies; and, finally, re-emphasise that, although 'development' has a number of very different dimensions, it must always be understood as an inescapably *political* process in which the purposive interaction of people, power and resources, in diverse cultural and historical contexts, shapes the pattern and the outcomes at any given point.

Milestones

Context

The rise and alleged fall of 'development studies' has been well documented. Most of the major accounts concur that, as a field of academic concern, the study of 'development' was essentially a postwar phenomenon, though it had been one of the central concerns of the classical political economists.[13] In the field of economics, at least, it represented the emergence of what came to be a subdiscipline, which was in part a reaction to the 'one theory fits all'[14] approach that was typical of mainstream economics. As John Toye has pointed out, development economics was characterised by 'its exploration of the problem of government engineered economic transformation'.[15] Accordingly, influenced theoretically by Keynesian economics, practically by the experience of Marshall aid to Europe after the Second World War, and politically by the need to elaborate viable alternative and 'non-communist' programmes[16] (or 'manifestos' in W. W. Rostow's terms), development theory, policy and practice based itself on a number of (not entirely unrealistic) assumptions about the character of the economies in the newly independent ex-colonies. Whereas colonial economic policy had been concerned largely with how to 'develop' the natural rather than the human resources of the colonies, the postwar consensus focused on how and where governments could act to promote economic growth and, indeed, establish the conditions for economic growth which were held to be seriously lacking.[17]

It was this focus on concerted state action which marked development theory off from mainstream economic theory which, from the end of the

19th century, had broken with its roots in classical political economy and sought thereafter to deal with mainly advanced, or advancing, capitalist market economies.[18] In the latter, though most varied in respect of their state-economy relationships (compare postwar France, the United States and Japan[19]), one might generally find stable and longstanding states, or at least largely consolidated ones, which had arisen endogenously, at least in the European context, though not without often intense internal struggle and external conflict,[20] where functioning markets and established property rights were supported by a range of juridical and governmental institutions. These, in turn, were underpinned by a broad and expanding ideological, if not philosophical, consensus about freedom, individualism, individual (and especially property) rights and enterprise[21] – though often challenged, and in due course often qualified, by the requirement for corrective redistributive action and social welfare provision by the state in the form of more or less social democracy.

Although the levels and forms of socioeconomic development varied widely in the West – consider how Italy, Spain and much of Central-East Europe had 'lagged' behind in the first half of the twentieth century – the newly independent former colonies evinced few of the characteristics of the 'settled' or emerging capitalist societies, especially in Africa, the Middle East and Asia, and large swathes of rural Latin America even after long periods of Iberian colonial rule. Generally, in the developing world (though it differed from continent to continent and within them) markets in factors and commodities were either non-existent or more often small, local and highly limited with regard to what was produced and exchanged.[22] Moreover, all forms of capital were sparse or weakly developed and infrastructure (Rostow's social overhead capital) non-existent or deficient, perhaps with the exception of the situation at, or around, some of the many extractive cores.

Often, too, fragmented and plural political cultures reflecting various forms of regional or ethnic conflict, expressed commonly in the form of patronage, clientelism, *caudillismo, caciquismo*, sultanism (in its Weberian sense) or 'big man-ism', persisted behind the official bureaucratic structures and seeped through the interstices of externally imposed colonial and post-colonial state systems.[23] At worst, and often in the context of failed states, various types of 'shadow state' emerged, in which formally elected leaders linked up, more or less surreptitiously, with powerful private individuals and interests (local and foreign) to form an illicit and self-serving alternative, or 'shadow', structure of power, behind that of the formal state.[24] Individualism and the conception of both individual rights and entrepreneurship was weak in many places. Varying principles and forms of social structure organised people in the 'new states' into diverse categories of identity and unequal opportunity, in uneasy and often conflict-ridden patterns of 'differential incorporation'[25] from clans and kin to estates, castes and classes, as well as gender, ethnolinguistic, regional and religious groupings. Given these circumstances, the task of development theory was to propose policies and practices that could, in the words of one of the classic texts on the subject, 'bring about *rapid* (at least by historical standards) and *large-scale improvements* in levels of living for the masses of poverty-stricken, malnourished and illiterate peoples of Africa, Asia and Latin America'.[26]

Planning

Against this background, the focused and deliberate promotion of national development became a distinctive and pervasive feature of the twentieth century. Few elites, on the eve of independence, did not promise to bring a new dawn of progressive development for their people. Each elite, like Martin Luther King Jr., had a dream, or at least said it did. In the event, the dreams of most turned out to be very different to the reality. Although in the course of the 19th century development of Europe and North America, states had actively adopted a variety of measures to promote and protect national economies on a scale far more widespread than has conventionally been appreciated,[27] none (except, perhaps, Japan after 1870 and the Soviet Union after 1917) had formulated the kind of coherent and integrated programmes for national 'development', which were to be the hallmark of the twentieth century. Before the Second World War, the dominant form of more or less total planning was of course that of the Soviet Union, through *Gosplan and Gosbank* in particular. But, after the war, and outside the Soviet bloc, and especially in the wake of the depression years, the state's role in promoting and regulating economic growth became almost universally expressed in the form of planning, to the extent that 'almost every country in the world, from Britain and Bolivia to Finland and Fiji, has had a national plan'.[28] Certainly, in the developing world, the planning process became the central mechanism for defining and shaping developmental goals and activities and it was through the plans – usually five-year plans – that the increasing flow of aid was directed, both bilaterally and multilaterally.

Planning was the process through which the whole gamut of policies, programmes and developmental fashions were delivered, whether they flowed from the policy implications of modernisation theory or the autonomous distancing requirements of dependency theory; whether they were top-down or bottom-up; whether they predicted 'trickle down', urged redistribution with growth or the satisfaction of basic human needs; or whether they took the concrete form of integrated rural development programmes, support for import-substituting industrialisation, the protection of infant industries or export promotion. In the 1960s and well into the 1970s, planning became the central mechanism for the promotion of national development, within the framework of the nation-state, by regimes on the left, the centre and on the right, by those committed (at least rhetorically) to various local forms of democratic socialism (as in India, Tanzania and Jamaica when under the rule of the People's National Party) and those (as in South Korea, Malaysia and

Ivory Coast) which were not, and whether they nationalised foreign-owned enterprises or not.

State institutions

The preoccupation with planning, however, had presupposed the power and legitimacy of consolidated state institutions and systems of governance capable of preparing and administering plans, implementing them and building further plans on the basis of evaluations of the results. Although there were those (often in the field of public administration), even in the late 1960s and early 1970s, who began to question the efficacy of planning,[29] the *political interpretation* of why so many states in the developing world were failing in their developmental aims and claims was slow to emerge. It is true that there were early warnings. But many of these early analyses came to focus more on the class nature of state elites and less on the bleak developmental implications of such weak states.[30] Some examples will help to anchor the point.

In the 1950s Paul A. Baran identified what he referred to as the 'comprador administrations' which, he argued, managed the ex-colonies on behalf of capitalist countries and interests. Whether that was true or not, he noted perceptively that 'waste, corruption, squandering of vast sums on the maintenance of sprawling bureaucracies and military establishments, the sole function of which is to keep the comprador regimes in power, characterize all of the countries in question'.[31] André Gunder Frank, influenced by Baran's work, developed a similar and more complex explanation for underdevelopment in Latin America, housing his approach in a much wider narrative about global metropolis-satellite relations.[32] Aristide Zolberg, drawing on Weber rather than Marx, was one of the first political scientists to identify the neopatrimonial character of West African polities in the 1960s,[33] a theme followed by many others well into the 1990s and beyond.[34] Class analysis of the emerging African states by other scholars, such as Richard Sklar, Issa Shivji and Claude Meillassoux, focused on the implications for power and politics.[35] In Asia, while Gunnar Myrdal and others discussed the 'soft states', Hamza Alavi explored the provenance of what he called the 'overdeveloped state'.[36] Both forms of state, they argued, were characterised – and hence compromised as formal Weberian states – by webs of patronage, coalitions of vested interests and a lack of 'social discipline' (according to Myrdal) within society.[37]

Political science and development

It is not altogether surprising that political scientists tended to overlook the developmental implications of emerging political patterns.[38] After all, many members of the discipline with interests in the developing world in the postwar years had largely been schooled in analytical and comparative questions to do with nationalism and the independence movements,[39] the emergence and character of new political parties, issues of 'nation-building', 'political development', and 'political order in changing societies' (the title of Samuel Huntington's classic study which always bears re-reading),[40] the military in politics, modernisation and cultural change, to mention but some.[41]

Where economists, and development economists in particular, had lost sight of the political, social and cultural institutional contexts of economic behaviour (or simply did not know how to deal with them), political scientists paid inadequate attention to the developmental implications of the political problems of many new states, or the complex webs of institutional inter-actions that defined the conflicts, configurations and uses of power, although it would be fair to say that it had taken some time for the underlying patterns to emerge. Even then, it was very difficult, by their very nature, to disclose, trace and analyse them. Nonetheless, expectations of the new states and their elites – radical in their pre-independence pronouncements – had been far too high. The infectious optimism of the speeches and writings of Julius Nyerere, and Nehru's 'tryst with destiny' speech on independence night, 14 August 1947, are good examples of this.[42] By the early 1980s, battered by the oil shocks of the previous decade and the ensuing debt crises (especially in Latin America), many developing countries evinced a picture of painfully slow (and, in many cases, negative) growth;[43] deepening inequalities within them, between them and between them and the developed countries; authoritarian military rule (grotesque, repressive and bloody in some cases); personal rule (especially in Africa[44]), burgeoning corruption and political exclusion or suppression – all of which were graphically illustrated in Latin America.[45]

It is important to qualify this generally bad news with the fact that, glob-ally, overall life expectancy had risen, more children were in school for longer and that literacy rates were improving. Moreover, there had been some remarkable growth success stories which had emerged, including the East Asian newly industrialising countries (Korea, Hong Kong, Taiwan), the Southeast Asian states of Thailand, Malaysia and Singapore, as well as two African states, Mauritius and Botswana.[46] Post-Maoist China was to record dramatic gains in growth in the two decades after 1980 and dramatic reduc-tions in poverty. While few of these were especially admirable from a demo-cratic, liberal, socialist or human rights point of view, they nonetheless bucked the downward or static developmental trend so widespread elsewhere. Because each of these pursued very different sets of policies in contexts of extreme historical, institutional and endowment diversity – compare China with Botswana and Mauritius with Korea – it was beginning to be clear that what mattered was less regime type (democracy or not) or constitutional form (union or federation), but rather the character and capacity of the regime, that is, the legitimate authority and consolidated power of the state, its politi-cal will, developmental determination and bureaucratic capacity. In short (though few were to say it explicitly at the time), *politics* was what mattered. However, the full implications of this has only just begun to register in both theory and policy, and I shall return to the point later.

The neoclassical 'counter revolution'

Although there were many other international and national political factors involved, it was the generally weak economic performance of many developing countries which was to put wind in the sails of the neoclassical 'counter-revolution'[47] when it arrived at the end of the 1970s. Its success was rapid and far-reaching.[48] Its policy implications had long been foreshadowed in the work of economists such as P. T. Bauer, Deepak Lal, Bela Balassa, A. O. Krueger, Milton Friedman and I. M. D. Little.[49] The counter-revolution had two central strands in its political economy: a clear and strongly theoretical antagonism to state action in the promotion of development, and a clear preference for markets and enterprise as the universal engines of development. As Lal was to put it, a 'necessarily imperfect market mechanism' was always preferable to a 'necessarily imperfect planning mechanism'.[50]

First expressed in policy terms in the form of structural adjustment conditionality in the early 1980s,[51] the new focus of aid and overseas development policy by the international institutions and major donors had blossomed by the end of the decade into what came to be called (somewhat crudely) the Washington Consensus. With its emphasis on fiscal discipline, a redirection of public expenditure (e.g. to primary education and health care), tax reform, liberalisation of interest rates, a competitive exchange rate, liberalisation of trade and foreign direct investment, privatisation, deregulation and secure property rights, the Washington Consensus became the broad template for the elaboration of conditional policies which were increasingly attached, more or less, to bilateral and multilateral loans. Although Williamson has justifiably made clear that, as the luckless originator of the label Washington Consensus, his ideas have been misrepresented,[52] the fact remains that, from the late 1980s until the start of the new millennium, the broad thrust of these policy ideas has been central to overseas aid and development policies pursued not only by the major bilateral donors but also by the World Bank, International Monetary Fund and the World Trade Organization. Where planning and state-led development had dominated developmental ideas and policies in the period 1950–80, from the 1990s such notions were barely mentioned and attempts at comprehensive planning have been rare. However, planning is not completely dead and in places (for example Vietnam[53]) national plans are still very effectively deployed for development objectives. It is also becoming clear that planning must and will play a major part in pro-poor growth strategies, which I deal with later. Elsewhere, as in South Africa for instance, strategic planning is less concerned with economic and developmental issues than it is with the orchestration and improvement of policy implementation and making governance more effective and democratic across national and subnational governments. Similar concerns informed the 74th Amendment to the Indian Constitution in 1992.[54]

Nonetheless, broadly market solutions (involving many features of the Washington Consensus, sometimes underpinned by even more hawkish expressions of neoliberal theory, although not always) for the problems of failed, stalled or poor development records were being sought. As the World Bank's *World Development Report* of 1991 put it, 'there is clear evidence . . . that it is better not to ask governments to manage development in detail'. While government intervention was 'essential' for some aspects of development (property rights protection, judicial and legal systems, improving the civil service), it was preferable for 'governments to do less in those areas where markets work, or can be made to work, reasonably well'.[55] The new orthodoxy was part of the acceleration in the politics and economics of globalisation, reviewed so effectively in *New Political Economy* in June 2004,[56] and explored in countless articles and books as an aspect of both political and economic international relations (especially its impact on state autonomy and capacity, and on national economic policy, practice and prospects).[57]

Governance and democracy

It is interesting to note that nowhere in Williamson's 1989 formulation of the Washington Consensus was there any mention of 'governance' or the role of institutions (though by 1997 when he revised his 'agenda', the question of institutional innovation had appeared[58]) or of power – and certainly not of politics. This is not to say that the question of governance had not appeared on the research, policy or theory agenda: it had. In its 1989 report on Sub-Saharan Africa, the World Bank had observed that 'underlying the litany of Africa's development problems is a crisis of governance. By governance is meant the exercise of political power to manage a nation's affairs.'[59] Thereafter, there was a deluge of pronouncements and research on governance, ranging from the Nordic Ministers of Development through to the Organization for African Unity. Initially, ideas about governance were broad, very much along the lines of the Bank's formulation above. Some, such as that developed in the Cotonou Agreement of 2000 between the European Union and the 77 African, Caribbean and Pacific countries, omitted any specific reference to democracy; it did, however, use the notion of 'participation' as a rather loose proxy concept, and defined good governance as:

> The transparent and accountable management of human, natural, economic and financial resources for the purposes of equitable and sustainable development. It entails clear decision-making procedures at the level of public authorities, transparent and accountable institutions, the primacy of law in the management and distribution of resources and capacity building for elaborating and implementing measures aiming in particular at preventing and combating corruption.[60]

The emphasis on the *public* domain in this conception of governance needs to be balanced by a more nuanced understanding of governance that spans the public and private domains. This was spelled out in one of the recent and more comprehensive accounts of governance in the academic literature, that by Hyden, Court and Mease, who argue that 'governance refers to the formation and stewardship of the formal and informal rules that regulate the public realm, the arena in which state as well as economic and societal actors interact to make decisions'.[61] Others were more explicit about the need for democracy (seldom defined or specified), notably the United Nations Development Programme, the Organisation for Economic Cooperation and Development and individual ministers of state responsible for aid or foreign policy.[62] The government of the United Kingdom set up the Westminster Foundation for Democracy, a joint-party affair, to promote pluralist democratic institutions abroad.[63] Other Western countries did the same and the requirement for democratisation, or steps towards it, became one of the new political conditions attached to (mainly) bilateral loans, although this was very patchily applied.[64]

The case for democratisation, in theory, was tied to the case for economic liberalisation.[65] For, if incompetent, undemocratic, authoritarian and often kleptocratic regimes, and clumsy state intervention in the economy, were central to the developmental malaise, then democratisation would surely ensure that they would no longer be able to get away with it, or so the argument went.[66] On the contrary, democratisation would see that they would be held to account and, if necessary, removed from office, leaving both the economic and political markets to perform their efficient magic in a sparse but effective institutional environment.

But, as the confident decade of the post-Cold War 1990s progressed – confident, because Western neoliberalism appeared so triumphant – it became apparent that the good governance agenda was really an intimate part of the emerging political economy of the new world order. As I have written elsewhere, it was also clear that 'the barely submerged structural model and ideal of politics, economics and society on which all notions of good governance rests is nothing less than that of western liberal (or social democratic) capitalist democracy – the focal concern and teleological terminus of much modernization theory'.[67] This was clear in the enthusiastic welcome given by the leaders of the Group of Seven at their Houston summit in the summer of 1990 to the 'renaissance of democracy throughout much of the world . . . and the increased recognition of the principles of the open and competitive economy . . . and the encouragement of enterprise . . . (and) of incentives for individual initiative and innovation'.[68] While Samuel Huntington recorded the 'third wave' of democratisation,[69] Francis Fukuyama's confident and celebratory announcement went much further – that liberal economic and political systems together constituted the 'final form' of development, thereby strengthening the view of Michael Doyle, expressed some years earlier, that liberal democracies did not go to war with each other.[70] In political

science, the 1990s were characterised by an explosion of studies on democracy and democratisation in the developing world, plus the emergence of
new journals devoted to the subject, such as the *Journal of Democracy* and
Democratisation.[71]

Institutions

Along with these two prongs of economic and political liberalism went an
emerging concern for 'institution building'.[72] For, if effective governance was
to be achieved in societies in which market economies were the engines of
development, then (it was now realised) the (formal) institutions (if they were
not present or if they had decayed) for facilitating and managing such economies needed to be built, or re-built. In its earliest formulation, institution
building was associated essentially with improving the 'management of a
country's economic and social resources for development' and with the 'capacity to design, formulate and implement policies and discharge functions'.[73]
This approach focused heavily on the organisations and personnel involved in
economic analysis, policy formulation and implementation, on strengthening
the 'offices' of such personnel and – at least in the desperate African context –
sought to 'build . . . a critical mass of professional African policy analysts
and managers who will be able to better manage the development process,
and to ensure the more effective utilization of already trained African analysts and managers'.[74] By its own admission, there was unquestionably a
strongly technocratic, administrative and managerial tone to such conceptions of both governance and how to improve the institutions of governance
in the early days.[75] Open, accountable, well-trained and transparent policy-
making bodies (sometimes with the insistence that they be 'democratic' and
elected, sometimes not); accountable executives; reliable, competent and
effective public bureaucracies on the Weberian model; and fair and independent courts applying the law impartially were held to be the core institutions
for good governance.[76]

Given this somewhat managerial and administrative focus on the formal
institutions of governance, and the personnel who worked within them, it is
hardly surprising that in the early days of institutional reform what was said
to be required was 'capacity building' to enhance their efficacy – which
involved training, experience, materials and resources. But such an approach
reflected a strongly top-down approach to development, a very limited conception of 'institutions' and the naive belief that such institutions could be
replicated, implemented or built anywhere – across space and time, and
irrespective of prevailing cultures and distributions of power.

Nonetheless, this realisation that institutions mattered was an important
change in the official political economy of development thinking in both the
international and national development agencies. It seemed to acknowledge
that 'sound' economic policy (whatever it may be) was not enough, and that
the institutional context could not be ignored. Even though it was still argued

officially that the state should not attempt to do what markets did better, the state was still needed to provide the formal institutional framework within which effective and developmental economic activities could safely, securely and peacefully proceed. The *World Development Report* of 1997, entitled *The State in a Changing* World (in which the treatment of the state contrasted sharply with the earlier 1991 *World Development Report*, entitled *The Challenge of Development*), was said to have been the culmination of much thinking inside the Bank 'about the centrality of institutions for development', a notion stressed again three years later in its *Reforming Public Institutions and Strengthening Governance*.[77]

Implications and outcomes

Before turning to the developmental preoccupations and theoretical bearings of the first decade of the twenty-first century, there are a number of important points to note here. The first is that this rediscovery of institutions in development theory and policy – and, especially, the institutions of the state – had been presaged in the work of economists such as D. C. North[78] (who built on a much deeper tradition of institutionalist economic analysis going back to List and the German historical school[79]), as well as political scientists such as James March and Johan Olsen (not in a developmental context, however).[80] This interest in institutions was subsequently to be developed from the late 1990s onwards in a rich vein of theoretical and empirical work by many scholars, such as Dani Rodrik and others,[81] and was to underline the need to deepen our understanding of the relationship between institutional legacies and structures, on the one hand, and economic behaviour (and hence developmental consequences), on the other. However, the full-frontal recognition of the need to engage analytically with the underlying realities of power and culture in shaping institutions was yet to be acknowledged and hence the process of bringing politics back in had only just begun. I shall return to the point later.

Second, in its initial expression, the idea of institutions was not only somewhat wooden, but often largely limited to formal institutions, sometimes understood as organisations or offices or agencies (within or outside the bureaucracies) whose 'capacity' needed to be beefed up; it was also sometimes badly confused with 'policy'. In the 'political' domain, these included institutions such as parties, legislatures, independent court systems, accountable and, especially, technically competent and non-corrupt bureaucracies; while in the economic sphere they generally referred to institutions concerned with the definition and protection of property rights, the enforcement of contracts, the establishment and regulation of reliable financial and credit institutions, the promotion and regulation of competitive markets, and so on.[82]

It is of course true that this new concern with governance and the structure and capacity of institutions was to open the door to a fuller political understanding of development. Moreover, very important studies showed a clear correlation between public bureaucracies which conformed to 'Weberian' characteristics and economic growth,[83] and that different governance institutions seemed closely associated with different developmental performances.[84] But it was to be some time before more sophisticated and comprehensive analyses of governance – and especially the *politics of development* – were to emerge, both within the international and national development agencies and in the wider scholarly community. Discussion of institution-building in the agencies remained couched in a highly technocratic, managerial and administrative language and was profoundly and almost determinedly non-political, or even anti-political in its implications and tone. In general, there was a strong tendency to take a Lego-like approach to institution building. If enough of the right institutional pieces could be put in place together, the result would be the building of societies framed by liberal democratic polities and market economies which, together, would promote growth, freedom and prosperity and would not go to war with each other. There were echoes here of some of the crasser forms of modernisation theory and practice that had dominated much Western development thinking after the Second World War. Although there were important exceptions, as mentioned above,[85] these discussions of the 1990s on governance and institutions in the main paid little attention to the *political* processes underlying the formation, endurance and change of developmental institutions, or to the structures of power, patterns of culture and the kinds of coalition of interests which might resist or promote change in existing institutional configurations, or establish new ones, whether for good or for bad.

Third, as neoliberalism and structural adjustment as reform templates for growth and development began to accumulate their own anomalies, from which the institutional and (shortly) political critiques were later to emerge, a parallel critique was growing on the intellectual and political periphery, in the form of what can only loosely be called postmodernist and postcolonial scholarship, anchored in a wider, more popular and radical critique of Western colonial and imperial history and practices.[86] This is not the place to do justice to the rich range of analyses to be found in this tradition, anchored loosely in an equally diverse range of causes and (often grassroots) social movements broadly associated with the 'anti-globalisation movement', so-called, with its annual focus at the World Social Forum,[87] and the series of protests which have been organised at major international meetings. At the core of this critique, whose provenance could in part be traced to dependency theory, was the proposition that both the conception and practices of 'development' had been generated mainly in Western minds from within the experiences of Western societies, with Western (and often Western capitalist) interests at heart. Moreover, the critics assert, the practices of development have been almost exclusively designed and deployed by Western, Western-dominated or Western-influenced institutions – notably the IMF, the World Bank and the WTO – exercising enormous power and wealth and hence imposing Western notions and strategies of development on non-Western societies, at immense cost to those societies. In short, such critics have argued, 'development' as both idea and action represents a contemporary version of Western economic, political, cultural and ideological imperialism.[88] 'Western knowledge is inseparable from the exercise of Western power' and takes precedence over the 'value of alternative experiences and ways of knowing'. Accordingly, 'development discourse is thus rooted in the rise of the West, in the history of capitalism, in modernity, and the globalization of Western state institutions, disciplines, cultures and mechanisms of exploitation'.[89] Although forming a distinct discourse of dissent to Western global dominance and the dynamics of globalisation, the net political impact of these loosely associated social movements is much harder to evaluate and few of them articulate a clear alternative developmental strategy, though many act effectively on a local basis to advance the political and material interests of the poor in developing countries.[90]

Fourth, as the post-1990 processes of globalisation intensified, as their developmental implications became more stark, as protests against them spread, and as the former East European and East Asian communist states came in from the cold, a very positive, if haphazard, blurring and merging of disciplinary and subdisciplinary foci began to occur. In so far as it was ever able to do so, development studies could now no longer have as its sole focus the particular policies, programmes and problems of individual states and economies. Dependency theory and world system theory had, perhaps somewhat hysterically and with a determinism that was to prove their undoing, insisted on a global and historical approach to development. But now scholars working in international relations, globalisation, political science, economics, geography and sociology all began to find themselves (maybe much more comfortably than before, and productively) straying into each other's previously quite exclusive terrains – something reflected strongly in the literature of the 1990s and beyond. Whether they liked it or not, or had intended it or not, they found themselves unavoidably engaged in the study of development and underdevelopment. As the first editorial of *New Political Economy* argued, development was concerned 'with the structures and processes of the world system which produced distributional outcomes characterised by uneven development and wide variation in the wealth and poverty of particular regions, sectors, classes and states'.[91] Neither Adam Smith nor Karl Marx would have been surprised by this. After all, it had been Smith who had observed that the opening of the sea-route to India and the 'discovery' of the Americas had been the two greatest occurrences in recorded history. He wrote: 'by uniting, in some measure, the most distant parts of the world, by enabling them to relieve one another's wants, to increase one another's enjoyment, and to encourage one another's industry, their general tendency would seem to be beneficial'.[92]

Although optimistic about the 'objective' benefits of these processes, Smith (like Marx later) was not blind to the 'dreadful misfortunes' which these beneficial developments had brought to the people of the East and West

Indies. Marx himself was later to observe that these events had 'produced world history for the first time'.[93] Some political scientists, working in international relations, have come to argue that politics is now a 'global affair', that the distinction between domestic and international politics has become a 'conceptual fiction': indeed, the 'separation of the study of Politics from the study of International Relations' now represents a mythical 'Great Divide',[94] for what happens in the international (or regional) sphere impacts decisively on national politics and – more so in the case of the great and hegemonic powers – vice versa.[95] The growing field of international political economy reflects precisely these global concerns and the disappearing disciplinary boundaries, for instance, between international economics and international relations.[96]

Finally, the new interest in governance and the institutions of development had moved theory, debate and policy a long way from the heady days of planning optimism but also from the confident expectations of the neo-classical counter-revolution. Nevertheless, despite economic liberalisation and the best efforts to improve governance, build institutions and enhance capacity, it was to be the extremely poor growth performance of many developing societies – and particularly the slow progress in the elimination of poverty – that was to stimulate the beginning of a much more thoughtful analysis of governance, institutions and – just beginning – *politics*, in under-standing the political economy of both successful and unsuccessful (and especially pro-poor) development. It is to that that I turn now.

The new millennium and the re-birth of social science

Paradigm strain

As Thomas Kuhn observed in his classic study, *The Structure of Scientific Revolutions*, 'paradigm shift' is occasioned by the build-up of sufficient anomalies in a prevailing paradigm for it no longer to be able to generate plausible explanatory solutions.[97] Using that analogy, it is clear that, by the dawn of the new millennium in 2000, the results of the neoliberal reforms with respect to growth, employment and poverty reduction had, in John Williamson's words, been 'disappointing'.[98] At best, the results of two dec-ades of structural reform had been patchy. With certain important exceptions (notably in Asia), the global situation (especially in Latin America and par-ticularly Africa[99]) remained critical, though of course there were variations in each of the continents. Although global growth in per capita gross domestic product for the period 1990–2002 had been 1.2 per cent and for all developing countries had been 2.8 per cent (with Africa being close to zero, Latin America being 1.3 per cent and South Asia and East Asia being 3.2 per cent and 5.4 per cent respectively),[100] its impact on unemployment was not impres-sive. Global unemployment rose from 140 million in 1994 to 184 million (or 6.1 per cent) in 2004, with the figures for Africa, Latin America and the

Middle East being 10.1 per cent, 8.6 per cent and 11.7 per cent respectively –
all up on the situation in 1994. Youth unemployment rates ranged in 2004
from 21.3 per cent in the Middle East, 18.4 per cent in Sub-Saharan Africa,
17.6 per cent in Latin America to 10.9 per cent in South Asia (it was
14.2 per cent in the developed economies).[101]

With respect to poverty reduction, there is much debate about the figures
and the methodology. Some argue that the period from 1980 saw a sustained
reduction in poverty (much of which was accounted for by developments in
East and South Asia) which was 'unprecedented in human history'.[102] Others
question these claims, suggesting that, while the *proportion* of the world's
population in poverty may well have declined over this period (hardly surprising, given the sharp increase in global population), the *number* in poverty may
well have risen.[103] Whatever the true global trend, there is little disagreement
that *at least* 1.1 billion people – about a fifth of world population – currently
live on less than US$1 per day, and that, whereas poverty seems to have
declined in East and South Asia (though the bulk of the world's poor live
there), the absolute number and proportion of people in Africa and Latin
America who were in poverty rose between 1981 and 2000.[104] But even in
China, the great success story of East Asia, while the poverty rate overall
declined dramatically between 1981 and 2001, from 53 per cent to 8 per cent
(according to some figures), half of the decline came in the first few years
after the reforms of the 1980s, but appears to have stalled after 1996, leaving
212 million people in poverty, despite an average annual growth rate since
then of 7 per cent, while the distribution of improvements has been very
uneven across the provinces.[105] Moreover, in its *World Development Report* for
2006, according to a draft of 2005, the World Bank will report that, if China
and India are excluded, global inequality, both between and within countries,
rose over the past 20 years.[106] This will come as no surprise to students of
Latin America where, despite marginal changes in a few countries, inequality
remains deeply entrenched and the richest 10 per cent of the population
in most Latin American countries still take 40–47 per cent of total income
while the poorest 20 per cent take 2–4 per cent. Moreover, inequality of
access to health care, education, utilities and both political influence and
power remains profound.[107] These data and conclusions were confirmed
in a joint World Bank/Civil Society multi-country participatory assessment
of structural adjustment, though published alone by SAPRIN (Structural
Adjustment Participatory Review International Network) in 2002.[108]

It was in the context of these disappointing if not dismal empirics that the
international community rededicated itself to promoting developmental aims
through the Millennium Development Goals, set out at the United Nations in
September 2000,[109] very much in the tradition of the various development
decades of the 1960s and 1970s, epitomised 30 years earlier by the attack on
'absolute poverty' by Robert McNamara in his address to the Board of
Governors of the World Bank in Nairobi in 1973. But the impact of the
1990s, in particular, was to have an even more pronounced effect on the

theories of, and approaches to, economic growth and development. Although it would be grossly premature to talk of a paradigm shift of Kuhnian proportions, it is clear that from the end of the twentieth century anomalies were beginning to accumulate which could not be contained within the neo-liberal orthodox paradigm of developmental theory and policy. As the new millennium commenced, economists with close ties to (or positions within) the major international development institutions began to acknowledge these. In particular, they began to edge towards a more open recognition of the centrality of politics. There are countless examples, but a few seminal ones will illustrate the point.

In an authoritative analysis of the success and failure of some 220 structural adjustment programmes, Dollar and Svensson concluded that success or failure depended critically on 'domestic political-economy forces' within the reforming country and that 'development agencies need to devote resources to understanding the political economy of different countries and to find promising candidates to support'.[110] Virtually the same conclusions were reached by an IMF research group which analysed 170 IMF-supported programmes between 1992 and 1998:

> Failures in program implementation are associated with a small number of observable political indicators in borrowing countries, including the strength of special interests in parliament; lack of political cohesion in the government; ethnic fragmentation in broader society; and the combination of political instability and an inefficient bureaucracy.[111]

What was happening was beginning to become clear. In its search for parsimony and rigour, the neoclassical orthodoxy had simply failed to appreciate 'the complex causal nature of the social world, assuming that the components and processes of the economy are the same across countries', as Kenny and Williams argued in their very important paper published in *World Development* in 2001.[112] The empirical evidence, they showed, provided little 'firm guidance for the universal efficacy of any particular policy prescriptions'.[113] Instead of seeking to build 'abstract universal models, more energy should be directed to 'understanding the complex and varied inner workings of actual economies'.[114] What they meant by 'actual economies' is not self-evident, but I suggest that the only plausible way to understand the phrase is to interpret it as 'whole societies', for 'actual economies' are no more isolable from the sociopolitical and environmental context than flame is from fire.

The new institutionalism

The initial response to these anomalies, at least in some quarters of the multilateral and bilateral development institutions and some research scholars working in the field, came not in the form of a political analysis, but instead began to assimilate some of the implications of the New Institutional

Economics into development theory and policy. Drawing on the work of Douglass North and the earlier historical school, as well as imbibing the implications of Ronald Coase's contribution and the important paper by Sokoloff and Engerman on the different paths of development in the new world,[115] the new institutional economics sought (in North's words) 'to assert a much more fundamental role for institutions in societies; they are the underlying determinant of the long-run performance of economies'.[116] This was to be a view underlined by Rodrik, Subramanian and Trebbi in their classic paper, 'Institutions Rule: The Primacy of Institutions over Geography and Integration in Economic Development'.[117] But the conception of institutions used in the new approach was both different and more subtle than that which had been used a decade earlier in work on the theory and practice of 'institution building'. Whereas the earlier tradition tended to focus on improving, and 'training' staff for public organisations (such as bureaucracies, legislatures, courts and ministries), the new understanding defined institutions as the 'rules of the game in a society', the 'humanly devised constraints that shape human interaction' and therefore 'structure incentives in human exchange, whether political, social or economic'.[118] A slightly different take on this was that of the World Bank's analysis of 'public institutions' which 'create the incentives which shape the action of public officials'.[119] In short, institutions are not to be limited in meaning to organisations, or confused with policies, but need to be understood as the rules, norms, established procedures and conventions – formal and informal – which govern all behaviour.

The implications of this approach were profound for the rational choice basis of much neoliberal development theory and policy. For instead of assuming rational agents pursuing their respective utilities sublimely uncluttered in both space and time by different institutional encumbrances and different distributions of power and opportunity, the new institutional approach recognised that all agents and groups everywhere operate within historical and contemporaneous contexts. These contexts – essentially those of rules and power – are constituted by a variety of both formal and informal institutional arrangements, some of which promoted and some of which hindered economic growth and social development. For example, as both Charles Tilly and Robert Bates were to argue,[120] where people are confronted with insecure, uncertain or contested rules, or where their enforcement is somewhat random and unpredictable, thereby rendering them unable to protect (for instance) life, limb or property, they are hardly likely to invest for development purposes (as indeed Hobbes had argued in *Leviathan* in 1661). And where the authority and power of the state was unconsolidated and contested by subnational foci of military organisation and power (for instance, Chinese warlords in the interwar years or Somali and Afghan warlords more recently), then it would be unlikely to be able to define or enforce a set of agreed and legitimate institutional rules that would provide the incentives for economic development, whether by individuals or cooperatives, or by entrepreneurs or collective action. More concretely, the same or similar set of policies (e.g market liberalisation) has produced very different outcomes in very different institutional settings and hence it is hardly realistic to assume that a one-size-fits-all approach to the promotion of development can work. The interaction of different sets of rules – formal and informal; internal and external; social, political, cultural and economic – ultimately shapes developmental outcomes. Nor are there, in the real world, simple, pure and 'free' markets. All markets – whether they take the form of silent barter or the trading of shares on the stock exchange – are governed by more or less complex sets of institutional rules which shape behaviour and interaction. The trick, then, is how to devise, encourage or shape the institutions most likely to promote development, given very different historical and structural contexts, endowments, institutional legacies – and political possibilities.

While the Bank had begun to recognise the force of such arguments in early publications in the 1990s,[121] by 2002 it had taken them fully on board to the point where the *World Development Report* of that year was devoted to the role of institutions in development.[122] But the focus of this new concern with institutions has tended to be concerned with their role in support of markets. Indeed, 'institutional quality' still tends to be conceived and measured in terms of the extent to which institutions entrench and protect property rights, encourage entrepreneurship, attract investment and boost productivity in a context of political stability and predictability, legal consistency and efficacy (where the courts work fairly) and bureaucratic efficiency and probity.[123] In short, in assuming (correctly) that economic growth and development can only occur, if they are to occur at all, in the context of an interacting network of formal and informal institutions in all spheres of society, the deep purpose of much of the new institutional concern has, however, been how to build the socioeconomic and political matrix of institutions which define the formal structure of liberal (or possibly social democratic) capitalist societies, to which – on that view – there appear to be no alternative institutional scenarios. To that extent, much of the thinking in official and peri-official development research appears largely to be a sophisticated re-invention of earlier 'modernisation' theory, although it should be said that it need not be.

Institutional analysis and the role of governance

Parallel to these developments in the institutional analysis of economic development has been an intensifying interest in specifying and measuring the characteristics of governance and good governance in particular. From the rather simplistic and often highly normative concerns of the 1980s and the 1990s (accountability, sometimes meaning democracy; a proper legal framework; open information and transparency[124]), these concerns had moved forward to a sharper and more useful disaggregation of the characteristics of governance and their measurement. At the World Bank, for instance, the work of Daniel Kaufmann, Aart Kraay and Pablo Zoido-Lobatón on

'Governance Matters' defined six central characteristics of 'public' governance (focusing essentially on the institutions of the state) to be measured and evaluated: voice and accountability, political instability and violence, government effectiveness and regulatory burden, rule of law and graft. In a series of papers they sought to identify and compare governance across countries.[125] Other scholars, seeking also to define and measure the quality of governance, set out to deploy more inclusive conceptions of governance, cutting across the conventional public and private divide by defining governance as 'the formation and stewardship of the formal *and informal* rules that regulate the public realm, the arena in which state as *well as economic and societal actors* interact to make decisions'.[126] Hyden, Court and Mease thus identified six 'institutional arenas' in which rules were made and applied and which together constituted the overall framework of governance for development: civil society (private organisations), political society (parties and pressure groups), government, bureaucracy, economic society and the judicial system. In a comprehensive World Governance Survey, they sought to measure these in 16 developing countries.[127]

It should already be apparent how far mainstream development theory and policy had come to recognise that there was much more to the processes of development than the application of so-called 'first order economic principles' which had characterised so much of the neoliberal orthodoxy.[128] These, as with the abstract models, always come 'institution free', as Rodrik has so aptly described it. But in the real world of 'actual economies', such principles – or any other principles – are always deeply implicated in a web of interacting institutional practices which shape, modify, enhance or inhibit their operation. In short, mainstream theory had commenced the journey down the road that leads to the understanding that economic growth and development requires a social scientific approach – as it had always done for the founders – and, at the heart of this, a political analysis of possibilities and constraints, interests and coalitions. But theory has not reached that point yet. However, the events of 9/11 were to jolt both theorists and policy makers into recognising just how profound were the implications of politics for development – and vice versa.

Poverty, security and development

Just as the Brandt Commission had done 20 years before,[129] the Millennium Development Goals elaborated a moral and economic case for development and, especially, the reduction of poverty. But after the September 2001 attack on the twin towers in New York, and the wars in Afghanistan and Iraq that followed, the *political* case for development began to be made much more forcefully. Driven by the concerns (and funding opportunities) of national and international political elites in developed countries, and by the patchy and uneven record of growth and poverty reduction in the 1990s, academic researchers, too, began to focus more sharply on the political implications of both absolute and relative poverty, and unstable polities, from which, it was argued, there arose a profound security threat to liberal polities, Western interests, regional stabilities and the global economy. The case for under-standing the politics of development was now being made and research into this was, at last, beginning to be funded.[130] Even development economists, seeking to redraw the boundaries of their frameworks, began to talk now about widening 'the scope of economics to include political phenomena'.[131]

The underlying explanatory focus which could no longer be avoided was, then, politics. As a report entitled *The Causes of Conflict in Africa* by the Department for International Development (DfID) of the United Kingdom government observed, there was now a need for 'greater coherence between foreign policy, security and development objectives'.[132] The meaning and nature of 'politics' was seldom spelled out in such reports. But for present purposes here I understand politics to consist of 'all the activities of co-operation, negotiation and conflict, within and between societies, whereby people go about organizing the use, production or distribution of human, natural and other resources in the course of the production and reproduction of their biological and social life'.[133] This applies to interactions within and between the formal or informal institutions of all more or less formally structured human collectivities, whether in families or villages, bands of hunter-gatherers or nation-states, companies or intergovernmental political or regulatory organisations. It therefore entails the analysis of the relations of people, power and resources: in short, political economy. The two central and related preoccupations of research and policy development flowing from this increasing awareness of politics have been, first, the link between security and development and, second, concern for pro-poor growth.

States, security and development

The sudden interest in failing, failed and collapsed states, and their implica-tions for development and security, had already begun to develop momentum from the start of the new millennium, but gathered pace after the events of September 2001,[134] predicted (though not precisely) with terrifying prescience by the distinguished American political scientist Chalmers Johnson.[135] For instance, the academic work by Robert Rotberg and his associates, and the official reports by US government agencies,[136] all illustrate how seriously the issues are being taken in both academic and policy circles in the US where it has come to be widely argued that the 'drivers' of state failure were 'weak governance, poverty and violent conflict'.[137] In short, 'appreciating the nature of and responding to the dynamics of nation-state failure have become cen-tral to critical policy debates. How best to strengthen weak states and prevent state failure are amongst the urgent questions of the twenty-first century.'[138] DfID, in the United Kingdom, went further, making the link between pov-erty, fragile or failed states and security issues even closer, by pointing out that such states account for some 30 per cent of the world's poverty and that they are 'more likely to become unstable, to destabilise their neighbours, to create refugee flows, to spread disease and to be bases for terrorists',[139] a view also advanced by Francis Fukuyama at about the same time.[140]

In similar vein, the Prime Minister's Strategy Unit in the United Kingdom mounted a major inter-departmental research project aimed at developing a strategic approach towards countries at risk of instability. Its report argued explicitly for the association between deprivation, unstable states and global insecurity, again making clear the link between poverty and politics.[141] At the international level, the World Bank established a task-force to develop a strategy for what it called Low-Income Countries Under Stress which started from the premise that such countries were characterised by 'very weak policies, institutions and governance' and that strategies for their development would require reforms which were 'feasible in socio-political terms'.[142]

Overall, then, the opening years of the new millennium saw both national and international development agencies move quite sharply to a more open recognition of the importance of politics (often more cautiously described as political economy) across a whole range of developmental processes and goals. By 2003, in a remarkable report on *Inequality in Latin America and the Caribbean*, the Bank made clear that only 'deep reforms of political, social and economic institutions' could produce both better growth rates and also reduce poverty and inequality. Any such reforms (including land reform) would need to enhance access not only to education and opportunities, but also to political influence and power, thereby correcting a long historical process in the region.[143] By the time the *World Development Report* for 2006 is published, the World Bank will (at least formally) have acknowledged the centrality of politics in a manner which would not displease even Marx. Observing that 'high levels of political inequality can lead to the design of economic institutions and social arrangements that systematically favour the interests of those with more influence', it is argued that this is all the more damaging for development because 'economic, political and social inequalities tend to reproduce themselves over time and across generations'.[144] But, if political and security factors have strengthened the economic and moral case for addressing the enduring problems of poverty and inequality, what is the way forward?

Pro-poor growth

During the course of the last five years, interest in pro-poor growth has intensified, for, if growth does not benefit the poor, wider developmental and security problems are unlikely to be resolved. A research report from a consortium of national development agencies (from the United Kingdom, Germany and France, plus the World Bank) found that, through the 1990s, economic growth had been essential for reductions in poverty, though the net distribution of the benefits of growth as far as the poor were concerned varied considerably across the 14 countries in the study. It found that what best explained the differences were the institutional patterns deployed in each of the countries both to generate and distribute the benefits of growth. Crucially, the report argued, institutions which expanded the 'opportunities' for the poor were what mattered, but the meaning of 'opportunity' was also considerably widened to include 'asset endowments (including capital assets), wealth and power, market access and process fairness'.[145] This is a view now increasingly underlined by academic research which also shows that, for economic institutions to be good and growth-promoting, they need to provide 'relatively equal access to economic resources to a broad cross-section of society'.[146]

Once more it is possible to discern the slightly uncomfortable recognition of politics as critical for developmental and pro-poor processes, coupled with an almost palpable reluctance to talk about its messy complexity directly and a consequent need to disguise its salience in parsimonious and technical-sounding language. But it is not so disguised in some of the individual research reports which underpinned the consortium study. In the case of the Bolivian report, for instance, it was argued that, if pro-poor growth is to happen, it would be 'urgently necessary to confront some of the deep-seated inequalities in assets, opportunities, resources and power'.[147] But if institutions – the rules and conventions of the game which shape incentives – are central for growth and pro-poor growth, what determines the shape and outcome of the institutions themselves?

Institutions, power and politics

The answers to some of these questions are being developed amongst academic researchers who have been exploring the impact of institutions on growth, development and pro-poor growth in particular. There is now increasingly wide recognition that what shapes institutions is politics, though the point had been made with devastating simplicity by Douglass North as early as 1990: 'institutions are not necessarily or even usually created to be socially efficient; rather they, or at least the formal rules, are created to serve the interests of those with the bargaining power to devise new rules'.[148] The point was elaborated further by Mushtaq Khan in an important paper on state failure in developing countries, where he argued that the definition and especially enforcement of rules for developmental purposes (for example, in relation to land reform or redistribution) required an effective state and, further, that 'the distribution and disposition of political power in society is a key determinant of enforcement success and the emergence of high-growth states is therefore as much a task of political as it is of institutional engineering'.[149] John Harriss' work on the different developmental and pro-poor records of various Indian states underlines the point.[150] Moreover, the sheer incapacity of the Pakistan state in the 1970s, under the leadership of Bhutto, to implement land reform illustrates this graphically.[151]

This centrality of politics – reflecting the distribution of resources and power – in shaping both formal economic (and political) institutions has been recently demonstrated by Acemoglu, Johnson and Robinson in a major contribution to the understanding of institutions and development: 'whichever group has more political power is likely to secure the economic institutions that it prefers'.[152] The view is sustained, more or less explicitly, by many other individual and comparative studies.[153] In surveying this literature it is simply astounding to see how close much of it is to what used to be dismissed as Marxist political economy, with its characteristic insistence on regarding control – and struggle for the control – of economic resources as being critical in shaping both the informal and formal institutions of political power in all societies. The fundamental idea is the same. The main difference is that attempts are being made to define more precisely and to measure more comprehensively the interactions of these economic and political phenomena in the course of the developmental process. Moreover, there is the presumption that it is possible to devise incentives and institutions which will resolve collective choice problems in part by curtailing some power of the strong and the rich and in part by enhancing the stakes and opportunities of the weak and the poor in such a way that both benefit from the effects of growth.

Work by other political scientists and political economists, going back to the early 1990s, has reinforced and deepened these understandings. Simplistic distinctions between state, society and economy are rejected in favour of more nuanced understandings of their relations. We are encouraged instead to see their continuous interaction and mutual reshaping into a variety of state forms – and to note the profound developmental implications of each, whether 'predatory', 'developmental', 'intermediate' or 'shadow'.[154] As Migdal has observed, 'states are not fixed entities, nor are societies; they both change structure, goals, constituencies, rules, and social control in their processes of interaction. They are constantly becoming.'[155] The importance of this for issues of growth and pro-poor growth especially cannot be emphasised enough. Moreover, it is a reminder of the immense dangers of a monodisciplinary approach to developmental issues in both theory and policy areas. The way in which these interactions have shaped the capacity of states, and hence their ability to establish and sustain institutions, is of course profoundly political and of critical importance for the processes of development, as a steady stream of case studies has now demonstrated.[156]

State failure entails institutional failure, and institutional decay and disintegration is the measure of state failure – at least in its formal sense. There is evidence that, even under the most extreme conditions of state collapse (as in Somalia), anarchy does not always prevail, and that some semblance of socioeconomic exchange can continue.[157] But such situations are devoid of developmental potential, offering little security for innovation, saving or investment. Where (as in Somalia) insecurity and predation is the norm, as Bates has nicely observed, 'people may seek to increase their welfare by choosing to live in poverty'; in short, 'to forestall predation, they may simply choose to live without goods worth stealing. In such a setting, poverty becomes the price of peace.'[158] But this is the politics of sheer survival, not of development. There can be little doubt that, without an effective state, there is likely to be little growth and even less poverty reduction – especially in the African context, but elsewhere too.[159] An effective state will be one that is constituted by a structure of consistent and coherent institutional arrangements networked and interacting across the public-private divide. Its rules and conventions will be sustained by enough consensus, appropriate authority and power, and there will be sufficient incentives to hold people to the rules (especially in the field of public management) so as to avoid capture or pervasive corruption[160] (the 'politics of the belly' in Bayart's term[161]). Ultimately, of course, such a state will need to be sustained by a politics that is committed to developmental goals.

Conclusions: from 'institutions matter' to 'politics matters'

I have sought to show in this chapter how, at last, a recognition of the centrality of politics seems to have emerged in development theory and policy through a trajectory from its early focus on planning and state-led development, through neoliberalism and then concerns about governance and institutions. Let me make a few final points by way of conclusion.

Social science and development studies

First, from their inception, all the major branches of social science have recognised that human societies are essentially defined and constituted by the presence, variety and relations of their institutions, understood as the formal and informal rules and conventions governing social, political and economic interactions. Some institutional ensembles have promoted growth and equitable development better than others. Some have not achieved it at all. But the sharpest social scientists have always sought to explain the structure, character and performance of different societies, and the dynamics of change within them, at different levels of development, in terms of the interaction (internal and external) of these institutional ensembles, and that requires a multi- or crossdisciplinary approach. Even if it has in part been occasioned recently by questions of security, the emerging recognition amongst development policy makers and researchers of the centrality of politics is to be welcomed. This rediscovery of institutions, and also, slowly and crucially, of politics as the prime determinant of their shape, returns the study of development to where it should always have been: at the intersection of social, economic and political relations. Economic principles and practices do not, as Rodrik observes, come 'institution free'.[162] To understand why they do or do not work, a wider analysis is required of the set of institutional interactions that bear on them. As Barbara Harriss-White has put it: 'markets do not perform "subject to" institutions, they *are* bundles of institutions and are nested in others'.[163] More sharply, Chang has reminded us of the 'fundamentally political nature of markets'.[164] To the extent that this crossdisciplinary approach is happening already, development studies remains alive and well, anchored securely at the heart of social science with social science at the heart of development studies.

Beyond political economy and political science

Second, it is clear, too, that research into how institutions are formed, sustained and changed requires detailed historical, comparative and theoretical enquiry,[165] drawing on a wide range of disciplinary perspectives in which questions are asked not only about structures, but also about agents, leadership and ideas in politics.[166] Moreover, if it is now recognised that we require political explanations for the institutional characteristics which promote developmental success or failure, it will soon be realised that understanding the political ideas, interests and practices which shape such institutions also requires us to turn to the analysis of cultural and ideological phenomena. This will involve the insights of applied anthropology and sociology to supplement the economic and political approaches, as a number of contemporary papers already demonstrate.[167] Weber long ago sought to show the influence of Protestant ideas on capitalist development in his classic study.[168] Some more recent studies have sought to explicate the role of ideas, norms and values in promoting or hindering development in Asia and elsewhere,[169] while other research shows that cultural practices and norms can promote, restrain or be affected by development, as well as survive 'modernisation' processes.[170] To illustrate further, informal personal networks and connections, deeply embedded in the cultural institutions of Chinese society, appear to have played a significant part in resource allocation and the organisation of production, and can work beneath and against formal institutional arrangements, for good or for bad.[171] Likewise, informal institutions have been shown to be able to work with, against or parallel to the formal institutions of democracy,[172] while the 'values and practices of caste' in India have had important implications for economic behaviour, notably within and between the networks of the many powerful family businesses.[173] In many parts of Africa, the unavoidable pull of the loyalties of kin and the obligations of clan have been powerful factors which have challenged and undermined the operation of supposedly rule-governed public bureaucracies, allegedly crafted on Weberian lines.[174] Moreover, controversial as it is, recent work on trust and 'social capital' is a further illustration of how the analysis of cultural institutions and associated ideological or normative attributes has deepened debate and understanding about development issues.[175] For all these reasons, the often very different sets of social, cultural and political institutions which shape, and are shaped by economies, suggest that there may have to be many different institutional solutions to overcoming the problems of growth and poverty in different societies at different levels of

Development, politics and social science   187

development and with diverse endowments, historical legacies and structural features.

The return of the state

Third, what is also clear is that, if institutions are to be established which will promote not only development but more equitable development, through pro-poor growth strategies for instance, and if their undermining and corruption is to be avoided, then the macroinstitutional context of the state can be neither sidelined nor ignored. Though rolled back, limited and relegated largely to a minimalist role under the neoliberal ascendancy, it is being realised, once again, that it is necessary to bring the state back in.[176] The pervasive role of state involvement and direction of economic life which characterised the immediate postwar phase of development theory and practice in some countries certainly created inefficiencies, bottlenecks and disincentives for growth, plus immense opportunities for both rent-seeking and regulation. Of course, nothing like that is being recommended again. But what is now recognised is the requirement of the state to provide and sustain the public goods – primarily institutional but, in many areas, physical and social as well – that both make private economic activity possible, attractive and safe, and also appear to be necessary conditions for democratic survival. For it seems that democracy is most likely to survive in strong and effective states.

For whether one likes it or not, the story of modern 'development' and the immense progress that has been achieved as a result of it – not forgetting the human and environmental costs along the way – is intimately bound up with the story of the emergence of the institutions of the modern state.[177] Whether socialist or capitalist, social democratic, developmental or corporatist, the state has helped (and must continue to help) devise, sustain, adapt and enforce the institutional framework of rules and conventions which shape the context in which economic, political and social behaviour occurs.[178]

Developmental challenges – creating social democracy in the tropics

Fourth, the challenge of pro-poor growth and development is both constituted *and* complicated by two other challenges facing states in the developing world: the challenges of democracy and of redistribution – the two central problems which have everywhere accompanied growth in the history of Western development. How growth, democracy and redistribution – all profoundly disruptive and transformative processes – are integrated and reconciled is perhaps the greatest challenge of all. It is essentially a political challenge to be resolved politically, not through one-size-fits-all economic models. It is, after all, the problem of how to create social democracy in the tropics. But, as Kohli's point cited at the start of this chapter suggests, none of these challenges will be met until state power is first sufficiently concentrated, consolidated and legitimised in (at least partly) accountable state institutions. This is necessary before rules can be proposed, debated and instituted in such a way as to constitute public goods supported by all. International and national development agencies and independent researchers are beginning to recognise this in urging that 'political economy considerations' affect outcomes.[179] Indeed they do. They always have.

Bringing politics back in

It is primarily in their politics, as I have defined it and argued here, that the explanations for varying developmental performances of national societies are to be found, and where solutions need to be sought. If that is so, then from a policy point of view there are many profoundly important questions of a social scientific kind which need to be explored, with longstanding problems in political science and political economy at their core. Such questions include the following. What are the benefits and disadvantages of an 'early start' in state formation and how can the disadvantages be overcome or compensated?[180] Given that there is bound to be a range of developmental institutional ensembles for different contexts and conditions, under differing degrees of state capacity, or 'stateness',[181] how can institutional arrangements be devised and established which are consistent with the capacity of the state to manage and uphold them? Where, for example, there is low starting capacity, that is, currently low 'stateness' – and many states in Africa, especially, fall into this category – how much can be expected or required of such states? Should broken-backed and failed states be allowed to fail, their artificiality acknowledged and new states with better prospects – whether smaller or larger – be encouraged and assisted to form?[182] How is improved governance to be achieved in circumstances very different to those of the West when state formation was initially taking place? Are there degrees of governance ('good enough governance'[183]) appropriate for different degrees of 'stateness'? If states are unable to guarantee provision of necessary public goods, could these be delivered also by informal or private institutions, or in a mix of either or both with state institutions, in what is loosely referred to as 'co-production'?[184]

In the final analysis, both institutions and policies are shaped, sustained or changed by politics. And political outcomes, in turn, are the consequence of the distribution, deployment and interaction (conflicting or cooperative) of both formal and informal expressions of power, themselves embedded in and reflecting wider structures of economic and social relations. Whether you call it class conflict or not, those who currently benefit from particular policies and institutional arrangements will want to defend them, and those who do not will want to change them. Given this, can such conflict be converted into negotiation and bargaining between diverse interests, stakeholders and the state? Can that in turn be transformed into consensual and legitimate developmental institutions, either where states are weak and such interests strong – or vice versa? And, if so, how? In short, can the collective action problem, from a developmental point of view, be resolved without further bloodshed?

And how may various interests learn to trust that new institutions, once established, will be respected and maintained? Where groups of the poor are small and weak, how can their interests be accommodated and protected? At the risk of infringing principles of sovereignty, can that kind of politics be deepened by encouraging or sponsoring the emergence of groups and coalitions so that developmentally progressive institutional arrangements may emerge? How does the politics of taxation, for example, fit into this bargaining process at the heart of state formation and consolidation?[185] Once legitimate institutional arrangements are in place, the capacity for implementation – 'stateness' – will be deepened and enhanced. But there will be no quick fixes or universal solutions, for institutional innovation and change will vary, in its forms and particulars, from context to context. And it will usually be slow, and the old questions will always remain. What should be the appropriate structure, function, size and scope of the state, in general and with respect to the economy, in societies at very different levels of development and with very different state capacities?

It is clear that these are amongst the central issues for the future, that they are essentially political and that they will have very different resolutions in different societies. In-depth and case-by-case analyses will be required, adopting a broad-based and historically-informed social science approach in which it is understood that the politics of development is also the development of politics. For all these reasons, it should now be clear why politics is in command.

Notes

1 Atul Kohli, 'State, society and development', in: Ira Katnelson and Helen V. Milner (eds), *Political Science: The State of the Discipline* (W. W. Norton & Co., 2002), p. 117.

2 Dani Rodrik, 'Growth strategies', in: Philippe Aghion and Steve Durlauf (eds), *Handbook of Economic Growth* (North-Holland, forthcoming).

3 Marvin Harris, *Cows, Pigs, Wars and Witches* (Fontana, 1977), p. 8. Dudley Seers made essentially the same point in his classic paper, 'The Birth, Life and Death of Development Economics', *Development and Change*, Vol. 10, No. 4 (1979), pp. 707–19. He noted that 'we really all know now that the economic aspects of the central issues of development cannot be studied or taught in isolation from other factors – social, political and cultural'. *Ibid.*, p. 712.

4 Daron Acemoglu, Simon Johnson and James A. Robinson, *The Colonial Origins of Comparative Development: An Empirical Investigation*, Working Paper 7771, National Bureau of Economic Research, Cambridge, Mass., June 2000, available at http://www.nber.org/papers/w7771

5 By the 'greats' I mean of course Adam Smith at the end of the 18th century, Marx and Weber in the 19th and early twentieth century and the likes of Karl Polanyi, Joseph Schumpeter and Barrington Moore Jr. in the twentieth century. And there are others.

6 Anthony Shorrocks and Rolph van der Hoeven (eds), *Growth, Inequality, and Poverty: Prospects for Pro-poor Economic Development* (Oxford University Press, 2004).

7 A number of important contributions may be found in Joan M. Nelson *et al.*, *Fragile Coalitions: The Politics of Economic Adjustment* (Transaction Books, 1989); Joan M. Nelson (ed.), *Economic Crisis and Policy Choice* (Princeton University Press, 1990); Merilee Grindle, *Challenging the State: Crisis and Innovation in Africa and Latin America* (Cambridge University Press, 1996); Merilee Grindle, *In Quest of the Political: The Political Economy of Development Policy Making*, Working Paper No. 17, Center for International Development, Harvard University, Cambridge, Mass., June 1999.

8 *New Political Economy*, Vol. 1, No. 1 (1996), p. 6.

9 A. O. Hirschman, 'The rise and decline of development economics', in: his *Essays in Trespassing: Economics to Politics and Beyond* (Cambridge University Press, 1981), pp. 3–4.

10 Charles Kenny and David Williams, 'What Do We Know About Economic Growth? Or, Why Don't We Know Very Much', *World Development*, Vol. 29, No. 1 (2001), p. 3.

11 Dani Rodrik, 'Getting institutions right', unpublished paper, Harvard University, April 2004, available at http://ksghome.harvard.edu/~drodrik/papers.html

12 Despite the general opprobrium heaped on W. W. Rostow's theories, he was amongst the very first to recognise the primacy of politics in development. Discussing what he aeronautically referred to as take-off, he observed 'many of the most profound economic changes are viewed as the consequence of non-economic human motivations and aspirations', and 'a decisive feature was often political'. Moreover, 'governments must generally play an extremely important role in the process of building social overhead capital' (he drew particular attention to the role of the state in the US in investing in transport and communications). And, in discussing the requirement that there be a determined development-oriented leadership, he stressed the role of the political process in the transition'. See W. W. Rostow, *The Stages of Economic Growth* (Cambridge University Press, 1960), pp. 2, 7, 25 and 26.

13 Hirschman, 'The rise and decline of development economics'; Seers, 'The Birth, Life and Death of Development Economics'; David Apter, 'The Passing of Development Studies – Over the Shoulder with a Backward Glance', *Government and Opposition*, Vol. 15, No. 3/4 (1980), pp. 263–75; Deepak Lal, *The Poverty of 'Development Economics'* (Institute of Economic Affairs, 1983); John Toye, *Dilemmas of Development* (Blackwell, 1987); Peter Evans and John D. Stephens, 'Studying Development since the Sixties: The Emergence of a New Comparative Political Economy', *Theory and Society*, Vol. 17, No. 5 (1988), pp. 713–45; David B. Moore, 'Development discourse as hegemony: towards an ideological history', in: David B. Moore and Gerald J. Schmitz (eds), *Debating Development Discourse* (Macmillan, 1995), pp. 1–53; and Colin Leys, *The Rise and Fall of Development Theory* (James Currey, 1996). For an excellent new retrospective survey, see Gerald M. Meier, *Biography of a Subject: The Evolution of Development Economics* (Oxford University Press, 2005).

14 Geoffrey M. Hodgson, *How Economics Forgot History* (Routledge, 2001), p. xiii.

15 John Toye, 'Changing perspectives in development economics', in: Ha-Joon Chang (ed.), *Rethinking Development Economics* (Anthem Press, 2003), pp. 21–40.

16 R. A. Packenham, *Liberal America and the Third World: Political Development Ideas in Foreign Aid and Social Science* (Princeton University Press, 1973).

17 David Morawetz, *Twenty Five Years of Economic Development, 1950 to 1975* (World Bank, 1977), p. 12; and H. W. Arndt, 'Economic Development: A Semantic History', *Economic Development and Cultural Change*, Vol. 29, No. 3 (1981), pp. 457 and 466.

18 Roger E. Backhouse, *The Penguin History of Economics* (Penguin, 2002); and

Gary J. Miller, 'The Impact of Economics on Contemporary Political Science', *Journal of Economic Literature*, Vol. 35, No. 3 (1997), pp. 1173–204.

19 Andrew Shonfield, *Modern Capitalism* (Oxford University Press, 1965); and Linda Weiss and John M. Hobson, *States and Economic Development* (Polity, 1995).

20 Charles Tilly, *Coercion, Capital and European States, AD 990–1992* (Blackwell, 1992).

21 C. B. MacPherson, *The Political Theory of Possessive Individualism: Hobbes to Locke* (Oxford University Press, 1962).

22 Richard Hodges, *Primitive and Peasant Markets* (Blackwell, 1988).

23 Joel S. Migdal, *Strong Societies and Weak States* (Princeton University Press, 1988); and Bruce Berman, 'Ethnicity, Patronage and the African State: The Politics of Uncivil Nationalism', *African Affairs*, Vol. 97 (1998), pp. 243–61.

24 William Reno, *Corruption and State Politics in Sierra Leone* (Cambridge University Press, 1995); Nikki Funke and Hussein Solomon, *The Shadow State in Africa: A Discussion*, Development Policy Management Forum Occasional Paper No. 5, 2002, United Nations Economic Commission for Africa, available at http://www.dpmf.org/Occasionalpapers/occasionalpaper5.pdf; Rosaleen Duffy, 'Global governance, shadow states and the environment', unpublished manuscript, available at http://members.lycos.co.uk/ocnewsletter/SGOC0103/duffy.pdf; Rosaleen Duffy, 'Ecotourism, Corruption and State Politics in Belize', *Third World Quarterly*, Vol. 21, No. 3 (2000), pp. 549–65; and Barbara Harriss-White, *Informal Economic Order, Shadow States, Private Status States, States of Last Resort and Spinning States: A Speculative Discussion Based on South Asian Case Material*, Working Paper No. 6, 1997, Queen Elizabeth House Working Paper Series, available at http://www.qeh.ox.ac.uk/research/wpaction.html?jor_id=6

25 M. G. Smith, 'Some developments in the analytic framework of pluralism', in: Leo Kuper and M. G. Smith (eds), *Pluralism in Africa* (University of California Press, 1971), pp. 415–58.

26 Michael P. Todaro and Stephen C. Smith, *Economic Development*, 8th edition (Addison Wesley, 2003), p. 9.

27 Ha-Joon Chang, *Kicking Away the Ladder* (Anthem, 2002); Richard Kozul-Wright, 'The myth of Anglo-Saxon capitalism', in: Ha-Joon Chang and Robert Rowthorn (eds), *The Role of the State in Economic Change* (Clarendon, 1996), pp. 81–113; Weiss and Hobson, *States and Economic Development*; and Alexander Gerschenkron, 'Economic backwardness in historical perspective', in: his *Economic Backwardness in Historical Perspective* (Belknap Press, 1962), pp. 5–30.

28 A. F. Robertson, *People and the State: An Anthropology of Planned Development* (Cambridge University Press, 1984), pp. 7 and *ff.* Robertson points out that amongst the handful of countries which did not have plans were Hong Kong, Liechtenstein, Switzerland and the US. See also Tony Killick, 'The Possibilities of Development Planning', *Oxford Economic Papers*, No. 28 (1976), pp. 161–84. It should always be recalled how fashionable planning was in Europe (and especially the United Kingdom) after the Second World War. It was argued for and implemented by the Labour Government in the United Kingdom, and in particular pursued by Sir Stafford Cripps, Herbert Morrison, Ernest Bevin, Nye Bevan and many others. Many of the assumptions and arguments were easily carried over into aid and development policy in relation to the newly independent former colonies.

29 Albert Waterson, *Development Planning: Lessons from Experience* (Oxford University Press, 1966); and Mike Faber and Dudley Seers (eds), *The Crisis in Planning*, 2 vols (Chatto & Windus, 1972).

30 I have discussed this more fully in Adrian Leftwich, *States of Development* (Polity, 2000).

31 Paul A. Baran, *The Political Economy of Growth* (Monthly Review Press, 1967), p. 215.

32 André Gunder Frank, *Latin America: Underdevelopment or Revolution* (Monthly Review Press, 1969).

33 Aristide Zolberg, *Creating Political Order: The Party States of West Africa* (Rand McNally & Co., 1966).

34 Michael Bratton and Nicolas van de Walle, *Democratic Experiments in Africa* (Cambridge University Press, 1997).

35 Richard Sklar, 'The Nature of Class Domination in Africa', *Journal of Modern African Studies*, Vol. 17, No. 4 (1979), pp. 531–52; Issa Shivji, *Class Struggles in Tanzania* (Heinemann, 1966); and Claude Meillassoux, 'An Analysis of the Bureaucratic Process in Mali', *Journal of Development Studies*, Vol. 6, No. 2 (1970), pp. 97–110.

36 Hamza Alavi, 'The State in Post-colonial Societies: Pakistan and Bangladesh', *New Left Review*, No. 74, (1972), pp. 59–81.

37 Gunnar Myrdal, 'The "soft state" in underdeveloped countries', in: Paul Streeten (ed.), *Unfashionable Economics: Essays in Honour of Lord Balogh* (Weidenfeld & Nicolson, 1970), pp. 227–43.

38 I generalise here to make the wider point.

39 'I was committed to African nationalism and independence', wrote David Apter in his 'backward glance'. See Apter, 'The Passing of Development Studies', p. 267.

40 S. P. Huntington, *Political Order in Changing Societies* (Yale University Press, 1969).

41 Another classic collection of the time shows these kinds of preoccupations. See Clifford Geertz (ed.), *Old Societies and New States* (Free Press, 1963).

42 Julius Nyerere, *Freedom and Socialism (Uhuru Na Ujamaa): A Selection of Speeches and Writings, 1965–1967* (Oxford University Press, 1968). See the account of Nehru's speech in Frank Moraes, *Jawaharlal Nehru: A Biography* (Macmillan, 1957), pp. 1–2.

43 World Bank, *World Development Report 1991* (Oxford University Press, 1991), pp. 204–5. The annual average growth rate of gross national product per capita between 1965 and 1989 in Sub-Saharan Africa had been 0.3 per cent; for Latin America it had been 1.9 per cent;.for South Asia it had been 1.8 per cent; and for East Asia it had been 5.2 per cent. Many African rates were negative, as were some in Latin America, such as Peru, El Salvador, Argentina and Venezuela. Although there had been strong growth from 1950 into the 1970s in Latin America, the decade that followed saw an economic crisis across much of the continent. See R. Ffrench-Davies, O. Muňoz and G. Palma, 'The Latin American economies, 1950–1990', in: Leslie Bethell (ed.), *Latin America: Economy and Society since 1930* (Cambridge University Press, 1998), pp. 149–237.

44 Richard Sandbrook, *The Politics of Africa's Economic Stagnation* (Cambridge University Press, 1985); and Robert H. Jackson and Carl G. Rosberg, 'The political economy of African personal rule', in: David E. Apter and Carl G. Rosberg (eds), *Political Development and the New Realism in Sub-Saharan Africa* (University of Virginia Press, 1994), pp. 291–324.

45 Bethell, *Latin America*; and Ruth Berins Collier and David Collier, *Shaping the Political Arena: Critical Junctures, the Labour Movement and Regime Dynamics in Latin America* (University of Notre Dame Press, 2002).

46 Leftwich, *States of Development*, ch. 1.

47 Toye, *Dilemmas of Development*, p. 71.

48 *Ibid.*, pp. 71–9.

49 *Ibid.*; and Christopher Colclough, 'Structuralism versus neo-liberalism: an intro-

duction', in: Christopher Colclough and James Manor (eds), *States or Markets? Neo-liberalism and the Development Debate* (Clarendon, 1996), pp. 1–25.

50 Lal, *The Poverty of 'Development Economics'*, p. 106.

51 Paul Mosley, Jane Harrigan and John Toye, *Aid and Power: The World Bank and Policy-based Lending*, 2 vols (Routledge, 1991).

52 John Williamson, 'What Washington means by policy reform', in: John Williamson (ed.), *Latin American Adjustment: How Much Has Happened?* (Institute of International Economics, 1990), pp. 7–38; John Williamson, 'The Washington Consensus revisited', in: Louis Emmerij (ed.), *Economic and Social Development into the XXI Century* (InterAmerican Bank, 1997), pp. 48–61; and John Williamson, 'Did the Washingon Consensus fail?', Outline of Remarks at the Center for Strategic and International Studies, available at http://www.iie.com/publications/papers/williamson1102.htm. Williamson's point, quite simply, was that he had only sought to summarise 10 key areas of policy reform which some (but not all) Latin American countries should be undertaking in 1989 and which would command a consensus in the institutions of Washington during the presidency of George Bush.

53 J. Pincus and Nguyen Thang, *Country Study: Vietnam*, Centre for Development Policy and Research, School of Oriental and African Studies, London, February 2004.

54 Republic of South Africa, Department of Provincial and Local Government, *Strategic Plan, 2005–2010* (DPLG, 2004), available at: http://www.dplg.gov.za. See Constitution of India at http://mchacode.nic.in/coiweb/amend/amend74.htm

55 World Bank, *World Development Report 1991*, p. 9.

56 *New Political Economy*, Vol. 5, No. 2 (2004).

57 Among the more comprehensive, compelling or controversial have been Paul Hirst and Grahame Thompson, *Globalization in Question: The International Economy and the Possibilities of Governance* (Polity, 1996); Linda Weiss, *The Myth of the Powerless State: Governing the Economy in a Global Era* (Polity, 1998); David Held, Anthony McGrew, David Goldblatt and Jonathan Perraton, *Global Transformations: Politics, Economics and Culture* (Polity, 1999); Joseph Stiglitz, *Globalization and its Discontents* (Penguin, 2002); and World Bank, *Globalization, Growth and Poverty* (Oxford University Press, 2003).

58 Williamson, 'The Washington Consensus revisited', p. 58.

59 World Bank, *Sub-Saharan Africa: From Crisis to Sustainable Growth* (Oxford University Press, 1989), p. 60.

60 See Article 9, Paragraph 3 of the Cotonou Agreement, available at: http://europa.eu.int/comm/development/body/cotonou/agreement/agr06_en.htm

61 Goran Hyden, Julius Court and Kenneth Mease, *Making Sense of Governance* (Lynne Rienner, 2004), p. 16.

62 UNDP (United Nations Development Programme), *Re-conceptualising Governance*, Discussion Paper 2 (UNDP, 1997); OECD (Organization for Economic Cooperation and Development), *The Final Report of the DAC Ad Hoc Working Group on Participatory Development and Good Government* (OECD, 1997); and Douglas Hurd, 'Promoting Good Government', *Crossbow* (Autumn 1990), pp. 4–5. For a fuller account of these developments, see Adrian Leftwich, *States of Development*, chs 5 and 6.

63 See http://www.wfd.org/

64 Gordon Crawford, 'Foreign Aid and Political Conditionality: Issues of Effectiveness and Consistency', *Democratization*, Vol. 4, No. 3 (1997), pp. 69–108.

65 Milton Friedman and Rose Friedman, *Free To Choose* (Penguin, 1980).

66 Crawford Young, 'Democratization in Africa: the contradictions of a political imperative', in: Jennifer A. Widner (ed.), *Economic Change and Political Liberalization in Sub-Saharan Africa* (Johns Hopkins University Press, 1994), pp. 230–50.

67 Leftwich, *States of Development*, p. 121; see also D. Williams and T. Young, 'Governance, the World Bank and Liberal Theory', *Political Studies*, Vol. 42, No. 1 (1994), pp. 84–100.

68 *New York Times*, 12 July 1990.

69 Samuel Huntington, *The Third Wave: Democratization in the Late Twentieth Century* (University of Oklahoma Press, 1991).

70 Francis Fukuyama, 'The End of History', *National Interest*, Summer 1989, pp. 3–18; and Michael W. Doyle, 'Kant, Liberal Legacies and Foreign Affairs', *Philosophy and Public Affairs*, Vol. 12, No. 3 (1983), pp. 205–35.

71 For instance, see Larry Diamond, *Developing Democracy: Towards Consolidation* (Johns Hopkins University Press, 1999); and Adam Przeworski *et al.*, *Sustainable Democracy* (Cambridge University Press, 1995) for good surveys of the literature and issues of the 1990s.

72 See the excellent survey by Mick Moore, Sheila Stewart and Ann Hudock, *Institution Building as a Development Assistance Method: A Review of Literature and Ideas* (Swedish International Development Authority, 1995).

73 World Bank, *Governance: The World Bank's Experience* (World Bank, 1994), p. xiv.

74 World Bank, *The African Capacity Building Initiative* (World Bank, 1991), p. 5.

75 World Bank, *Reforming Public Institutions and Strengthening Governance* (World Bank, 2000), p. xiii.

76 *Ibid.*

77 *Ibid.*, p. 15.

78 The seminal works by North are Douglass North and Robert Thomas, *The Rise of the Western World* (Cambridge University Press, 1973); Douglass North, *Structure and Change in Economic History* (W. W. Norton, 1981); Douglass C. North, *Institutions, Institutional Change and Economic Performance* (Cambridge University Press, 1990); and a host of papers. In particular, see his 'Institutions and Economic Growth: An Historical Introduction', *World Development*, Vol. 17. No. 9 (1989), pp. 1319–32.

79 Hodgson, *How Economics Forgot History*.

80 James G. March and Johan P. Olsen, *Rediscovering Institutions: The Organizational Basis of Politics* (Free Press, 1989); see also the good surveys in B. Guy Peters, *Institutional Theory in Political Science* (Continuum Press, 1999); and P. Hall and C. R. Taylor, 'Political Science and the Three New Institutionalisms', *Political Studies*, Vol. 44, No. 4 (1996), pp. 936–57.

81 See Rodrik's many papers on his website and, in particular, Dani Rodrik (ed.), *In Search of Prosperity* (Princeton University Press, 2003). The various papers in that volume provide a rich set of references to studies and work done by economists, mainly in the US, on the role of institutions in development. See Acemoglu *et al.*, *The Colonial Origins of Comparative Development*. See also the important earlier collection of papers in John Harriss, Janet Hunter and Colin M. Lewis (eds), *The New Institutional Economics and Third World Development* (Routledge, 1995), in which there is a very interesting paper by Robert H. Bates exploring the origins and sources of the new institutionalism and its implications for development theory. See also Christopher Clague (ed.), *Institutions and Economic Development: Growth and Governance in Less-Developed and Post-Socialist Countries* (Johns Hopkins University Press, 1997). One of the seminal papers was R. E. Hall and C. I. Jones, 'Why do Some Countries Produce So Much More Output per Worker than Others?', *Quarterly Journal of Economics*, Vol. 114, No. 1 (1999), pp. 83–116, which drew attention to the centrality of institutions in determining output and growth.

82 World Bank, *World Development Report 1997: The State in a Changing World* (Oxford University Press, 1947), chs 5 and 6.

Development, politics and social science   195

83 Peter Evans and James E. Rauch, 'Bureaucracy and Growth: A Cross-National Analysis of the Effects of "Weberian" State Structures on Economic Growth', *American Sociological Review*, Vol. 64, No. 5 (1999), pp. 748–65; and James E. Rauch and Peter B. Evans, 'Bureaucratic Structure and Bureaucratic Perform-ance in Less Developed Countries', *Journal of Public Economics*, Vol. 75, No. 1 (2000), pp. 49–71.
84 Nauro F. Campos and Jeffrey B. Nugent, 'Development Performance and the Institutions of Governance: Evidence from East Asia and Latin America', *World Development*, Vol. 27, No. 3 (1999), pp. 439–52.
85 Nelson *et al.*, *Fragile Coalitions*; Nelson, *Economic Crisis and Policy Choice*; Grindle, *Challenging the State*; and Grindle, *In Quest of the Political*.
86 'Postcolonial – or tricontinental – critique is united by a common political and moral consensus towards the history and legacy of western colonialism . . . The assumption of postcolonial studies is that many of the wrongs, if not crimes, against humanity are a product of the economic dominance of the north over the south', observes Robert J. C. Young in *Postcolonialism: An Historical Introduction* (Blackwell, 2001), pp. 5–6.
87 See http://en.wikipedia.org/wiki/Anti-globalization_movement for a good survey of the range of movements, causes and themes under the umbrella of anti-globalisation.
88 J. Crush, 'Imagining development' in: J. Crush (ed.), *Power of Development* (Routledge, 1995), pp. 1–23; Arturo Escobar, 'Reflections on "Development": Grassroots Approaches and Alternative Politics in the Third World', *Future*, Vol. 24, No. 5 (1992), pp. 411–36; Arturo Escobar, 'Imagining a Post-Development Era', in: Crush, *Power of Development*, pp. 211–27; Arturo Escobar, *Encountering Development: The Making and Unmaking of the Third World* (Princeton University Press, 1995); and W. Sachs, 'The Archaeology of The Development Idea', *Interculture*, Vol. XXIII, No. 4 (1990), pp. 6–25.
89 Crush, 'Imagining development', p. 11.
90 Robin Cohen and Shirin Rai (eds), *Global Social Movements* (Athlone Press, 2000); and Dong-Sook S. Gills, 'The political economy of globalization and grass roots movements', in: Anthony McGrew and Nana Poku (eds), *Globalization, Development and Human Security* (Polity, forthcoming).
91 Editorial, *New Political Economy*, Vol. 1, No. 1 (1996), p. 10.
92 Adam Smith, *The Wealth of Nations* (1776) (Routledge, 1892), Book IV, p. 488.
93 Karl Marx and Friedrich Engels, *The German Ideology* (Lawrence & Wishart, 1965), p. 76.
94 Anthony McGrew, 'Politics as distorted global politics', in: Adrian Leftwich (ed.), *What is Politics?* (Polity, 2004), p. 166.
95 See also Jeffrey Haynes, *Comparative Politics in a Globalizing World* (Polity, 2005).
96 Susan Strange, 'International Economics and International Relations: A Case of Mutual Neglect', *International Affairs*, Vol. 46, No. 2 (1970), pp. 304–15. For a good survey of these developments and concerns, see Anthony Payne, 'Rethink-ing development inside International Political Economy', in: Anthony Payne (ed.), *The New Regional Politics of Development* (Palgrave, 2004), pp. 1–28.
97 Thomas S. Kuhn, *The Structure of Scientific Revolutions*, 2nd edition (University of Chicago Press, 1970).
98 Williamson, 'Did the Washington Consensus fail?'.
99 Commission for Africa, *Our Common Interest: Report of the Commission for Africa* (Commission for Africa, 2005).
100 United Nations Development Programme (UNDP), *Human Development Report 2004* (Oxford University Press, 2004), pp. 186–7.

Adrian Leftwich

101 International Labour Office, *Global Employment Trends Briefing* (International Labour Office, 2005), pp. 7–8.

102 David Dollar, *Globalization, Poverty and Inequality since 1980*, World Bank Policy Research Paper 3333, World Bank, 2004, p. 18; and World Bank, *Globalization, Growth and Poverty* (Oxford University Press, 2002).

103 Robert Hunter Wade, 'On the Causes of Increasing World Poverty and Inequality, or Why the Matthew Effect Prevails', *New Political Economy*, Vol. 9, No. 2 (2004), pp. 163–88. See also the debate between Robert Wade and Martin Wolf in their 'Are global poverty and inequality getting worse?', in: David Held and Anthony McGrew (eds), *The Global Transformations Reader*, 2nd edition (Polity, 2003), pp. 440–6.

104 Arne Bigsten and Jörgen Levin, 'Growth, income distribution and poverty: a review', in: Shorrocks and van der Hoeven, *Growth, Inequality, and Poverty*, pp. 251–76.

105 Martin Ravallion and Shaohua Chen, *China's (Uneven) Progress Against Poverty*, World Bank Policy Research Paper 3408, World Bank, 2004; Jan Vandemoortele, 'Ending World Poverty: Is the Debate Settled?', *One Pager*, No. 12 (United Nations Development Programme, International Poverty Centre, 2005); and Alejandro Grinspun, 'Chinese Boxes: What Happened to Poverty', *One Pager*, No. 13 (United Nations Development Programme, International Poverty Centre, 2005). The problems of defining poverty levels and obtaining and interpreting data is illustrated in a claim in a recent report that poverty in China fell from 29.6 per cent in 1990 to 14.94 per cent in 2000. See World Bank (Operationalising Pro-poor Growth Research Program), *Pro-poor Growth in the 90s: Lessons and Insights from 14 Countries* (World Bank, 2005), p. 16.

106 World Bank, *World Development Report 2006*, Draft (World Bank, 2005), p. 31.

107 World Bank, *Inequality in Latin America and the Caribbean* (World Bank, 2003), p. 3.

108 SAPRIN (Structural Adjustment Participatory Review International Network), *The Policy Roots of Economic Crisis and Poverty* (SAPRIN, 2002).

109 United Nations General Assembly, Resolution 55/2, September 2000. There were eight goals: to halve world poverty by 2015; to achieve universal primary education; to promote gender equality; to reduce infant mortality; to enhance maternal health; to combat AIDS; to work for environmental sustainability; and to develop a global partnership for development.

110 David Dollar and Jakob Svensson, 'What Explains the Success or Failure of Structural Adjustment Programmes?', *The Economic Journal*, Vol. 110, Issue 466 (2000), pp. 895–6.

111 Anna Ivanova, Wolfgang Mayer, Alex Mourmouras and George Anayiotos, *What Determines the Implementation of IMF-Supported Programs?*, IMF Working Paper, WP/03/8, International Monetary Fund, 2003, p. 39.

112 Kenny and Williams, 'What Do We Know About Economic Growth?', p. 1. This echoed very much the view put forward by Ronald Coase, a decade before, that much of contemporary economics studied 'a system which lives in the minds of economists, but not on earth'. Ronald Coase, 'The Institutional Structure of Production', *American Economic Review*, Vol. 82, No. 4 (1992), p. 714.

113 Kenny and Williams, 'What Do We Know About Economic Growth', p. 1.

114 *Ibid.*, p. 16.

115 Ronald Coase, 'The Nature of the Firm', *Economica*, Vol. 4, No. 3 (1937), pp. 386–405, and 'The Problem of Social Cost', *Journal of Law and Economics*, Vol. 3, No. 1 (1960), pp. 1–44; and Kenneth L. Sokoloff and Stanley L. Engerman, 'History Lessons: Institutions, Factor Endowments, and Paths of Development

in the New World', *Journal of Economic Perspectives*, Vol. 14, No. 3 (2000), pp. 217–32.

116 North, *Institutions, Institutional Change and Economic Performance*, p. 107.

117 Dani Rodrik, Arvind Subramanian and Francesco Trebbi, *Institutions Rule: The Primacy of Institutions over Geography and Integration in Economic Development*, CID Working Paper 97, Center for International Development, Harvard University, October 2002.

118 *Ibid.*, p. 3.

119 World Bank, *Reforming Public Institutions and Strengthening Governance*, pp. xii, 2.

120 Tilly, *Coercion, Capital and European States*; and Robert H. Bates, *Prosperity and Violence: The Political Economy of Development* (W. W. Norton, 2001).

121 Janine Aron, 'Growth and Institutions: A Review of the Evidence', *The World Bank Research Observer*, Vol. 15, No. 1 (2000), pp. 99–135.

122 World Bank, *World Development Report 2002: Building Institutions for Markets* (Oxford University Press, 2002).

123 *Ibid.*; and Dani Rodrik, 'What do we learn from country narratives?', in: Rodrik, *In Search of Prosperity*, pp. 1–19. See also the detailed survey of the literature by Johannes Jütting, *Institutions and Development: A Critical Review*, Technical Paper No. 210, OECD Development Center (OECD, 2003); Aron, 'Growth and Institutions', pp. 128–30; and Rodrik *et al.*, *Institutions Rule*.

124 Leftwich, *States of Development*, p. 121.

125 Daniel Kaufmann, Aart Kraay and Pablo Zoido-Lobatón, *Governance Matters*, Policy Research Working Paper 2196, World Bank Institute, 1999; and related papers at the Governance website of the Bank.

126 Goran Hyden, Julius Court and Kenneth Mease, *Making Sense of Governance* (Lynne Rienner, 2004), p. 16. My emphasis.

127 *Ibid.*, pp. 7–33.

128 Dani Rodrik, 'Growth strategies', in: Aghion and Durlauf, *Handbook of Economic Growth*.

129 *North-South: A Programme For Survival*, Report of the Independent Commission on International Development Issues under the Chairmanship of Willy Brandt (Pan, 1980); and *Common Crisis: North-South: Cooperation for World Recovery* (Pan, 1983).

130 See the work and publications of the Centre for the Future State, at the Institute of Development Studies, University of Sussex, led by Mick Moore, available at: http://www.ids.ac.uk/gdr/cfs/; and also that of the Crisis State Research Centre, at the London School of Economics, also funded by DfID, and led by James Putzel, available at: http://www.crisisstates.com. See, in particular, The Centre for the Future State, *Signposts to More Effective States* (Institute for Development Studies, 2005).

131 Christopher Clague, 'Introduction', in: Clague, *Institutions and Economic Development*, p. 2. Though political economists from Smith onwards have always focused on the relations between economics and politics, as *New Political Economy* exemplifies, the notion that economics would or should *include* the 'political', and that economic principle and analysis could apply to political phenomena, was one which is associated with contemporary rational and public choice theory, and its disciplinary imperialism, best and most mischievously expressed in Gary Becker's essay, 'The economic approach to human behaviour', in: Jon Elster (ed.), *Rational Choice* (Blackwell, 1986), pp. 108–22.

132 DfID (Department for International Development), *The Causes of Conflict in Africa* (DfID, 2001), p. 20.

133 Adrian Leftwich, 'The political approach to human behaviour: people, resources and power', in: Leftwich, *What is Politics?*, p. 103.
134 Jack Straw, 'Failed and failing states', Speech at European Research Institute, University of Birmingham, 6 September 2002, available at http://www. eri.bham.ac.uk/eventsjstraw.htm
135 Chalmers Johnson, *Blowback: The Costs and Consequences of American Empire* (Henry Holt & Co., 2000).
136 Robert I. Rotberg (ed.), *State Failure and State Weakness in a Time of Terror* (Brookings Institution, 2003); and Robert I. Rotberg (ed.), *When States Fail* (Princeton University Press, 2004); see, also, Robert H. Bates, *Political Insecurity and State Failure in Contemporary Africa*, Working Paper 115, Center for International Development, Harvard University, Cambridge, Mass., January 2005, available at http://www.cid.harvard.edu/cidwp/115.htm
137 USAID, *Fragile States Strategy* (USAID, 2005). Similar, but not so sharply focused, concerns had already been expressed in the report of the National Intelligence Council, *Global Trends 2015* (National Intelligence Council, 2000).
138 Robert I. Rotberg, 'Failed states, collapsed states, weak states: causes and indicators', in Rotberg, *State Failure and State Weakness in a Time of Terror*, p. 1.
139 DfID (Department for International Development), *Why We Need to Work More Effectively in Fragile States* (DfID, 2005), p. 5.
140 Francis Fukuyama, *State Building: Governance and World Order in the Twenty-First Century* (Profile Books, 2005).
141 The Prime Minister's Strategy Unit of the Cabinet Office, *Investing in Prevention: An International Strategy to Manage Risks of Instability and Improve Crisis Response* (The Strategy Unit, 2005).
142 World Bank, *World Bank Group Work in Low-Income Countries Under Stress: A Task Force Report* (World Bank, 2002), p. iii.
143 World Bank, *Inequality in Latin America and the Caribbean* (World Bank, 2003), pp. 1–24.
144 World Bank, *World Development Report 2006*, draft, p. 1.
145 World Bank, *Pro-poor Growth in the 90s*, p. 12.
146 Daron Acemoglu, Simon Johnson and James Robinson, 'Institutions as the fundamental cause of long-run growth', in: Aghion and Durlauf, *Handbook of Economic Growth*.
147 Stephen Klasen, Melanie Grosse, Rainer Thiele, Jann Lay, Julius Spatz and Manfred Wiebelt, 'Operationalising Pro-Poor Growth: A Country Case Study on Bolivia', available at: http://www.dfid.gov.uk/search/proxy/query. html?col=dfid&qt=propoor+growth+bolivia&charset=iso8859-1
148 North, *Institutions, Institutional Change and Economic Performance*, p. 16.
149 Mushtaq Khan, 'State failure in developing countries and strategies of institutional reform', in: B. Tungodden, N. Stern and I. Kolstrad (eds), *Toward Pro-Poor Policies: Aid, Institutions and Globalization* (Oxford University Press/World Bank, 2004), p. 178.
150 John Harriss, 'Do political regimes matter? Poverty reduction and regime differences across Indian states', in: Peter Houtzager and Mick Moore (eds), *Changing Paths: International Development and the New Politics of Inclusion* (University of Michigan Press, 2003), pp. 204–32. He says: 'the structure and functioning of local (agrarian) power and the relations of local and state-level power holders exercise a significant influence on policy processes and development outcomes. They show that politics does "make a difference" ', p. 228.
151 R. J. Herring, 'Zulfikar Ali Bhutto and the "Eradication of Feudalism" in Pakistan', *Comparative Studies in Society and History*, Vol. 21, No. 4 (1979), pp. 519–57.

152 Acemoglu *et al.*, 'Institutions as the fundamental cause of long-run growth'.
153 Meredith Woo-Cumings (ed.), *The Developmental State* (Cornell University Press, 1999); Clague, *Institutions and Economic Development*; and Rodrik, *In Search of Prosperity*.
154 Peter Evans, *Embedded Autonomy: States and Industrial Transformation* (Princeton University Press, 1995); and Funke and Solomon, *The Shadow State in Africa*.
155 Joel S. Migdal, *State in Society: Studying How States and Societies Transform and Constitute One Another* (Cambridge University Press, 2001), p. 57.
156 Joel S. Migdal, Atul Kohli and Vivienne Shue (eds), *State Power and Social Forces: Domination and Transformation in the Third World* (Cambridge University Press, 1994).
157 Sabrina Grosse-Kettler, *External Actors in Stateless Somalia: A War Economy and its Promoters*, Paper 39, Bonn International Centre for Conversion, Bonn, 2004.
158 Bates, *Prosperity and Violence*, p. 47.
159 Crawford Young, *The African Colonial State in Comparative Perspective* (Yale University Press, 1994); John Iliffe, *Africans: The History of a Continent* (Cambridge University Press, 1995); Jeffrey Herbst, *States and Power in Africa: Comparative Lessons in Authority and Control* (Princeton University Press, 2000); and Berman, 'Ethnicity, Patronage and the African State'.
160 Joel S. Hellman, Geraint Jones and Daniel Kaufmann, *Seize the State, Seize the Day*, World Bank Policy Research Working Paper 2444, World Bank, 2000.
161 Jean-François Bayart, *The State in Africa: The Politics of the Belly* (Longman, 1993).
162 Rodrik, 'Growth strategies'.
163 Barbara Harriss-White, 'The market, the state and institutions of economic development', in: Chang, *Rethinking Development Economics*, p. 481. Author's emphasis.
164 Ha-Joon Chang, 'Breaking the Mould: An Institutionalist Political Economy Alternative to the Neoliberal Theory of the Market and the State', *Cambridge Journal of Economics*, Vol. 16, No. 5 (2002), p. 557.
165 For a good discussion and some interesting (but non-developmental) cases, see Sven Steinmo, Kathleen Thelen and Frank Longstreth (eds), *Structuring Politics: Historical Institutionalism in Comparative Analysis* (Cambridge University Press, 1992).
166 Grindle, *In Quest of the Political*.
167 Jean-Philippe Platteau, 'Behind the Market Stage Where Real Societies Exist', Parts 1 and 2, *Journal of Development Studies* Vol. 30, No. 3 (1994), pp. 533–77 and Vol. 30, No. 4 (1994), pp. 754–817; John Harriss, 'The Case for Cross-Disciplinary Approaches in International Development', *World Development*, Vol. 30, No. 3 (2002), pp. 487–96; John Harriss, *Institutions, Politics and Culture: A Case for Old Institutionalism in the Study of Historical Change*, Working Paper No. 34, 2002, Development Studies Institute, London School of Economics; and Manoj Srivastava, *Moving Beyond 'Institutions Matter': Some Reflections on How The 'Rules of the Game' Evolve and Change*, Discussion Paper No. 4, Crisis States Development Research Centre, London School of Economics, 2004.
168 Max Weber, *The Protestant Ethic and the Spirit of Capitalism* (George, Allen & Unwin, 1965).
169 Winston Davis, 'Religion and development: Weber and the East Asian experience', in: Myron Weiner and S. P. Huntington (eds), *Understanding Political Development* (Little, Brown & Co., 1987), pp. 221–80.
170 Ronald Inglehart and Wayne E. Baker, 'Modernization, Cultural Change and the

Persistence of Traditional Values', *American Sociological Review*, Vol. 65, No. 1 (2000), pp. 19–51.

171 Hongying Wang, 'Informal Institutions and Foreign Investment in China', *The Pacific Review*, Vol. 13, No. 4 (2000), pp. 525–56.

172 Hans-Joachim Lauth, 'Informal Institutions and Democracy', *Democratization*, Vol. 7, No. 4 (2000), pp. 21–50.

173 John Harriss, *On Trust, and Trust in Indian Business: Ethnographic Exploration*, Working Paper No. 35, Development Studies Institute, London School of Economics, 2002.

174 Robert M. Price, *Society and Bureaucracy in Contemporary Ghana* (University of California Press, 1975).

175 Edward C. Banfield, *The Moral Basis of a Backward Society* (Free Press, 1958); Robert D. Putnam, *Making Democracy Work: Civic Traditions in Modern Italy* (Princeton University Press, 1993); Michael Woolcock, 'Social Capital and Economic Development: Toward a Theoretical Synthesis and Policy Framework', *Theory and Society*, Vol. 27, No. 2 (1998), pp. 151–208; M. Woolcock and D. Narayan, 'Social Capital: Implications for Development Theory, Research, and Policy', *The World Bank Research Observer*, Vol. 15, No. 2 (2000), pp. 225–49; and David Halpern, *Social Capital* (Polity, 2005).

176 In the academic community, the work being done, for instance, at the Centre for the Future State at the Institute of Development Studies at the University of Sussex and at the Crisis States Development Research Centre at the London School of Economics is an indication of the importance of this.

177 Karl Polanyi, *The Great Transformation: The Political and Economic Origins of Our Time* (Beacon Press, 1957); Tilly, *Coercion, Capital and European States*; and Fukuyama, *State Building*.

178 Weiss and Hobson, *States and Economic Development*; Chang, *Kicking Away the Ladder*; and Weiss, *The Myth of the Powerless State*.

179 The work of the researchers within the international aid and development agencies has in many ways been more significant and imaginative in trying to develop solutions to the problems, if more controversial, than the generally critical accounts of the independent academic researchers.

180 Valerie Bockstette, Areendam Chanda and Louis Putterman, 'States and Markets: The Advantage of an Early Start', *Journal of Economic Growth*, Vol. 7, No. 2 (2002), pp. 347–69.

181 Fukuyama, *State Building*, p. 8.

182 Jeffrey Herbst, 'Let them fail: state failure in theory and practice', in: Rotberg, *When States Fail*, pp. 302–18.

183 Merilee Grindle, 'Good Enough Governance: Poverty Reduction and Reform in Developing Countries', *Governance*, Vol. 17, No. 4 (2000), pp. 525–48.

184 Peter Evans, 'Introduction: Development Strategies across the Public-Private Divide', *World Development*, Vol. 24, No. 6 (1996), pp. 1033–7; Elinor Ostrom, 'Crossing the Great Divide: Co-production, Synergy, and Development', *World Development*, Vol. 24, No. 6 (1996), pp. 1073–87; A. Joshi and M. Moore, 'Institutionalised Co-production: Unorthodox Public Service Delivery in Challenging Environments', *Journal of Development Studies*, Vol. 40, No. 4 (2004), pp. 31–49; Centre for the Future State, *Signposts to More Effective States*; and the report of a conference, organised by the Centre, on 'New Challenges in State Building', on 21 June 2005, available at http://www.grc-xchange.org/docs/EB104.pdf

185 Mick Moore, 'Revenues, State Formation and the Quality of Governance in Developing Countries', *International Political Science Review*, Vol. 25, No. 3, pp. 297–319. See also Tilly, *Coercion, Capital and European States*.

Index

Acemoglu, D. 184
Afghanistan 178, 180
Africa 167, 169, 171, 188; poverty 184–5
Alavi, H. 166
Albert, M. 12, 14, 19
Alter, C. 22
Amable, B. 21–2
anti-globalisation movement 173, 174
APEC (Asia–Pacific Economic Cooperation) 137, 143, 150, 152
APT (ASEAN Plus Three) countries 138
ASEAN (Association of Southeast Asian Nations) 137, 138, 145, 150
ASEM (Asia-Europe Meeting) 150
Asian financial crisis 137–8
AU (African Union) 143, 153
Austria 18, 21
autonomism 45–6
Axline, A. 130, 132, 153

Balassa, B. 132, 168
Baran, P. 5, 166
Bates, R. 178, 184
Bauer, P.T. 168
Bayart, J.-F. 185
Berkhout, F. 65, 69
Bertoldi, M. 16
Beyer, J. 24
Bhagwati, J. 36–40
Bhutto, Z.A. 183
borders/bordering 8–9, 108, 114; disembedding from national 116–19; multiple dimensions 116; multiple locations 114; national and subnational 113–19; novel 106–20; positioning of economic sites 115–16
Boserup, E. 81
Boyer, R. 16–17, 25
Breslin, S. 153

Bretherton, C. 142
Bull, H. 146
Bush, George H.W. 148
Bush, George W. 9, 49–50, 154
business systems 21
Buzan, B. 139

Cable, V. 135
Calmfors, L. 19
Campbell, J.L. 14
capital flows 113–14
capitalism 4, 8, 34; models of 7–8, 11–27; recombinant 8, 25–7
capitalist diversity 7, 11–12, 13; CMEs 15, 16–17, 18–19, 22; conservative continental model 20, 21; dualist approach 12–19; free-market model 12–13, 19; geocultural models 20–2; and governance 22, 23–4; hybridisation 23; LMEs 15–16, 17–18, 19; market, managed and state 19–20; Mediterranean group 18–19; nation-state-based analysis 23–5; neoclassical analysis 13–14, 16; neoinstitutionalism on 11–12, 13–19, 23, 24, 25–7; Rhenish model 12–13
Castles, F.G. 20
Chang, H.-J. 186
Chen, X. 113
China 167, 176, 178, 186
cities, global 112
civilisation 153
class 41, 44, 166; conflict 46, 188–9
climate change 57, 59, 60, 71, 74
Clinton, Bill 151
Coase, R. 178
Coates, D. 13
Cold War era 5, 152
colonial globality 42–4, 45

Payne, A. 1–10, 130, 135, 146
Pedersen, O. 13, 14
Peterson, V. S. 8, 79–105
Phillips, N. 7
planning, national 165–6, 168
Polanyi, K. 4, 133
political economy 2, 5, 6, 184; as
    androcentric 81, 84, 88–9; and gender
    8, 80–3, 84–7; new 1–9
political integration 132
politics 50–1; and development 166–7,
    172, 173, 187–9
poverty 162, 165, 180–2, 184–5;
    feminisation of 91; numbers in 176;
    security and development 180–3
power 44; gendered 39, 42, 83, 86;
    social 50, 51
Prebisch, R. 137
private sphere, feminised 92
privatisation 87, 168; gender effects 91,
    93
pro-poor growth 182–3, 184, 187
productive economy, gendered 89–92
property rights 164, 168
public interest 68
public-private partnerships 72

racial inequality 41
Radice, H. 24–5
Ragin, C. 17
redistribution 187
regime theory and environment 60–1, 69
region: building 131; core, peripheral
    and intermediate 135, 143; definitions
    129, 130; as socially constructed 129
regional integration 130, 132, 152;
    European 132, 133, 152–3
regional security complex 139, 140, 147–8
regionalisation 130–1; actors in regional
    area 140–1; and state 72, 140, 141
regionalism 9, 130, 132, 133–5, 152;
    dimensions 136, 139–40, 153; early
    debate 131–2; and functionalism 131,
    152; higher level 144–6; lower levels
    143–4; old and new 128, 132, 133, 134,
    152; region as actor 141–3; US
    approach to 151–2; and world order
    146–52, 154; *see also* multiregionalism
regionness 133–4, 135; and actorness
    142
reproductive economy 41, 92–4, 98
resistance to globalism 36–7; *see also*
    anti-globalisation movement;
    multitude

Ricardo, D. 2
Robinson, J. 184
Rodrik, D. 172, 178, 180, 185
Rostow, W.W. 163, 164
Rotberg, R. 181
Rotmans, J. 62–3
Rupert, M. 8, 32–56

SADC (Southern African Development
    Community) 138, 145, 153
Said, E. 37
Sassen, S. 8, 106–27
Scandinavia 13, 20
Schmidt, V. 19–20, 23
Schmitter, P. 132
Schumpeter, J. 4
Scott, W.R. 22, 25
security 49–50, 180–2
security regionalism 136, 139–40, 147–8,
    153
Sen, A. 86
September 11 attacks 147, 149, 180; and
    US neoliberalism 49
service sector employment 90, 94
Shivji, I. 166
Shonfield, A. 11
Sklar, R. 166
Smith, Adam 2, 161, 174
Smith, Adrian 65, 69
social change and environment 70, 71
social democracy 13, 15, 164, 187
social life and decentring of rule 45
social reproduction 81, 95
social science and development 9, 161–2,
    175–7, 180, 185–6, 188–9
Solingen, E. 140
Solokoff, K.L. 178
Somalia 178, 184–5
Söderbaum, F. 141
Soskice, D. 14, 15, 16, 17–19
sovereignty 36, 119, 130
state 72, 73–4, 187, 188; capacity 188,
    189; decline in power of 71–2;
    failure 164, 181, 183, 184, 188;
    security and development 181–2;
    see also nation-state
Steger, M. 35
Stirling, A. 65, 69
structural adjustment programmes 49,
    173; conditionality 168; gender
    effects 91; patchy results 175–6
Subramanian, A. 178
subregionalism 143
sustainable development 59, 62, 68